THE MAGILL BIBLIOGRAPHIES

The American Presidents, by Norman S. Cohen, 1989
Black American Women Novelists, by Craig Werner, 1989
Classical Greek and Roman Drama, by Robert J. Forman, 1989
Contemporary Latin American Fiction, by Keith H. Brower, 1989
Masters of Mystery and Detective Fiction, by J. Randolph Cox, 1989
Nineteenth Century American Poetry, by Philip K. Jason, 1989
Restoration Drama, by Thomas J. Taylor, 1989
Twentieth Century European Short Story, by Charles E. May, 1989
The Victorian Novel, by Laurence W. Mazzeno, 1989
Women's Issues, by Laura Stempel Mumford, 1989
America in Space, by Russell R. Tobias, 1991
The American Constitution, by Robert J. Janosik, 1991
The Classical Epic, by Thomas J. Sienkewicz, 1991
English Romantic Poetry, by Bryan Aubrey, 1991
Ethics, by John K. Roth, 1991
The Immigrant Experience, by Paul D. Mageli, 1991
The Modern American Novel, by Steven G. Kellman, 1991
Native Americans, by Frederick E. Hoxie and Harvey Markowitz, 1991
American Drama: 1918-1960, by R. Baird Shuman, 1992
American Ethnic Literatures, by David R. Peck, 1992
American Theatre History, by Thomas J. Taylor, 1992
The Atomic Bomb, by Hans G. Graetzer and Larry M. Browning, 1992
Biography, by Carl Rollyson, 1992
The History of Science, by Gordon L. Miller, 1992
The Origin and Evolution of Life on Earth, by David W. Hollar, 1992
Pan-Africanism, by Michael W. Williams, 1992
Resources for Writers, by R. Baird Shuman, 1992
Shakespeare, by Joseph Rosenblum, 1992
The Vietnam War in Literature, by Philip K. Jason, 1992
Contemporary Southern Women Fiction Writers, by Rosemary M.
    Canfield Reisman and Christopher J. Canfield, 1994
Cycles in Humans and Nature, by John T. Burns, 1994
Environmental Studies, by Diane M. Fortner, 1994
Poverty in America, by Steven Pressman, 1994

The Short Story in English: Britain and North America, by Dean Baldwin and Gregory L. Morris, 1994

Victorian Poetry, by Laurence W. Mazzeno, 1995

Human Rights in Theory and Practice, by Gregory J. Walters, 1995

Energy, by Joseph R. Rudolph, Jr., 1995

A Bibliographic History of the Book, by Joseph Rosenblum, 1995

The Search for Economics as a Science, by the Editors of Salem Press (Lynn Turgeon, Consulting Editor), 1995

Psychology, by the Editors of Salem Press (Susan E. Beers, Consulting Editor), 1995

World Mythology, by Thomas J. Sienkewicz, 1996

Art, Truth, and High Politics: A Bibliographic Study of the Official Lives of Queen Victoria's Ministers in Cabinet, 1843-1969, by John Powell, 1996

Popular Physics and Astronomy, by Roger Smith, 1996

Paradise Lost, by P. J. Klemp, 1996

Social Movement Theory and Research, by Roberta Garner and John Tenuto, 1996

Propaganda in Twentieth Century War and Politics, by Robert Cole, 1996

The Kings of Medieval England, c. 560-1485, by Larry W. Usilton, 1996

The British Novel 1680-1832, by Laurence W. Mazzeno, 1997

The Impact of Napoleon, 1800-1815, by Leigh Ann Whaley, 1997

Cosmic Influences on Humans, Animals, and Plants, by John T. Burns, 1997

One Hundred Years of American Women Writing, 1848-1948, by Jane Missner Barstow, 1997

Vietnam Studies, by Carl Singleton, 1997

British Women Writers, 1700-1850, by Barbara J. Horwitz, 1997

The United States and Latin America, by John A. Britton, 1997

Reinterpreting Russia, by Steve D. Boilard, 1997

British Women Writers, 1700–1850

British Women Writers, 1700–1850

An Annotated Bibliography of Their Works and Works about Them

Barbara J. Horwitz

Magill Bibliographies

The Scarecrow Press, Inc.
Lanham, Md., & London
and
Salem Press
Pasadena, Calif., & Englewood Cliffs, N.J.
1997

SCARECROW PRESS, INC.

Published in the United States of America
by Scarecrow Press, Inc.
4720 Boston Way
Lanham, Maryland 20706

4 Pleydell Gardens, Folkestone
Kent CT20 2DN, England

British Library Cataloguing in Publication Information Available

Library of Congress Cataloging-in-Publication Data

Horwitz, Barbara Joan.
    British women writers, 1700–1850 : an annotated bibliography of their works and
works about them / Barbara J. Horwitz.
        p.   cm. — (Magill bibliographies)
    Includes bibliographical references and index.
    ISBN 0-8108-3315-8 (alk. paper)
        1. English literature—Women authors—History and criticism—Bibliography.
    2. Women and literature—Great Britain—History—18th century—Bibliography.
    3. Women and literature—Great Britain—History—19th century—Bibliography.
    4. English literature—18th century—History and criticism—Bibliography. 5.
    English literature—19th century—History and criticism—Bibliography. 6. English
    literature—Women authors—Bibliography. 7. English literature—18th century—
    Bibliography. 8. English literature—19th century—Bibliography. I. Title.
    II. Series.
    Z2013.5.W6H67   1997
    [PR111] 016.8208'09287—dc21   97–5001

ISBN 0–8108–3315–8 (cloth : alk. paper)

⊖™ The paper used in this publication meets the minimum requirements of
American National Standard for Information Sciences—Permanence of
Paper for Printed Library Materials, ANSI Z39.48–1984.
Manufactured in the United States of America.

For Ted

Contents

Acknowledgments

I am grateful to the Research Committee of the C. W. Post Campus of Long Island University for the time they granted me to complete this project. I am also indebted to the Reference Department at the B. Davis Schwartz Library of the C. W. Post Campus of Long Island University, particularly Louis Pisha and Jacqueline Elsas, for an unfailingly cheerful willingness to help. Finally, I must express my deepest gratitude to Theodore Horwitz for his technological support and unfailing encouragement.

INTRODUCTION

Interest in works written by women during the eighteenth and nineteenth centuries is growing. Many of these works are now being reprinted and studied in literature courses as well as in women's studies courses. Scholars and critics have been evaluating, analyzing, and reevaluating these works in light of the events and ideas of the eighteenth and nineteenth centuries and current literary theories. Clearly, a guide to these authors, their works, and the writing about them should be of great help to students, researchers, and others interested in the subject. This bibliography lists works by British women dramatists, poets, and novelists who wrote between 1700 and 1850. Some of these authors, such as Jane Austen and the Brontës, are very well known. The writing of other authors, popular during their era, is just now being rediscovered and reprinted. This bibliography mentions accessible editions of the works, as well as recent biographies of the authors. In addition, the scholarship concerning these writers and their works is listed and described, emphasizing features likely to be most useful to undergraduates, graduate students, and other interested readers.

The first chapter outlines political events in England from 1700 to 1850, from the time of the Glorious Revolution, which brought William and Mary to the throne, through the reign of the Hanoverians, the American Revolution, the French Revolution, the wars against the French, the beginnings of the Industrial Revolution, and the early years of the reign of Queen Victoria. It also describes the change in the cultural climate from the wit, satire, and intellectualism of the Neoclassic Age through the age of sensibility, which indulged in emotion and pity for the vulnerable, to the revolutionary fervor and the subjectivity of the Romantics, and finally to the moral seriousness of the Evangelicals, industrialists, and philanthropists of the Victorian Age. A list of sources for further reading is included.

This chapter also discusses literary history. The period was dominated by classically educated male authors who felt a strong kinship with the Latin writers who wrote when Augustus ruled Rome. The Romantics, who succeeded them, preferred to express themselves in more colloquial language and wrote in different forms, to express their own sense of the cosmos. A new form of writing, the novel, developed during this time.

The second chapter discusses the history of women's writing in light of the tension between the necessity for self-expression, financial or psychological, on the part of women, and the culture's insistence that such self-expression not only was unseemly in a woman but also gave probable evidence of untrammeled female sexuality. Anthologies, bibliographies, and guides to women's writing are described. This chapter also discusses current criticism of women's novels, poetry, drama, and other writing and supplies a descriptive bibliography of the most helpful of those works.

The third chapter presents biographical information for individual women authors, born after 1700 in Great Britain, whose most significant work was done by 1850. The chapter lists their works and describes writing about them which is accessible, recent, and most important, helpful to students of literature, students of women's place in society, and to students of the age.

Those interested in the most current information about these women and their work, should also consult recent issues of *The Bibliography of the Modern Language Association* for journal articles discussing these authors. Computer enthusiasts will find information concerning many of the better-known women writers, such as Jane Austen, on the Internet.

Chapter 1

ENGLAND, 1700-1850:

POLITICAL TURMOIL AND ITS RESOLUTION

In the year 1700, William and Mary ruled England. William of Orange was a Dutch Protestant who had been asked to rule England when James II lost the country's support for policies which were seen to be too favorable toward Roman Catholics. King James fled to France, but his supporters remained a force in European politics for the next fifty years.

Indeed, Louis XIV of France declared James's son king of England in 1701, thus precipitating a war with England which lasted until the Treaty of Utrecht was signed in 1713. Meanwhile, in 1702, James's Protestant daughter Anne succeeded to the throne. Because of the war and the fact that money to finance it could only be raised through acts of Parliament, she had to cede power to her ministers and to Parliament. Her ministers negotiated the Act of Union with Scotland in 1707, making Scotland an integral part of Great Britain. The war with France caused great controversy. The Whigs, the party representing the Dissenters, who were Protestant heirs of the Puritans, and commercial interests, pressed for its continuance while the Tories, the party representing agricultural interests and the Church of England, wished to end it. When Anne died in 1714, the Tories joined with the Whigs in accepting the accession to the throne of George I, a Hanoverian Protestant.

George I was never a beloved figure (he did not even speak English), but the government was stable and the country prospered under his Whig ministers. The Jacobite Rebellion, an attempt to restore the Stuarts to the throne, failed, increasing Whig power.

As the chief minister, Robert Walpole gained the support of George II and much of the population by maintaining peace abroad and prosperity at home. His skill at using patronage to ensure the loyalty of his supporters eventually led to charges of corruption, however. This, as well as impatience with his reluctance to pursue European wars, led to calls for his resignation in 1742.

Prince Charles Edward, the son of the Stuart Pretender to the throne, invaded Scotland and England in 1745, but his troops received little support from the populace and were defeated overwhelmingly at Culloden in 1746. England's brutal pacification of the Scotland's Highlands destroyed the clan system, caused great hardship, and increased migration to America. Wars in Europe, North America, and India, primarily with the French, persisted. William Pitt the Elder took office in 1757 to pursue the war in order to promote England's commercial interests. England was successful, particularly in Canada and India, but also in Africa, gaining a colonial empire.

When George III succeeded to the throne in 1760, England had become a world power, but the return of peace brought unemployment and resentment of taxation. Indeed, imposition of taxes on the American colonies caused resentment that eventually led to the American Revolution. In England, calls for reform accompanied great political unrest. The government's wish to increase the rights of Roman Catholics led to the Gordon Riots in 1780. The following year, the American colonies succeeded in separating themselves from Great Britain. National humiliation caused by that defeat increased the influence of the Evangelicals, who wished to end slavery and the slave trade and improve the moral tone of the nation.

In 1784, William Pitt the Younger became prime minister with the support of George III and rural interests. Pitt undertook to reduce government corruption and decrease the national debt. As his reforms succeeded, he became an increasingly powerful figure.

During this period population grew, particularly in urban areas. London's population increased greatly as did that of other cities such as Manchester. New methods of agriculture were introduced and technology began to develop. An increase in commercial activity led to calls for better roads and the development of canals. It also led to the rise of a class of merchants and manufacturers, many as wealthy as the landed aristocracy. The professional class grew, and factory workers joined agricultural laborers on the bottom of the social ladder.

The major event of the end of the eighteenth century was the French Revolution. Greeted at first with approval by the English, who had looked on the French government as tyrannical, it soon aroused fear and hatred. Edmund Burke wrote against it. The execution of King Louis XVI and Queen Marie Antoinette shocked England and led to war with France. The writings of sympathizers with the revolution, such as Thomas Paine, were suppressed; indeed, the British government passed laws suppressing dissent, because of its fear that the revolution would spread to the British poor, who were suffering from the inflationary effects of a poor harvest and war.

As a consequence of its greater sea power and economic power, Britain ultimately defeated France under Napoleon. The Prince of Wales became regent in 1811, subsequent to the apparent insanity of George III. (Scholars later surmised that the king suffered from porphyria, a physical disease that contributed to the king's mental decline.) Victory over Napoleon was gained in 1814 and England emerged as the richest country in the world. Britain's war with the United States from 1812 to 1814 was opposed by the commercial interests, whose strength continued to grow. Workers and the poor were strongly disaffected by the introduction of machinery that increased unemployment and the price of bread. Riots and other disturbances took place between 1816 and 1819. Government attempts to repress them led to the Peterloo Massacre in Birmingham. An agricultural depression also took place in the early 1820's.

All this, as well as the accession of William IV to the throne in 1830, spurred interest in political reform. In 1832, a bill was passed giving the wealthier members of the middle class and the new industrial areas greater representation in Parliament. This bill was the first of a series of laws widening the electorate. The Parliament elected under these reforms made further reforms.

By the beginning of the nineteenth century, laws improving the status of Roman Catholics were introduced, and laws extending rights to Jews were subsequently passed.

Queen Victoria came to the throne in 1837 during a period of economic depression which led to demands for changes in government by the Chartists and the Anti-Corn Law league. The Chartists argued for a widening of the electorate; the Anti-Corn Law league wanted to end taxes on the importation of grain in order to lower its price. The Chartists did not succeed for many years, but the Corn Laws were repealed in 1846. This change, together with the growth of British industry and the growth of Britain's colonial empire, ushered in a period of prosperity, social unity, and optimism that culminated in the Great Exhibition of 1851, during which Britain displayed its technological achievements.

SOCIAL CHANGE

What was life like for the mass of the population during this period? Nearly half the population of the country was very poor. These people formed a mobile labor pool that landlords and manufacturers employed for financial gain but feared. Those who provided work for the poor were applauded. The poor who could not find work were afforded aid only in their own parish and only under the most severe terms. By the end of the eighteenth century, increasing concern for the problems of poverty led to exhortations that the poor avoid drunkenness, gambling, and sexual activity in order to better themselves. Other reformers advocated educating members of the laboring class so they could benefit from religious instruction but not so much that they would be dissatisfied with their position in life. Poverty was seen as a moral fault on the part of the poor themselves. Thomas Malthus warned that philanthropic efforts to feed the poor would only increase their numbers and worsen their situation.

The children of the poor suffered from inadequate food and clothing, and infant mortality was high. Babies were often fed gin to pacify them. If jobs were available, children were sent out to work even when they were younger than five years old. The children of the wealthy were less likely to be hungry, but they tended to be dressed uncomfortably and to receive little affection since cuddling was frowned upon until the second half of the eighteenth century. About that same time, collections of nursery rhymes began appearing, followed by children's stories.

Some children were treated badly at home during this period, but most children were treated brutally at school. In fashionable schools, younger boys were bullied and beaten by older ones, as well as by their schoolmasters. Their education was primarily devoted to the study of Greek and Latin. Calls for educational reform began toward the end of the century. Girls' schools, where young ladies were taught manners, morals, and ladylike accomplishments, were problematic. They were suspected of instilling dangerous ideas of upward mobility into the daughters of the middle class and of valuing elegance over morality as far as the daughters of the rich were concerned.

The education of women was an issue often discussed during the period. Although it was generally agreed that women needed some education in order to bring up their children responsibly, it was believed that anything resembling academic learning would make them less desirable as wives and mothers. Many people believed that the most important quality to instill in women was cheerful self-sacrifice. Women had almost no power, whatever their social status. George I imprisoned his wife for life. Judge John Buller ruled that wife-beating was not illegal. Women writers were ridiculed. Some women, however, did manage to become educated and many women began to write during this period. Some of these women writers, such as Jane West, excused their writing on the grounds that it was necessary for them to engage in this occupation in order to support their families. They insisted on a domestic and a subordinate role for women, and because such writing supported the established order, it seemed a natural extension of woman's role as teacher of the young or dispenser of charity, and was accepted. During the 1790's, however, writers such as Mary Wollstonecraft and Mary Hays protested against the unfair treatment of women, the reaction against their writing was so great that other women writers became far more circumspect. In many of the conduct books written for women by women into the first decades of the nineteenth century, authors proclaimed that they had no interest in promoting the rights of women, only their well-being, which, they insisted, could best be served by selflessness.

There was less religious than political turmoil during the eighteenth century and the first half of the nineteenth century. At the beginning of this period, the great majority of the British public adhered to the Church of England, although some remained Roman Catholic and others were Dissenters, descendants of the Puritans. Most people were tired of the religious "enthusiasm" that had caused such dissension in the country during the seventeenth century. The Church stressed a rational Christianity, God as Creator and First Cause. Like ordinary citizens, the clergy enjoyed gambling, hunting, dancing, and the theater. A reaction against this lifestyle set in when John Wesley and his followers preached a more emotional religion to the poor beginning in 1739. The inroads made by these Methodists was a factor causing some adherents of the Church of England to take their spiritual lives and their duties to the poor more seriously; such individuals became known as Evangelicals. Among these Evangelicals, William Wilberforce was instrumental in the struggle to abolish the slave trade and Hannah More helped establish Sunday Schools in order to teach the poor to read.

The use of propaganda grew at this time. The government had launched an extensive propaganda campaign against democratic principles during the wars with France. Evangelicals and the heirs of the Dissenters continued to propagandize against drunkenness, the theater, and other forms of amusement. Even before Victoria ascended the throne, the prudery and Puritanism that became known as hallmarks of Victorianism distinguished English life, as did strict Sabbath observance. Although the Industrial Revolution transformed English life and the Reform Bill of 1832 and its successors extended the franchise to men of the middle class, the revolution in manners had the greatest immediate effect on England in the early nineteenth century.

Political Histories of Great Britain

Briggs, Asa. *The Making of Modern England, 1783-1867: The Age of Improvement.* New York: Harper & Row, 1965.
    Briggs provides a clear description of the changes in political, social and economic conditions that produced what the author sees as the transformation of England.

Colley, Linda. *Forging the Nation 1707-1837*. New Haven, Conn.: Yale University Press, 1992.
Colley's work provides a fascinating discussion of the factors influencing the development of Great Britain during the period. The book uses illustrations extensively and includes a chapter about the growing political power of women.

Derry, John W. *A Short History of Nineteenth Century England: 1793-1868*. New York: Mentor Books, 1963.
This brief political history of the period supplies a chronology and a reading list.

Webb, R. K. *Modern England From the Eighteenth Century to the Present*. New York: Dodd, Mead, 1980.
Webb's work is a complete, readable introduction to the period that stresses major political events in England without ignoring economic and social factors. A separate list of kings and queens of England and descriptions of the peerage, the Church of England, and the courts are supplied, as well as a bibliography and maps.

Williams, Glyn, and John Ramsden. *Ruling Britannia: A Political History of Britain 1688-1988*. London: Longman, 1990.
Williams and Ramsden provide a straightforward political history with maps and a valuable bibliography.

Social and Intellectual Histories

Anderson, Amanda. *Tainted Souls and Painted Faces: The Rhetoric of Fallenness in Victorian Culture*. Ithaca, N.Y.: Cornell University Press, 1993.
Anderson argues that images of fallen women pervaded British culture from about 1840 to 1860 because the fallen woman's lack of autonomy reflected the pervasive anxiety of the culture over tensions between materialism and idealism, selfhood and agency, purity and fallenness. She illustrates her ideas by discussions of novels, poetry, and essays.

Burton, Elizabeth. *The Pageant of Early Victorian England 1837- 1861*. New York: Charles Scribner's Sons, 1972.
An informal account of life during the period, describing Queen Victoria's life as well as the food, furniture, recreation, and medical care of her subjects.

Houghton, Walter E. *The Victorian Frame of Mind 1830-1870*. New Haven, Conn.: Yale University Press, 1975.
Houghton describes the characteristic attitudes that have become known as Victorianism, particularly its dogmatism, earnestness, hypocrisy and sexual prudery. It is a fascinating book enlivened by many quotations from the Victorians themselves.

Jarrett, Derek. *England in the Age of Hogarth*. New Haven, Conn.: Yale University Press, 1992.
Jarrett uses pictures by Hogarth to show how ordinary people lived during this era. He focuses on patriotism, bravery, earning a living, the use of leisure time, religious practices and the condition of women and children. There is a complete bibliography.

Levine, Joseph. *The Battle of the Books: History and Literature in the Augustan Age*. Ithaca, N.Y.: Cornell University Press, 1991.
Levine's book is narrowly focused on the dispute over the relative value of the Greek and Roman classics and sixteenth and seventeenth century literature and scholarship. It includes information about Madame Dacier, an early eighteenth century classical scholar, a very unusual figure for the age.

Plumb, J. H. *England in the Eighteenth Century: A Study of the Development of English Society*. Vol. 7 of *The Pelican History of England*. Baltimore: Penguin Books, 1952.
Plumb provides a clear, succinct discussion of events in England during the period.

_____. *Georgian Delights*. Boston: Little, Brown, 1980.
Copiously illustrated, this volume shows the prosperous middle classes enjoying themselves by decorating their houses and gardens, reading, attending the theater, concerts, and sporting events, and traveling, all for pleasure.

Pool, Daniel. *What Jane Austen Ate and Charles Dickens Knew: From Fox Hunting to Whist—The Facts of Daily Life in Nineteenth-Century England*. New York: Simon & Schuster, 1983.
Pool's entertaining book explains money, geography, manners, the courts, clothing, games—many of the facets of life in the nineteenth century that might puzzle modern readers. It also includes a glossary of terms that are no longer familiar to current readers.

Quinlan, Maurice J. *Victorian Prelude: A History of English Manners 1700-1830.* Hamden, Conn.: Archon Books, 1965.
A readable book documenting crucial changes in taste and behavior that occurred during the period. There is a particularly valuable chapter on women's issues and a bibliography.

Reed, Michael. *The Georgian Triumph 1700-1830.* London: Routledge & Kegan Paul, 1983.
This illustrated volume stresses man's interaction with his environment in terms of geography, architecture, agriculture and the growing industrialization of the time. Very informative chapters describe Britain at the beginning and at the end of this period. In addition, an extensive bibliography is provided.

Rogers, Pat, ed. *The Context of English Literature: The Eighteenth Century.* New York: Holmes & Meier, 1978.
Politics, religion, science and art are discussed in relation to literature. The excellent introduction discusses the influence of classical literature and French literature on the writing of the time, as well as the economics of publishing. In addition, the book traces the development of the essay, the novel, and literary criticism. It is particularly valuable for its discussions of women writers. It is illustrated and provides a helpful time line and extensive bibliographies.

Sambrook, James. *The Eighteenth Century: The Intellectual and Cultural Context of English Literature, 1700-1789.* London: Longman, 1986
Sambrook provides a rather dense discussion of the scientific, religious, political, and aesthetic ideas of the era. His bibliography is extensive, and its chronology is helpful, but it ignores the condition of women and their writing. Illustrated.

LITERATURE: A NEW AUDIENCE AND A NEW GENRE

Great changes in literature as a mode of expression occurred during this period. Early in the eighteenth century, classically educated male writers wrote primarily for the relatively small group who also were familiar with the Latin and Greek classics that had been the staple of a gentlemen's education since the Renaissance. These authors patterned their work on the work of Latin poets such as Virgil, Horace, and Juvenal. They also attempted to follow what they conceived to be classical rules of decorum in poetry and drama. Satire was an important mode of expression whose best-known practitioners were Jonathan Swift and Alexander Pope. Women were often their target. Pope was also a translator of a very popular version of Homer's *Iliad* and *Odyssey*.

The essay, as practiced by Joseph Addison, Richard Steele, and Samuel Johnson, became a very popular form and new periodicals featuring them were founded. The Neoclassic insistence on rules encouraged Johnson to compile his *Dictionary*. The success of these works, and the increase in literacy during the period undermined the importance of aristocratic patrons as more and more authors could achieve financial (and literary) independence by writing.

The drama enjoyed great success. Playwrights such as John Dryden attempted to follow what they believed to be Aristotle's prescriptions for the drama and even revised Shakespeare's plays to fit the taste of the age. When censorship forced Henry Fielding to stop writing for the stage, he turned to the newest literary form, the novel.

The success of the novel, heralded by the publication of Samuel Richardson's *Pamela* and *Clarissa*, as well as Henry Fielding's *Joseph Andrews* and *Tom Jones*, was partially the result of its appeal to women and the newly important middle classes. Women had published essays in the periodicals and by the end of the century they were producing novels and poetry as well.

By the end of the eighteenth century, the tastes of the age had shifted from delight in the artificial, the intellectual, and the classic to an interest in emotion, nature, the insane, the child. The age of sensibility and its stress on feelings, prepared the way for Romanticism, with its insistence on the importance of freedom, the imagination, and spontaneity.

Histories of English Literature

Barrell, John. *English Literature in History 1730-80: An Equal, Wide Survey*. New York: St. Martin's Press, 1983.
Barrell discusses how literary figures saw their era, its diversity, philosophy, and language. Women writers receive almost no mention.

Bredvold, Louis. *The Literature of the Restoration and the Eighteenth Century 1660-1798*. London: Collier-Macmillan, 1950.
A valuable discussion of major figures and of the beginnings of Romanticism, particularly the importance of sensibility as it relates to the eighteenth century novel.

Butler, Marilyn. *Romantics, Rebels and Reactionaries: English Literature and Its Background 1760-1830*. New York: Oxford University Press, 1982.
  Butler reviews the history of criticism of Romanticism and goes on to analyze it in political terms, asserting that the earlier secular-minded Romantics rebelled against the established order, causing a strong reaction against rebellion. Women authors such as Mary Wollstonecraft, Maria Edgeworth, Ann Radcliffe, and Jane Austen are given significant coverage. An excellent chronology is provided.

Butt, John. *The Mid-Eighteenth Century*. Edited by Geoffrey Carnall. Oxford: Clarendon Press, 1979.
  A fairly complete survey of the literature of the period. Its reading lists are particularly helpful for research on lesser-known writers.

Cambridge History of English Literature. Vols. 9 and 10. Edited by A. D. Ward and A. R. Walker. Cambridge, England: Cambridge University Press, 1912.
  Although quite dated, this survey is very complete and provides at least basic information on almost everyone who wrote during the nineteenth century.

Chambers, Robert. *Chambers's Cyclopaedia of English Literature. Vol. 2: The Eighteenth Century*. Edited by David Patrick and revised by J. Liddell Geddie. 1938. Reprint. Detroit: Gale Research, 1978.
  The language here is dated but the book's coverage is wide, as it quotes from the work of even the most obscure writers.

Churchill, Reginald C. *English Literature of the Nineteenth Century*. Reprint. Freeport, N.Y.: Books for Libraries Press, 1970.
  First published in 1951, Churchill's work is a straightforward, if dated, history of nineteenth century literature concentrating on the major figures but also discussing the periodicals, the journalists, and other writers.

Curran, Stuart, ed. *Cambridge Companion to British Romanticism*. Cambridge, England: Cambridge University Press, 1993.
  This book provides a particularly valuable series of essays on various aspects of Romanticism including critical theory and the relationship of Romanticism to political events, philosophy, and art. A revisionist and more accurate view of the writing of the age results from a study of popular writing and periodicals. Women writers are treated in a

separate chapter but are also mentioned throughout the book, which includes a very complete chronology and bibliography.

Elton, Oliver. *A Survey of English Literature 1730-1780*. London: Edward Arnold, 1928.
Although Elton's work is dated, it contains useful information on obscure authors.

Ford, Boris, ed. *The Pelican Guide to English Literature: Vol. 4 From Dryden to Johnson*. Harmondsworth, Middlesex, England: Penguin Books, 1973.
This literary guide provides a helpful introduction and informative chapters on the social currents, the literary scene, and language of the times. Individual essays are limited to major male figures for the most part.

Sampson, George. *Cambridge Concise History of English Literature*. 3d ed. Edited and revised by R. C. Churchill. London: Cambridge University Press, 1970.
A convenient, concise history providing basic information such as names and dates.

Todd, Janet. *Sensibility: An Introduction*. London: Methuen, 1986.
Todd provides a clear, complete discussion of sensibility in drama, poetry, and fiction. She discusses the meaning of the term and its relationship to seventeenth and eighteenth century philosophy. At its height, the cult of sensibility attracted women writers and well as a female audience. Therefore, it is crucial to a study of women's literature. Men and women playwrights, poets, and novelists are discussed. The attacks on the literature of sensibility are noted as well as its continued existence in melodrama and the popular novel. The bibliography is dated.

Tucker, Martin, ed. *The Critical Temper: A Survey of Modern Criticism on English and American Literature from the Beginnings to the Twentieth Century*. New York: Continuum, 1985.
This series provides excerpts from current criticism of major writers of the age, providing insight into the relationship between writers and their modern interpreters.

Vinson, James, ed. *St. James Reference Guide to English Literature. Vol. 2: The Restoration and Eighteenth Century*. Chicago: St. James Press, 1985.

A fine introduction to the period, this book describes the characteristics of the Augustan age as far as literature is concerned. It also discusses Neoclassic aesthetics and the important (male) writers, and provides an excellent reading list.

_____, ed. *St. James Reference Guide to English Literature: Vol. 3: The Romantic and Victorian Periods.* Chicago: St. James Press, 1985.
This guide explains Romanticism and discusses its major (male) figures. It also provides reading lists.

_____, ed. *St. James Reference Guide to English Literature. Vol. 4: The Novel to 1900.* Chicago: St. James Press, 1985.
A helpful history of the novel that also provides an excellent reading list.

Wilson, Carol Shiner, and Joel Haefner, eds. *Re-Visioning Romanticism: British Women Writers, 1776-1837.* Philadelphia: University of Pennsylvania Press, 1994.
In their introduction, Wilson and Haefner provide an excellent survey of the history of criticism of romantic literature. They document the shifts in the canon and show how women writers deleted from the canon are now being restored to it. They believe that in the future "Romanticisms" will be studied and the critic will identify his own ideology. They also believe that works will be rediscovered and added to the canon.

A Brief Chronology of Major Events

1700	William and Mary ruled England.
1701	War with France began.
1702	Anne became queen of England.
1707	England and Scotland became the United Kingdom.
1714	George I, of Hanover in Germany, became king of England.
1715	Robert Walpole became prime minister.
1745	Prince Charles Edward, the grandson of James II, invaded Scotland and England.
1746	After Charles Edward Stuart was defeated at Culloden, England wreaked its vengeance on the Scots Highlanders, destroying the clan system and much of the countryside.
1756	The Seven Years' War with France began.

1757	William Pitt became prime minister and pursued wars with France in North America and India. England became a colonial power in Africa as well.

1757   William Pitt became prime minister and pursued wars with France in North America and India. England became a colonial power in Africa as well.

1760   George III became king.

1776   America declared its independence.

1780   The Gordon Riots, during which the population demonstrated against extending rights to Roman Catholics, took place.

1789   The French Revolution began.

1793   War with France began.

1811   The Prince of Wales became Regent.

1815   Napoleon was defeated.

1819   The Peterloo Massacre, during which government forces killed protesters, took place.

1832   The Reform Bill was passed, extending the vote to some middle-class men and beginning a period of electoral reforms that eventually widened suffrage to most men.

1837   Victoria became queen.

1841   Robert Peel became prime minister and promoted social and economic reforms.

1846   The Corn Laws, which favored agricultural interests over city dwellers, were repealed.

1851   The Great Exhibition took place, allowing Great Britain to display its technological achievements.

Chapter 2

LITERATURE WRITTEN BY WOMEN, 1700-1850

English women have been writing in the face of constant discouragement since the Middle Ages. The Renaissance saw an increase in the number of educated women and not surprisingly, an increase in female authorship. In the seventeenth century, some women preached and wrote on religious subjects.

Professional women writers became important after the Restoration in 1660. The first, Aphra Behn, wrote fourteen plays, many poems, and important prose fiction. She was denounced for irregularities in her personal life, and died in poverty. Nevertheless, she was followed by many other women writers. Their prose fiction developed into the novel.

The second half of the eighteenth century saw an increase in the number of women readers and women writers. The latter were tolerated as long as they avoided traditional masculine subjects such as theology and philosophy, or what were considered masculine forms such as satire or the epic. Since nearly all women lacked "learning," a knowledge of the Greek and Latin classics, they were advised not to write on serious subjects. Nevertheless, they were permitted to indulge themselves in writing less substantial literature, such as the periodical article or the novel. The growing popularity of the cult of sensibility, which extolled feeling over reason, sympathy for the oppressed, the poor, children, animals, a love for nature and the domestic, afforded them a clear field.

Male and female novelists provided different portraits of female characters. Samuel Richardson, who published *Clarissa* in 1747-1748, glorified the suffering woman, vulnerable not only to tears and blushes but also to sexual violation and death. Henry Fielding's *Amelia* (1751) glorified the long-suffering, but thoroughly loyal wife. Some women novelists created heroines who used submissive rhetoric but whose very passivity gave them power over their husbands, despite their vulnerability. Others, however, stressed the power of mothers. This emphasis seemed more plausible to most readers and enabled the writers to avoid confronting women's deplorably inferior legal and social status.

The American and French Revolutions gave an added dimension to the novel of sensibility as villains became representatives of the corrupt aristocratic culture or the repressive older generation. Mary Wollstonecraft, Helen Maria Williams, and Mary Hays are best known for portraying such exploitation of the vulnerable. Radical thinkers, who often were

Dissenters rather than members of the Established Church and middle class rather than aristocrats, identified women as members of an oppressed class, and hoped that the blessings of liberty could spread from France and America to British women. They believed that the idea of liberty was British and had influenced the American and French Revolutions in the first place.

With the arrest of the French royal family and the persecution of the aristocrats, English public opinion changed. The French revolutionaries, and those who sided with them in England, were denounced as evil and immoral destroyers. Many women writers were condemned, particularly Mary Wollstonecraft and Mary Hays who wrote in favor of women's rights. Conservative women writers denounced them, or any woman who would stray from the domestic sphere and renounce the ideology of patriarchy. This ideology insisted on the primacy of the male head of the household because he was more rational and, therefore, more fit to rule. The woman's role involved pleasing her husband by running his household efficiently, bearing his children and bringing them up properly. Ironically, the very conservative women writers who advocated this ideology were often neither wives nor mothers, and became very influential in the public sphere.

By the end of the 1790's, the English were concerned with the spread of the Revolution in Europe under Napoleon and France's imperialist designs on the rest of the world. British citizens who sympathized with the French were harassed; censorship was increased. Economic hardships caused by the war with France worsened. Corruption and vice were attacked as weakening England in its struggle. Women writers continued to grow in importance, some attacking patriarchy, most defending it but undermining it by their own success. Women authors such as Ann Radcliffe produced gothic novels, involving the persecution of a blameless heroine. Others wrote books of advice on conduct and novels which were also meant to teach proper behavior. Fanny Burney achieved literary fame with *Evelina* (1778), a novel of a young girl's entrance into society.

Middle-class women became active in charity and educational work among the poor. Despite being excluded from political life, women were seen as constituting the moral foundation of the nation. This moral stature was thought to entitle women to increased educational opportunities and an improved social position. A backlash against the increased cultural power of women, and the political conservatism of the 1790's, led to vicious attacks on women writers. This hostility discouraged many women from publishing under their own names, from writing professionally as journalists or editors, or from attempting to write in the "important" genres.

Women did not publish work in the sciences except as popularizers or writers for children. Most of their history writing took the form of novels and biographies. Lives and letters of women writers began to appear, primarily to demonstrate that domesticity was compatible with female authorship. Also, religious autobiographies were published, as well as fictionalized biographies of prostitutes, criminals, and a woman soldier, Susannah Cope. Women also produced travel writing.

During the nineteenth century, critics writing for the highly influential periodicals became more likely to attack women writers whom they saw as either puritanical or immoral. During the 1790's, male Romantic poets, including William Wordsworth and Samuel Taylor Coleridge, appropriated genres used by women poets, such as the verse narrative and the personal lyric, as well as topics heretofore considered feminine, such as tales of heroism in everyday life and descriptions of places. They also used techniques developed by women: personal expression, loose form, domestic realism, and the use of allusions to everyday events rather than classical allusions. Women continued to dominate as novelists until Sir Walter Scott turned from poetry and began to publish novels in 1814.

One province of women writers had been the subjective. They had written about feelings, but this came to be seen as egotistic individualism. After 1800, few women writers wrote about passion because (male) critics insisted that they limit themselves to the domestic and the didactic. Nevertheless, women novelists, writing about women for women, constituted a significant proportion of writers. Their work was acceptable because it could be performed at home. It was educational, and teaching was an approved female function, and it was done for the good of others. Any financial rewards were presumed to be necessary for the support of impoverished relatives. As long as women novelists apologized sufficiently and upheld patriarchal ideology, their work, condescended to by male critics, was approved chivalrously.

Women novelists often discussed the conflict between the demands of society and the needs of the self, usually advocating repression as a necessity. The greatest novelist of the period, Jane Austen, demonstrated how her heroines were able to forge a community, if a very limited one, in which the legitimate demands of the self could be met. In her novels, humor replaced didacticism. Other novelists, such as Maria Edgeworth, helped unify the nation by writing about local language, history, and culture while subsuming the local into the national as represented by the narrator and the reader. Historical novels became popular, and the concept of chivalry was refigured by stressing the chivalric virtues rather than social status.

The most popular poet of the time, Felicia Hemans, began by writing patriotic poetry, but when she began to doubt that Britain was always the favorite of history, she too wrote about nature, subjectivity, and domesticity. The work of other women poets was very popular, but their publications, like those of nearly all the women writers of the early nineteenth century, came to be associated with popular culture, fit only for the young and the less educated. Toward the middle of the nineteenth century, serious women writers such as the Brontës and George Eliot believed they needed to publish under men's names in order to be taken seriously.

ANTHOLOGIES OF WRITING BY WOMEN

Ferguson, Moira, ed. *First Feminists: British Women Writers 1578-1799*. Bloomington: Indiana University Press, 1985.

An anthology of writing by twenty-eight women who protest against the subordination of women and the slave trade. These women came from different backgrounds and wrote in different genres, but they were united in defending women against charges of vanity and insisted on their right to speak. Biographical head notes and brief bibliographies are included. The anthology includes a list of works by women of the period that are not excerpted but that also promote women's rights and the antislavery movement.

Gilbert, Sandra M., and Susan Gubar, eds. *The Norton Anthology of Literature by Women: The Tradition in English*. New York: W. W. Norton, 1985. 2d ed. New York: W. W. Norton, 1996.

A fairly complete anthology with helpful introductions to the period and head notes about the English and American authors whose work is included.

Galleons, Joan, ed. *By a Woman Writt: Literature from Six Centuries By and About Women*. Indianapolis: Bobbs-Merrill, 1973.

This collection provides selected excerpts from works by fairly well known women writers accompanied by their picture and a brief head note giving biographical information.

Rogers, Katherine M., and William McCarthy, eds. *The Meridian Anthology of Early Women Writers: British Literary Women from Aphra Behn to Maria Edgeworth 1660-1800*. New York: New American Library, 1987.

The introduction to this anthology discusses all the disabilities discouraging women from writing during this period. They lacked education, financial independence, experience outside the home, self-confidence. Nevertheless, by the end of this period, women writers could compete successfully with men. Selections from the works of Aphra Behn, Mary Astell, Elizabeth Manley, Mary Wortley Montagu, Hester Piozzi, Anna Laetitia Barbauld, Frances Burney, Mary Hays, Maria Edgeworth, Katherine Philips, "Ephelia," Anne Killigrew, Mary Collyer, Elizabeth Carter, Mary Leapor, Hannah More, Charlotte Smith, and Ann Yearsley are included, headed by a brief description of each writer's life and works. The editors also provide a bibliography.

BIBLIOGRAPHIES OF WOMEN'S WRITING

Alston, R. C. *A Checklist of Women Writers, 1801-1900: Fiction, Verse, Drama.* Boston: G. K. Hall, 1990.
Alston lists more than seventeen thousand texts written in English by women and published in the British Isles of other British territory. She supplies the name of the author, as well as the title of the book and the city and year in which it was published. She does not include translations or children's literature.

Backscheider, Paula, Felicity Nussbaum, and Philip Anderson. *An Annotated Bibliography of Twentieth Century Critical Studies of Women and Literature 1660-1800.* New York: Garland, 1977.
The compilers list scholarly and critical books and articles published between 1900 and 1975. One section is devoted to general criticism, another organizes the articles according to the genre of the work discussed, while yet another is devoted to the opinions of women that appeared in writings of the major male authors of the time. The last section lists criticism of individual women writers.

de Jackson, J. R. *Romantic Poetry by Women 1770-1835: A Bibliography.* Oxford: Clarendon Press, 1993.
This bibliography lists all books of poetry by women written during the period. These books are listed in order of publication, and the bibliography includes poetry by American as well as British women. De Jackson's work is valuable because it includes the works of obscure poets. Biographical information on the poets is included.

Schwartz, Marda Lacey. *Articles on British Women Writers 1960-1975: A Bibliography.* Santa Barbara, Calif.: ABC-Clio, 1977.
Schwartz lists articles published in English-speaking countries, giving the names of the women writers, their nationality, and their birth and death dates, if known. In the section concerned with general works, the articles are listed according to critic. The section devoted to individual authors lists their works and the works published about them. Writers are included if they had at least one article published about them between 1960 and 1975.

_____. *Articles on British Women Writers 1976-1984: A Bibliography.* Santa Barbara, Calif.: ABC-Clio, 1986.
A sequel to the work by Schwartz cited above, this volume lists articles covering the period from 1975 to 1985, which the compiler notes was a very fruitful time for women's studies.

GUIDES TO WOMEN'S LITERATURE

Blain, Virginia, Isobel Grundy, and Patricia Clements. *The Feminist Companion to Literature in English.* New Haven, Conn.: Yale University Press, 1990.
A useful literary guide including pertinent topics relating to women's literature as well as biographical information about women authors. Each entry is, by necessity, fairly brief.

Schlueter, Paul, and June Schlueter. *An Encyclopedia of British Woman Writers.* New York: Garland, 1988.
This guide lists women authors, their works, and provides a very short list of material about them.

Shattuck, Joanne. *The Oxford Guide to British Woman Writers.* New York: Oxford University Press, 1993.
Part of the noted Oxford series of literary guides, this work includes biographical information and also provides a brief guide to further reading.

Todd, Janet. *A Dictionary of British and American Women Writers 1660-1800.* Totowa, N.J.: Rowman & Allanheld, 1985.
Compiled by a noted scholar, this dictionary contains brief entries that describe the life and work of women writers.

WOMEN'S LITERATURE: HISTORY AND CRITICISM

Adburgham, Alison. *Women in Print: Writing Women and Women's Magazines From the Restoration to the Accession of Victoria.* London: Allen
& Unwin, 1972.
This history of writing by women primarily for women discusses not
only fiction but also books and articles giving advice, cookbooks, and
articles about fashion. It also discusses women printers and book
sellers of the time as well as the role of circulating libraries. This
illustrated work also supplies a chronological list of English periodicals.

Agress, Lynne. *The Feminine Irony: Women on Women in Early Nineteenth Century English Literature.* Lanham, Md.: University Press of
America, 1984.
Agress describes the political, social and economic conditions that
caused women to become readers and writers from about 1750 on,
asserting that most women accepted their subordinate position in
society. She also shows the connections between women's roles and
the domestic and gothic novel forms.

Alexander, Meena. *Woman in Romanticism: Mary Wollstonecraft,
Dorothy Wordsworth and Mary Shelley.* Savage, Md.: Barnes & Noble,
1989.
The introduction gives a clear picture of the pressures against which
women had to struggle to write during this period. The author maintains, for example, that women authors either needed to renounce the
world and write meditatively or confront authority violently, using
imagery related to their own bodies, maternity, and nurture of the
young. Because they were women, they were not permitted to exalt the
individual vision that sustained and inspired male Romantic poets. As
a result, they were forced into other roles.

Anderson, Amanda. *Tainted Souls and Painted Faces: The Rhetoric of
Fallenness in Victorian Culture.* Ithaca, N.Y.: Cornell University Press,
1993.
The author has found that women's writing treats the problem of the
fallen woman and its solutions differently from texts written by men.
Women writers believed that both pure and fallen women had much in
common. They both lacked power and a strong sense of identity;
neither was sexually voracious. Elizabeth Gaskell, who believed in
individual charitable efforts, shows fallen women rescued by good

women in *Ruth* and in *Mary Barton*. Anderson believes she hopes her readers will be inspired to help others. In the subplot of *Aurora Leigh*, Elizabeth Barrett Browning focuses on a fallen woman with whom the female artist must come to terms. The plot attempts to bring together art and philanthropy, literature and social action.

Auerbach, Nina. *Romantic Imprisonment: Women and Other Glorified Outcasts*. New York: Columbia University Press, 1985.

Auerbach sees woman's lot, particularly the woman writer's lot, in terms of tension between security and imprisonment. She asserts that romantic fiction is obsessed with prisons or prison-type settings as well as themes and forms that imprison both characters and readers. She also writes about the relationships between women and children in fiction.

Ballaster, Ros. *Seductive Forms: Women's Amatory Fiction from 1684-1740*. Oxford: Clarendon Press, 1992.

This book provides a history of critical theories about literature, then asserts that the literature concerned with love written by women concerns delayed sexual gratification and therefore, has a porno-graphic effect. The book sees the act of reading someone else's letters in epistolary novels to be the symbolic equivalent of rape and also finds that domestic novels represented a revolt against the sexuality of the earlier epistolary novels.

Barreca, Regina. *Last Laughs: Perspectives on Women and Comedy*. New York: Gordon & Breach, 1988.

Barreca asserts that women's comedy differs from men's comedy in that it is based on aggression and rage. This difference, as well as its method of attacking patriarchy covertly, makes women's comedy difficult for male critics to understand. She also finds a different use of language and different endings in women's literature, involving recognition rather than resolution, as well as a lesser degree of didac-ticism.

Basham, Diana. *The Trial of Women: Feminism and the Occult Sciences in Victorian Literature and Society*. London: Macmillan, 1992.

Basham contends that the revival of interest in the occult was con-nected with an interest in what was considered to be woman's myste-rious nature. To show that they were not naturally evil, women turned to philanthropy and women writers asserted that women's suffering had spiritual significance. The author believes that Mary Shelley would not allow Dr. Frankenstein to create a female monster because she did not want to portray an evil woman. Basham believes that other novels combined realism with fantasy to show that reality can have a fantastic quality.

Blake, Katherine. *Love and the Woman Question in Victorian Literature: The Art of Self-Postponement.* Sussex, N.J.: Harvester Press, 1983.
Blake believes that Victorian heroines do not act because they are waiting for either love or salvation. In Christina Rossetti's poems they do not come in time, but she accepts this. George Eliot, through Dorothea Brooke, protests it. Charlotte Brontë shows how self-postponement operates in *Villette*. Victorian writers, for example, George Eliot and Elizabeth Barrett Browning, show women torn between love and art. George Gissing, Thomas Hardy, and Olive Schreiner are also discussed using a feminist and neo-Freudian critical approach.

Craft-Fairchild, Catherine. *Masquerade and Gender: Disguise and Female Identity in Eighteenth-Century Fictions by Women.* University Park: Pennsylvania State University Press, 1993.
According to Craft-Fairchild, male writers believed that the masquerade liberated women. Women disagreed, but the book asserts that the masquerade was related to the eighteenth century idea of femininity. The change from fiction involving a female rake to the domestic novel during the time is noted. The author makes use of psychoanalytic theory in her argument.

Cross, Nigel. "The Female Drudge: Women Novelists and Their Publishers." In *The Common Writer: Life in Nineteenth Century Grub Street.* New York: Cambridge University Press, 1985.
The author maintains that twenty percent of nineteenth century writers were women. Because of their lack of education and their minimal employment opportunities they wrote fiction. They and their readers were assumed to be inferior and the attacks on them must have discouraged many women from writing. Records of the Literary Fund, which was established to provide financial aid for impoverished writers, show that many women writers needed charity as they faced old age. Despite their economic plight, most of these novelists were conservative politically.

Curran, Stuart. "The I Altered." In *Romanticism and Feminism*, edited by Anne K. Mellor, pp. 185-207. Bloomington: Indiana University Press, 1988.
Curran's essay discusses the women writers who were very popular during the late eighteenth and early nineteenth centuries and have

begun to be rediscovered. Women writers actually dominated the field and made their living by writing. They used colloquial diction and minute observation of daily life to express a moral vision and compassion for their subjects. Asserting women's ability to think as well as to feel, they overcame the enormous difficulties of their own lives by writing. Their influence on later writers is significant even though it has been undervalued.

Ezell, Margaret. *Writing Women's Literary History*. Baltimore: The Johns Hopkins University Press, 1993.
Ezell's work discusses critical theory as it relates to the establishment of the literary canon. It laments the neglect of women's writing before the eighteenth century, which Ezell attributes to a devaluing of what the late twentieth century considers private writing. Two interesting chapters discuss eighteenth and nineteenth century anthologies of earlier women's writing, which were characterized by apologies for the inadequacy of either the author or the work.

Favret, Mary A. *Romantic Correspondence: Women, Politics, and the Fiction of Letters*. New York: Cambridge University Press, 1993.
According to Favret, letters have conventionally been associated in eighteenth century fiction with sentimental heroines, seductive villains, interiors, and sexual vulnerability, but later in the century they become political. As they are a tool available to almost anyone, letters can be used to incite class conflict, social upheaval, even civil war.

Ferguson, Moira. *Colonialism and Gender Relations from Mary Wollstonecraft to Jamaica Kincaid*. New York: Columbia University Press, 1993.
The author connects antislavery agitation to agitation for women's rights by radical women writers and moral improvement of the British upper classes on the part of more conservative women writers.

_____. *Subject to Others: British Women Writers and Colonial Slavery 1670-1834*. New York: Routledge, 1992.
In this work, Ferguson asserts that English women wrote against the cruelty of slavery until the French Revolution, when they began to write about the right to be free. After 1793, when Britain fought France, talk of political rights for black people was replaced by a sentimental view of those blacks who would accept European control. Antislavery agitation provided an impetus for the struggle for women's rights, but the women involved had no real knowledge of or respect for blacks.

Figes, Eva. *Sex and Subterfuge: Women Writers to 1850.* London: Macmillan, 1982. Reprint. New York: Persea Books, 1988.

Figes shows how women novelists transformed their disabilities as women novelists into assets as they transformed the novel from the picaresque to the gothic and the sentimental novel to the courtship novel.

Gilbert, Sandra M., and Susan Gubar. *The Madwoman in the Attic: The Woman Writer and the Nineteenth Century Literary Imagination.* New Haven, Conn.: Yale University Press, 1979.

An invaluable guide to women's literature in general and a seminal work in feminist critical theory. The authors assert that women's writing was strongly affected by anxiety over whether it was proper for women to write at all as well as rage over women's position in society.

_____. "Literature of the Seventeenth and Eighteenth Centuries." In *The Norton Anthology of Literature by Women: The Tradition in English.* New York: W. W. Norton, 1985.

This chapter provides a brief but informative discussion of the history of the period, in America as well as in England, discussing the political background, Puritanism, the new science, urbanization, contemporary images of women, the realities of women's lives, and writing as a profession for women.

_____. "Literature of the Nineteenth Century." In *The Norton Anthology of Literature by Women: The Tradition in English.* New York: W. W. Norton, 1985.

This chapter discusses how revolution, reform, industrialism, imperialism, and religious doubts affected both England and America. It also discusses the widening of woman's sphere and the movement for women's rights. Very briefly, it explores the relationship of women's writing to men's writing of the period.

Krueger, Christine. *The Reader's Repentance: Women Preachers, Women Writers and Nineteenth Century Social Discourse.* Chicago: University of Chicago Press, 1992.

Krueger's work demonstrates how women preachers, who were far more common during the nineteenth century than scholars used to believe, gave women writers the authority to speak, to use scriptural language, and to characterize male exploitation of women as sin. Since they were Evangelicals, they took their rhetoric from that movement. They attributed their authority to divine inspiration and they saw their audience as potential converts. Their relationship to patriarchal ideology was complex, but the mere existence of such famous preachers as Mary Bosanquet Fletcher, Sarah Crosby, and Joanna Southcott prepared the way for Hannah More who influenced Charlotte Elizabeth Tonna who, in turn, influenced Elizabeth Gaskell. Their principle contribution to women's writing was to cast social problems in moral terms.

Gorsky, Susan R. *Femininity to Feminism: Women and Literature in the Nineteenth Century*. New York: Twayne, 1992.
Gorsky asserts that nineteenth century literature not only gave a fairly realistic picture of life but also attempted to teach readers how to live, idealizing the family and the role of the housewife. The book discusses the realities of women's lives: marriage, children, education, death, divorce, involvement in feminist issues, and compares them with their representation in books. A helpful chronology of events in women's history and literature is provided.

Homans, Margaret. "Representation, Reproduction, and Women's Place in Language." In *Bearing the Word: Language and Female Experience in Nineteenth-Century Women's Writing*. Chicago: University of Chicago Press, 1986.
Homans attempts a revision of Jacques Lacan's theory of writing that sees writing as a male act deriving from the separation of the baby boy from his mother and his receiving symbolic language as a recompense. She bases her work on Nancy Chodorow's revision of the Lacanian myth, in which Chodorow sees writing as a form of motherhood. Homans realizes, however, that nineteenth century women's writing might best be understood by its reaction to the appropriation of language by an androcentric culture that devalues the maternal and the literal, all that has to do with the female.

Kelly, Gary. *Women, Writing and Revolution 1790-1827*. Oxford: Clarendon Press, 1993.
A valuable discussion of the impact of the cultural revolution affecting literature during the period and how women authors reacted to it. Kelly provides helpful analyses of the effect of historical events and contemporary reviews on literary form as well as content, and he shows how, by the end of the period, women's writing had become marginalized and trivialized.

Lane, Maggie. *Literary Daughters*. New York: St. Martin's Press, 1989.

Lane believes that many women authors, particularly Fanny Burney, Maria Edgeworth, Elizabeth Barrett Browning, Charlotte Brontë, and George Eliot, were emotionally dependent on their fathers. She also discusses the relationships of other women authors with their fathers.

Mellor, Anne K., ed. *Romanticism and Feminism*. Bloomington: Indiana University Press, 1988.
Mellor attempts to explain how male poets appropriated Romanticism for themselves. Men not only controlled publishing and reviewing and claimed ownership of the intellectual realm but also took over the realm of feelings by writing sensibility novels. Some men even saw themselves as having maternal qualities. Mellor asserts that Romanticism itself is historically masculine in its insistence that emotions and ideas are powerful.

Mermin, Dorothy. *Godiva's Ride: Women of Letters in England, 1830-1880*. Bloomington: Indiana University Press, 1993.
Merman asserts that British culture caused women writers to be apologetic about their work, and shy about exposing themselves. For the most part, however, reviewers condescended toward them, valuing their work for its sincerity and morality. Because of this fear of exposure, few women wrote lyric poetry. Lack of education and the censure of women who were educated, discouraged women from writing serious nonfiction prose, except for religious works. These works were tolerated because religion was were seen as women's province. By the end of the nineteenth century, women's writing was derided for a lack of artistry.

Messenger, Ann. *His and Hers: Essays in Restoration and Eighteenth Century Literature*. Lexington: University Press of Kentucky, 1986.
Messenger compares selected women poets, dramatists and essayists with their better known male contemporaries in order to show that both used traditional forms and conventional genres to confront similar issues. Because women's experience was different, the author feels their writing was in some ways more original and deserves a reappraisal. Her appendix includes selected poems by Ann Pettigrew (1660-1685), Ann Finch, Countess of Winshilsea (1661-1720), and Anna Laetitia Barbauld (1743-1825).

Moers, Ellen. *Literary Women*. Garden City, N.Y.: Doubleday, 1976.
This classic study connects the major late eighteenth and nineteenth century English women novelists and poets: Jane Austen, Fanny Burney, Ann Radcliffe, the Brontës, Mrs. Gaskell, Elizabeth Barrett

Browning, and Christina Rossetti, with their counterparts in America and France as well as with twentieth century American women writers. For example, the influence of Mme de Genlis on Jane Austen as well as the influence of Mme de Staël on George Eliot is discussed, as are the lives and works of Harriet Beecher Stowe, Louisa May Alcott, and Emily Dickinson. Indeed, women writers are shown to share many concerns and experiences and to have strongly influenced each other. The bibliography is particularly helpful.

Newton, Judith L. *Women, Power and Subversion: Social Strategies in British Fiction 1778-1860*. Athens: University of Georgia Press, 1986. Patriarchal ideology denies women power but concedes them influence in the domestic arena if they are selfless, according to Newton. Reflecting their authors' experience, many heroines seek power but in the end limit themselves to influence. This concern for power may be a result of capitalism creating opportunities for economic advancement for men but limiting those for women. Newton contends that even though most fiction by women contained a conservative message, the fact that women writers insisted power relationships were not immutable was ultimately revolutionary.

Poovey, Mary. "The Proper Lady." In *The Proper Lady and the Woman Writer: Ideology as Style in the Works of Mary Wollstonecraft, Mary Shelley, and Jane Austen*. Chicago: University of Chicago Press, 1984. In this chapter, Poovey traces the change in British culture from misogyny to an idealization of women, which it attributes in part to capitalism and the influence of Puritanism and, later, the Evangelicals. As industry moved out of the home, women lost economic power, but they gained the occupation of helping the poor. Capitalism increased women's power as consumers, as negotiable entities in marriage, and as indoctrinators of their children. The idealization of modesty and self-restraint urged by social pressures began to seem natural. Nevertheless, these traits needed constant cultivation, which women received from conduct books, the books of advice on behavior addressed to young ladies. The French Revolution, while it increased calls for female equality, engendered a backlash against it. Women, particularly women writers, did assert their right to publish, but they excused their writing on the grounds of their own ignorance, or their desire to help others, or financial need. Poovey asserts convincingly that their literary style, particularly the styles of Jane Austen, Mary Wollstonecraft, and Mary Shelley, was affected by the authors' need to harmonize the ideals of "the proper lady and the woman writer."

Richardson, Alan. "Romanticism and the Colonization of the Feminine."
In *Romanticism and Feminism*, edited by Anne K. Mellor, pp. 13-25.
Bloomington: Indiana University Press, 1988.
This essay describes how women were shut out of the literary tradition
not only because of their lack of education and opportunities to publish
but also because the male writers of the period had appropriated
feminine qualities such as sensibility and nurturing for themselves.

Rogers, Katherine M. *Feminism in Eighteenth Century England*. Urbana:
University of Illinois Press, 1982.
Rogers discusses the change in the position of women during the
eighteenth century due to a new emphasis on marriages based on love,
and the increase in female education. These factors increased the
amount of reading and writing by women. She discusses the influence
of Locke and rationalism on women as well as the influence of the new
emphasis on "feeling." Rogers describes the limitations on women in
a patriarchal society and how that led them to write novels. She also
discusses the influence of Samuel Richardson on women as well as the
rise in writing by and for women in the periodicals. Restoration drama
and the work of Jonathan Swift, Daniel Defoe, and Mary Astell are
mentioned, as is the work of other seventeenth century women writers.
The work of both the radical women writers of the eighteenth century
such as Mary Wollstonecraft is evaluated, as is the work of the
conservative women writers such as Hannah More. Rogers maintains
that certain terms, such as modesty and chastity, were particularly
important for women writers as were a suspicion of the imagination
and academic knowledge, an acknowledgement of the importance of
women's education, and a preference for fathers rather than mothers.
Rogers supplies a list of eighteenth century women writers together
with very brief biographies.

Ross, Marlon B. "Romantic Quest and Conquest." In *Romanticism and
Feminism*, edited by Anne K. Mellor, pp. 26-51. Bloomington: Indiana
University Press, 1988.
Ross believes that Romanticism is, historically, a male phenomenon
involving the warfare of ideas, an arena in which the poet sees himself
as a knightly defender of humanity. The poet is also compared to the
scientist, the capitalist, and the mountain climber, figures impossible
for the women of the time to attempt to emulate.

Scheuermann, Mona. *Her Bread to Earn: Women, Money, and Society
from Defoe to Austen*. Lexington: University Press of Kentucky, 1993.

This book asserts that both men and women authors saw women characters as capable individuals, finding Daniel Defoe most positive in his view of women and Samuel Richardson least. Scheuermann also finds that Jane Austen was more conservative in her stance than Mary Wollstonecraft. The author demonstrates that female characters do not die as often as had been believed in fiction, and that women characters are primarily concerned with money and courtship.

Shaffer, Julie. "The High Cost of Female Virtue: The Sexualization of Female Agency in Late Eighteenth- and Early Nineteenth-Century Texts." In *Misogyny in Literature: An Essay Collection*, edited by Katherine Anne Ackley, pp. 105-142. New York: Garland, 1992.
Shaffer points out that loss of reputation replaced loss of virginity as the greatest danger to the heroine of the late eighteenth century novel. To maintain their reputation and their marriageability, heroines must be silent according to conduct books and fiction of the period. To achieve some sense that they were in control, women silenced themselves. Novels such as Fanny Burney's *Evelina* showed that the situation of young women was problematic.

Shevelow, Kathryn. *Women and Print Culture: The Construction of Femininity in the Early Periodical*. London: Routledge, 1989.
In this book, Shevelow discusses how the early periodicals such as *The Tattler*, *Spectator*, *Athenian Mercury*, *The Free Thinker*, *The Female Spectator*, and *The Lady's Museum* were established and how they formed their audience. They were addressed at least partly to women, but they did not express feminist concerns. Instead they worked at imparting patriarchal ideology to their readers, convincing them to limit themselves to a purely domestic role.

Singley, Carol J. "Experiencing Anxious Power." In *Anxious Power: Reading, Writing and Ambivalence in Narrative by Women*, edited by Carol J. Singley and Susan Elizabeth Sweeney, pp. 3-18. Albany: State University of New York Press, 1993.
According to Singley, feminist criticism asserts that the culture forces women to be anxious about reading and writing. This anxiety leads to writer's block, constant apologies, and denial.

Todd, Janet. *Gender, Art, and Death*. New York: Continuum, 1993.
Todd's work discusses the development of feminist criticism since the 1970's and its relation to the new historicism, many of whose features it deplores.

_____. *The Sign of Angellica: Women, Writing, and Fiction, 1660-1800*. New York: Columbia University Press, 1989.
Todd describes the experiences of early women writers who learned that they would be attacked if they did not write anonymously. They apologized for writing at all by claiming a desire to educate or financial necessity. Although outwardly they supported the ideology of patriarchy, they created a fictional realm where deserving young women were rewarded. Todd defends the fiction of the time even though it does not conform to what has become the dominant aesthetic because it is sentimental and didactic, and she is particularly interested in how the writers of the time vindicated themselves for daring to write at all. Todd's work is an extremely informative history of women's writing in relation to the history of the era.

Turner, Cheryl. *Living By the Pen: Women Writers in the Eighteenth Century*. London: Routledge, 1992.
This rather technical work reviews previous work in the field, and examines the social and economic conditions which underlay the writing of women. She discusses the financial and class status of women writers, the changes in copyright laws and in the publishing industry, as well as the practice of literary patronage. She examines the unpublished as well as the published writings of women, literature for children, and religious literature. She describes women's poetry, drama, and translations as well as the role of education, circulating libraries, and serialization in the promoting women's writing. In addition, she provides a catalogue of women's fictions in book form from 1696 to 1796 and a chronological list of women authors for the same period.

Vallone, Lynne. *Disciplines of Virtue: Girls' Culture in the Eighteenth and Nineteenth Centuries*. New Haven, Conn.: Yale University Press, 1995.
According to Vallone, fiction and conduct books reinforced the ideology of the time which insisted on rewarding virtuous girls and punishing those who engaged in sexual misconduct. A dirty environment is connected with sexuality. These books also reinforce the idea that domestic life is preferable for women. Later nineteenth century agitation for women's suffrage, the growth of the field of domestic science, and the treatment of female delinquents, particularly in America, is also discussed.

Yaeger, Patricia. *Honey-Mad Women: Emancipating Strategies in Women's Writing*. New York: Columbia University Press, 1988.

Yaeger provides a highly theoretical account of how women appropriate men's language for their own use.

THE NOVEL

Auerbach, Nina. *Communities of Women: An Idea in Fiction.* Cambridge, Mass.: Harvard University Press, 1978.
The author traces the idea of women living in groups and acting in concert through myth and literature. This idea negates the more conventional concept of the role of women as daughters, wives, and mothers, existing only in relation to men. In myth, women living only with other women were thought to be powerful but mutilated and are ultimately defeated. In the novel, communities of women in Jane Austen's *Pride and Prejudice* and Louisa May Alcott's *Little Women* ultimately dissolve to admit men. Charlotte Brontë and Elizabeth Gaskell show communities of women who are free from family ties and demands. Later communities of women enter, possibly to dominate, the male world.

_____. *Woman and the Demon: The Life of a Victorian Myth.* Cambridge, Mass.: Harvard University Press, 1982.
The author discusses popular Victorian female archetypes: the angel, the demon, the old maid, and the fallen woman. She shows that even the outcasts are considered powerful in fiction and in art and notes that women were powerful despite their limited legal rights. They were dynamic and immortal and controlled the world. Queen Victoria symbolized their power.

Battestin, Martin. *British Novelists 1600-1800.* 2 vols. Detroit: Gale Research, 1985.
This two-volume study is part of the *Dictionary of Literary Biography*. An introduction discusses the history of the novel, maintaining that the earliest novelists although they differed in many ways were alike in that they wished to copy nature accurately and they believed in the importance of the individual and the necessity to sympathize with him or her. Battestin provides a list of works, a biography, and critical and historical information as well as further references for the novelists it covers. A chapter listing novel criticism by novelists is also included.

Beer, Patricia. *Reader, I Married Him: A Study of the Women Characters of Jane Austen, Charlotte Brontë, Elizabeth Gaskell, and George Eliot.* New York: Barnes & Noble, 1974.

A pioneering study when it first appeared, this work discusses the lives and works of these novelists as it was affected by the disabilities they suffered as women. Now it seems dated.

Boone, Joseph Allen. *Tradition Counter Tradition: Love and the Form of Fiction.* Chicago: University of Chicago Press, 1987.

According to Boone, the Anglo-American ideal of romantic love leading to marriage is an integral part of the novel. Narrative structure reinforces the ideal. The happy ending involves marriage; the tragic ending is a result of seduction. Also, men and women often seem to be members of different species. The author examines the problem of maintaining female identity in marriage in *Pamela, Pride and Prejudice, Clarissa, Tess of the D'Urbervilles, Amelia* and the novels of Sarah Scott, the Brontës, George Eliot, Elizabeth Gaskell, and twentieth century British and American novelists. His argument is dense and based on feminist literary theory.

Brophy, Bridget. *Women's Lives and the Nineteenth Century English Novel.* Tampa: University of South Florida Press, 1991.

Brophy examined unpublished diaries and letters by women and compared their accounts of their lives with novelistic accounts of life by Samuel Richardson, Henry Fielding, Sarah Fielding, Charlotte Lennox, Sarah Scott, Clara Reeve, and Fanny Burney to see if the novels were in fact realistic. She finds that women were considered intellectually inferior; their virtue, beauty, and willingness to please were their only important characteristics. Only novels made women important. The book also explores the role of courtship and discusses the stages of women's lives as daughters, wives, and widows. Brophy questions whether the novels tended to reinforce patriarchal ideology or incite rebellion against it. Although all the novels advocate education for women and better treatment of women, Brophy concludes that Samuel Richardson's novels advocate a greater respect for the abilities of women than the novels written by women do.

Brownstein, Rachel. *Becoming a Heroine: Reading About Women in Novels.* New York: Viking Press, 1982.

The writer asserts that young women pattern themselves on heroines in novels—a tendency that can be either liberating or imprisoning. She notes that novels are realistic, but their emphasis on young women is not. Her essays on Jane Austen's novels, on *Villette*, and on *Daniel Deronda* demonstrate the changes in the concept of women's role and how it is reflected in the heroine.

Cohen, Michael. "First Sisters in the British Novel: Charlotte Lennox to Susan Ferrier." In *The Significance of Sibling Relationships in Literature*, edited by Joanna Stephens Mink and Janet Doubler Ward, pp. 98-109. Bowling Green, Ohio: Bowling Green State University Popular Press, 1993.

Cohen credits Charlotte Lennox with the first use of sisters in the novel in *The History of Harriet and Sophia* (1761). The sisters are opposite in temperament and morals and rivals in love. The good sister marries a rich man and lives happily ever after while her less worthy sister marries less well and must emigrate. Susan Ferrier makes her characters who have sisters in marriage opposite in appearance, and dress as well as temperament and morality. Their differences result from differences in education. The exploration of relationships between sisters was a literary device used by many other novelists, including Fanny Burney, Maria Edgeworth, and Jane Austen.

Colby, Robert A. *Fiction with a Purpose: Major and Minor Nineteenth Century Novels.* Bloomington: Indiana University Press, 1968.

The author maintains that novels achieved respectability by being didactic. Nineteenth century novelists, who were critics as well, wrote about realistic characters in fairly realistic situations because they maintained that everyday life was more interesting than exotic tales. To enhance their realism, they alluded to current events. They often wrote about education, even setting their novels in schools or tracing the course of adolescence, in order to educate their readers. Characteristics of these novels include the omniscient narrator, a family group, and an address to a generalized audience about universals. They believed that novels should be didactic because life is didactic. The author does not differentiate between male and female writers in this regard.

Colby, Vineta. *Yesterday's Woman: Domestic Realism in the English Novel.* Princeton, N.J.: Princeton University Press, 1974.

Colby maintains that British novels written between 1818 and 1840, which are rarely read in the late twentieth century, are important in that they increased the prestige of the novel form and established the emphasis on domestic realism in the later Victorian novels. These later novels were home-centered and female-dominated works. She also

discusses changes in aristocratic society, religious practice, educational theory, and attitudes toward reality. Her argument is based on
work of Mrs. Gore, Maria Edgeworth, Susan Ferrier, Hannah More,
Charlotte Elizabeth Tonna, Elizabeth Sewell, and Charlotte Yonge.

Cosslett, Tess. *Woman to Woman: Female Friendship in Victorian Fiction.*
Atlantic Highlands, N.J.: Humanities Press International, 1988.
This book demonstrates how female friendship is often necessary to
resolve the conventional marriage plot, although it is never a substitute
for marriage nor does it allude to lesbianism. The subject of female
friendship does allow writers to explore different female identities and
it can be subversive, although until *Shirley* was written the novels about
it tend to uphold patriarchy. Such novels take place in an Edenic setting
and stress the maternal. They take three forms. In one, two female rivals
decide who will marry the man; in another the rebellious sister is
chastened by the angelic sister; in the third, a friendship occurs between
a pure woman and a fallen woman that causes the reformation of the
latter.

Daleski, H. M. *The Divided Heroine: A Recurrent Pattern in Six English
Novels.* New York: Holmes & Meier, 1985.
Daleski explores the situation, common to many novels, in which the
heroine is in love with two men.

David, Gail. *Female Heroism in the Pastoral.* New York: Garland, 1991.
According to David, women's pastoral, as opposed to men's, involves
a young woman's journey from a simple, rural environment to a
complex, urban environment which she must master. Her country
home has been pleasant and egalitarian. Her malign destination is the
court or the city, the locus of a tyrannical father or male-identified
mother. When she masters the masculine ways of this place, she can
go home, claiming her authority as a wife or queen or saint and
reasserting her bond with her mother and nature. Her journey is more
difficult than that of the male hero because she has to be both feminine
and masculine, retain her bond with her mother, and avoid sexual
misconduct. David refers to the works of Fanny Burney, Ann Radcliffe,
Jane Austen, Charlotte Brontë, George Eliot, and Elizabeth Gaskell.

Edwards, P. D. *Idyllic Realism from Mary Russell Mitford to Hardy.* New
York: St. Martin's Press, 1988.
According the author, all Victorian art and literature tends toward the
idyllic. He defines the term as a mixture of social concern, concern
with nature, pastoralism, human interest narratives, glimpses of evil,

and realistic details. In an idyll, all conflict is finally resolved, and the existence of tragedy or heroic passion is denied. This form attracted the Victorians because of their anxiety over industrialization, urbanization, loss of religious faith, class struggle, and change in general. He traces its origins to the work of Mary Russell Mitford, who influenced the novelists Elizabeth Gaskell, George Eliot, and Anthony Trollope, as well as the poets Alfred, Lord Tennyson and Arthur Hugh Clough.

Ferris, Ina. "From Trope to Code, The Novel and the Rhetoric of Gender in Nineteenth Century Critical Discourse." In *Rewriting the Victorians: Theory, History, and the Politics of Gender*, edited by Linda M. Shires, pp. 31-51. New York: Routledge, 1992.
The author asserts that because the novel was so closely associated with women writers and readers, it was thought to have some cultural power but no literary value. For the novel to be considered literature, women and narrativity had to be eliminated.

Fraiman, Susan. *Unbecoming Women: British Women Writers and the Novel of Development*. New York: Columbia University Press, 1993.
Fraiman asserts that women's novels of development, as a genre, differ from novels concerned with the development of men because the construction of femininity is more complex than the construction of masculinity. The male *Bildungsroman*, a novel about the education, in the broadest sense, of the hero, involves his choice of friends, a wife, an occupation. It rationalizes capitalism. Women's novels contain competing stories. The plot ends in marriage and motherhood, but the female hero must always beware of bad men because they make bad husbands, causing misery. She also needs female friends. Novels of female development maintain that education for women is desirable if it does not lead to pedantry. The author concludes that female novelists of the period were themselves middle-class conservatives, but there works are subversive of middle-class orthodoxy in many respects.

Gruner, Elisabeth Rose. "'Loving Differences': Sisters and Brothers from Frances Burney to Emily Brontë." In *The Significance of Sibling Relationships in Literature*, edited by Joanna Stephens Mink and Janet Doubler Ward, pp. 47-57. Bowling Green, Ohio: Bowling Green State University Popular Press, 1993.
Gruner maintains that Burney in *Camilla* and Austen in *Sense and Sensibility* use brothers when they want to condemn patriarchy while the heroes of the novels represent the desirable aspects of patriarchy. Gruner asserts, however, that even good marriages limit the freedom

of the heroine. In *Wuthering Heights*, she sees Heathcliff as a good brother who becomes an evil patriarch. To the older Catherine, Heathcliff is a fellow rebel against her brother Hindley and represents the freedom and power she enjoys in her childhood. Domesticity, in the form of marriage and childbirth, kills her. Her daughter Catherine enjoys domesticity. Young Catherine is deprived of her class and gender privileges when she moves from the Grange to Wuthering Heights, but she re-creates her mother's relationship to Heathcliff in her relationship to Hareton.

Hunt, Linda C. *A Woman's Portion: Ideology, Culture and the British Female Novel Tradition*. New York: Garland, 1988.
The nineteenth century saw women as selfless, controlled and naturally domestic, an antidote to the materialism of the age. Novels helped promote these ideas. George Eliot rendered the emotions and moral consciousness of her female characters. Jane Austen used the nineteenth century ideal of women in her characterization of Fanny Price, Emma, and Anne Elliot. Charlotte Brontë changed the novel form to accommodate her idea of the ideal woman.

Lawrence, Margaret. *The School of Femininity: A Book for and About Women as They Are Interpreted Through Feminist Writings of Yesterday and Today*. Port Washington, N.Y.: Kennikat Press, 1968.
The author asserts that women's writing differs from that of men in that it is born either out of resentment of or acquiescence to men's view of the world.

Levin, Amy K. *The Suppressed Sister: A Relationship in Novels by Nineteenth and Twentieth Century British Women*. Lewisburg, Ohio: Bucknell University Press, 1992.
Levin claims that nineteenth and twentieth century novels treat the sisterly relationship in a realistic manner. Basing her argument on psychoanalytic theory, the author asserts that sisters are rivals for the attention of their father and because their roles in the household are identical and interchangeable try to differentiate themselves, disturbing the harmony of the home. The author believes novels use sisters to enact the struggle between conformity and nonconformity. She asserts further that fiction is based on myth, particularly those myths relating to Cinderella, Cupid and Psyche, Antigone, Snow White, and King Lear. In many novels, because sisters are rivals for the love of the father, they mistake their suitors for brothers. Since the identities of these characters are not fixed, physical objects and jewelry help define their

roles. Sisters also need to learn who is trustworthy; their aunts may be evil. When sisters disentangle their lives, they marry and are separated by either geography or class. The nineteenth century works discussed are by Jane Austen, Elizabeth Gaskell, and George Eliot.

Kraft, Elizabeth. *Character and Consciousness in Eighteenth Century Comic Fiction*. Athens: University of Georgia Press, 1992.
Kraft explores eighteenth century concepts of identity and consciousness as they impinge on the novel. Fielding's *Tom Jones* and Sterne's *Tristram Shandy* are compared to *The Female Quixote* by Charlotte Lennox.

MacCarthy, B. G. *The Female Pen: Women Writers and Novelists 1621-1818*. Reprint. New York: New York University Press, 1994.
First published in 1946, MacCarthy's study is a highly informative, if dated, history of novels written by women, summarizing plots and supplying biographical data. It is complete and readable.

McCormick, Margaret. *Mothers in the English Novel: From Stereotype to Archetype*. New York: Garland, 1991.
McCormick asserts that mothers are important in novels because novels are realistic and based on the lives of middle-class individuals. In the nineteenth century novel, however, mothers have no identities beyond their motherhood. This lack of identity is shown by their lack of a first name. In the nineteenth century novel, most mothers are portrayed as either saintly or stupid. Their archetype is the Great Mother, once a powerful goddess, but now evil and weak. This limited characterization of mothers constitutes the most unrealistic aspect of these novels. At the same time that they represent the legal powerlessness of women, mothers in the nineteenth century novel also demonstrate the genuine power of mothers in real life.

Mei, Huang. *Transforming the Cinderella Dream: From Fanny Burney to Charlotte Brontë*. New Brunswick, N.J.: Rutgers University Press, 1990.
Mei offers a thorough examination of the fairy tale, and explains how various women novelists use elements of the Cinderella myth to fashion their heroines.

Mellor, Anne K. "A Criticism of Their Own: Romantic Women Literary Critics." In *Questioning Romanticism*, edited by John Beer, pp. 29-48. Baltimore: The Johns Hopkins University Press, 1995.

Mellor discusses the literary criticism of Joanna Baillie, Anna Laetitia Barbauld, Elizabeth Inchbald, Clara Reeve, Anna Seward, and Mary Wollstonecraft, maintaining that they developed a coherent literary theory different from that of the male Romantics. These female critics looked for a balance of reason and emotion. They disapproved of immorality, self-indulgence, and obscurity, and they approved of the education of women, egalitarian marriages, the family, the community. They disapproved of violent revolution, and they saw nature as a sister, rather than an outside force. They preferred novels, dramas, and poetry that celebrated an ordered life. They also believed that women were superior to men and that men should emulate women. Mellor notes that women dominated the production and consumption of literature during the time. These critics promoted didactic literature as the only education available to many women. They were interested in the response of their readers, ways of knowing peculiar to women, and their craft as writers. She quotes women writers to demonstrate these points.

Miles, Rosalind. *The Female Form: Women Writers and the Conquest of the Novel*. London: Routledge & Kegan Paul, 1987.
The author discusses why women began to write novels during the nineteenth century, and how the values and the situation of these women affected the development of the novel. Miles also discusses novels that confirm the prevailing ideology as well as those which argue against it.

Miller, Jane. *Women Writing About Men*. New York: Pantheon Books, 1986.
Women writers use the novel form to question men's versions of women's lives. Novels that end in marriage involve only a small part of a woman's life. The author also notes that men play many roles in novels written by women. She notes that Jane Austen, the Brontës, and George Eliot wrote about sexual inequities. Later writings questioning the sources of sexual inequity question whether narrative itself is a fit vehicle for female expression. Miller is also interested in the roles played by fathers and brothers in women's novels and how heroes created by women differ from heroes created by men. Her theoretical stance is feminist, and she is interested in her own development as a reader.

Mills, Sarah, Lynn Pearce, Sue Spanell, and Elaine Millard. *Feminist Readings/Feminist Reading*. Charlottesville: University Press of Virginia, 1989.

Feminist critical theory allows many readings of a novel. This book contains three readings of *Wuthering Heights*, a political reading, a realist reading, and a reading using the methods of French feminist criticism.

Mitchell, Sally. *The Fallen Angel: Chastity, Class and Woman's Reading 1838-1880*. Bowling Green, Ohio: Bowling Green University Press, 1981.

Because it guaranteed inheritance by one's rightful heir, and because women were considered property, female chastity was valued by the Victorians. Female purity was considered to be protected by ignorance, and was also considered fairly easy to protect since most Victorians believed women were naturally asexual. Nevertheless, both nonfiction and fiction tried to inculcate chastity and had a strong influence on their readers. Mitchell discusses the inexpensive magazines that circulated widely and novels that treated prostitution as a social problem. She also provides biographical material for little-known men and women authors who wrote about the fallen woman, as well as historical and critical background information.

Mudge, Bradford K., ed. *British Romantic Novelists 1789-1832*. Detroit: Gale Research, 1992.

An extensive introduction discusses the denigration of novels, their connection with women and the French and American Revolutions, and the Gothic novel. The book notes that even modern critics ignored nearly all the women novelists who are just now being rediscovered. The rise of the novel changed the literary marketplace as sales became more important than literary standards. The editor notes that the novel thrived during the romantic era but was overshadowed by poetry. He also notes that despite the popularity of novels most people could not afford to buy books. The book lists well-known male and female authors and their works, giving biographical and historical and critical information. Sources for further reading are also listed.

Parkin-Gounelas, Ruth. *Fictions of the Female Self*. New York: St. Martin's Press, 1991.

The (male) Romantic poets absorbed in the self as the site of meaning and source of knowledge. Modern feminists are preoccupied with questions of female identity. Charlotte Brontë was their precursor, but as a woman and as a Victorian she was ambivalent about writing about the self. The author also asserts that novels written by women are assumed to be autobiographical. Critics need to focus on the conventions women writers are subject to and how they accommodate to patriarchy.

Perry, Ruth. *Women, Letters and the Novel*. New York: AMS Press, 1980.
Perry explains how the personal letter developed into travel writing and eventually into epistolary fiction. It discusses the social situation and status of women as well as their sexual fantasies.

Rowbotham, Judith. *Good Girls Make Good Wives: Guidance for Girls in Victorian Fiction*. New York: Basil Blackwell, 1989.
According to the author, middle-class adults believed didactic fiction was important for girls and they could buy books because during the nineteenth century, they became less expensive. Books for young people were strongly gendered; books for boys were about adventure while books for girls encouraged domesticity and submission. Nevertheless, the fact that writing provided women with a profession undermined patriarchy. The most popular authors of these books were Charlotte Yonge, E. E. Green, L. T. Meade, and Mrs. George De Horne Vaizey. Historical novels were also popular because they taught history as well as morals. In them, girls inspired action although they did not act themselves. Girls' books also promoted colonialism; women characters did their duty and sacrificed themselves for their country. Later in the century, nineteenth century novels discussed work outside the home for girls. An extensive bibliography of girls' books is provided.

Sabiston, Elizabeth Jean. *The Prison of Womanhood: Four Provincial Heroines in Nineteenth Century Fiction*. New York: St. Martin's Press, 1989.
Sabiston sees the heroine of Jane Austen's *Emma* as providing the prototype for imaginative, intelligent yet ignorant and provincial heroines who desire self-fulfillment.

Sandock, Mollie. "Learned Ladies: Misogyny and the English Novel." In *Misogyny in Literature: An Essay Collection*, edited by Katherine Anne Ackley, pp. 143-164. New York: Garland, 1992.
Sandock maintains that literature through the early nineteenth century devalued learned women. Women writers, to ensure their own position, used exaggeratedly obnoxious female pedants as a "cover" that allowed them to present intelligent women characters.

Sanders, Valerie. *The Private Lives of Victorian Women: Autobiography in Nineteenth Century England*. New York: St. Martin's Press, 1989.

Sanders notes that nineteenth century women rarely wrote autobiographies because they were not supposed to be self-centered. She contends, however, that they inserted autobiographical material in conduct books and novels. She discusses women's autobiographical works from the time of Margery Kempe through the beginning of the twentieth century. She also discusses the use of the novelist's own childhood experiences in the works of the Brontës, Elizabeth Barrett Browning, and Harriet Martineau, among others.

Spacks, Patricia Meyer. *Desire and Truth: Functions of Plot in Eighteenth Century English Novels.* Chicago: University of Chicago Press, 1990. According to Spacks, fiction creates and conveys truth, but novels do not always convey what society expects them to convey. In that sense, they are subversive. The novels of the 1740's and 1750's, such as *Tom Jones*, are about power. The novels written during from 1760 to 1770, such as *Tristram Shandy*, are about the breakdown of plot. The novels of the 1770's are about relationships, a feminized plot. Later novels resolve the discourse of power into a harmony. Novels show ideological ferment and illuminate possibilities.

_____. *Gossip.* New York: Alfred A. Knopf, 1985.
Spacks maintains that gossip is thought to be a female fault, but once it is written down, gossip becomes stable enough to form biographies and novels. Here the author discusses Elizabeth Gaskell's *The Life of Charlotte Brontë* and *Cranford*, Burney's *Evelina*, and Austen's *Emma*.

_____. *Imagining a Self: Autobiography and Novel in Eighteenth Century England.* Cambridge, Mass.: Harvard University Press, 1976. Spacks tries to account for the fact that eighteenth century novels written by women (as most of them were) are apologetic, conventional, didactic, and dreary. Autobiographies of women during the age centered on relationships with men and seem to have been written to establish an identity for the women who wrote them.

Spencer, Jane. *The Rise of the Woman Novelist: From Aphra Behn to Jane Austen.* Oxford: Basil Blackwell, 1986.
Spencer notes that eighteenth century England accepted female novelists who promoted the ideology of femininity. This acceptance improved the social position of women writers relative to other women. The development of the novel accompanied the rise of the middle class and the increase in women writers, partly because women as well as most middle-class men were cut off from a classical education. Women

were barred from working outside the home, so they turned to writing. They were praised for writing about domestic life in a moral and sentimental way as long as they themselves led virtuous lives.

Spender, Dale. *Mothers of the Novel: One Hundred Good Women Writers Before Jane Austen*. London: Pandora, 1986
Spender wants to reclaim the great early novels and document women's subjugation by men. She provides a valuable list of women's novels written before Jane Austen, which she claims educated women. She sees the decline in female authorship as a result of men's imitating women's novels and then creating a backlash against them.

Todd, Janet. *Women's Friendship in Literature*. New York: Columbia University Press, 1980.
In this work, Todd provides an analysis of female friendship in French and English novels of the eighteenth and early nineteenth century written by both women and men. The motifs Todd identifies include virginity (or chastity), narcissism, money, illness, madness, and death. Todd asserts that female writers prefer their female characters to commit suicide rather than to be murdered, identify with their heroines, blame mothers, prefer sentimental to erotic female relationships, and companionate to passionate heterosexual relationships. She believes women's literature values the power of women and the help they give each other in adversity.

Tompkins, J. M. S. *The Popular Novel in England 1770-1800*. Lincoln: University of Nebraska Press, 1961.
This valuable study shows its age by apologizing for its subject. It discusses the financial and marketing aspects of the popular novel as well as how it was reviewed. The author notes that these novels were often written in the form of letters and were always didactic. There is a separate chapter on female novelists in which Tompkins notes that it was permissible for women to write if they were humble about their work. Tompkins also notes that these popular books, although often satiric, gave an accurate picture of life. Heroes as well as heroines are passive and the morality prudential. Their subject is generally the endurance of the pursued heroine. They advocate filial piety, submission by women, and the sacredness of motherhood. They mock learned women and old maids. The book also discusses Gothics, romances, and the philosophic novel.

Tuchman, Gaye, with Nina E. Fortin. *Edging Women Out: Victorian Novelists, Publishers and Social Change*. New Haven, Conn.: Yale University Press, 1989.

Using sociological methodology, including statistical analysis, the writers show how women's writing began to be seen as an aspect of popular culture while men's novels were considered serious and a part of high culture. It is noted that before 1840, half the novelists in England were women. By 1917, however, nearly all serious novelists were men.

Warhol, Robyn. *Gendered Interventions: Narrative Discourse in the Victorian Novel*. New Brunswick, N.J.: Rutgers University Press, 1989.

Contemporary scholars and critics devalue authorial intervention, which they consider intrusive, because it has been used by women authors. Warhol has studied it to see how women's writing differs from that of men and to learn how novels communicate. Her work is based on narratological theory and feminist contextual criticism.

Wheeler, Michael. *English Fiction of the Victorian Period 1830-1890*. New York: Longman, 1985.

Wheeler connects fiction with its historical context. He outlines the development of the novel and discusses its subgenres: sensation novels, problem novels, and social novels. He also discusses realism, romance, the novel as entertainment, didacticism, and sentimentality. He notes that the novel reflects the conflict between the self and society and often uses imprisonment as a metaphor. He sees the novel turning from optimism to pessimism as the Victorian world loses its stability. Extensive bibliographies and a detailed chronology are very helpful.

Yeazell, Ruth Bernard. *Fictions of Modesty: Women and Courtship in the English Novel*. Chicago: University of Chicago Press, 1991.

Yeazell maintains that men set the terms of debate regarding female modesty and it was a popular subject. Yet the heroine's resistance to sex, beginning with Richardson's novels, centered the novel on the female consciousness. The author contends that women who do not realize they need love are modest. She believes that while Fanny Burney understood the political aspects of relationships, Jane Austen moralized about them. She also believes Charlotte Brontë wrote about the psychology of modesty and Elizabeth Gaskell wrote about it naturalistically. Modesty in novels is rational according to the author and she discusses verbal and physical signs of modesty in the novel as well as repression and ignorance of one's own heart.

POETRY BY WOMEN

Anthologies

Bax, Clifford, and Meum Steward, eds. *The Distaff Muse: An Anthology of Poetry Written By Women.* London: Hollis and Carter, 1949.
This old-fashioned, chatty book supplies biographies and one or two poems written by eighteenth and nineteenth century women poets.

Breen, Jennifer. *Women Romantic Poets 1785-1832: An Anthology.* London: J. M. Dent & Sons, 1992.
The introduction to this anthology describes why women poets wrote and the conditions under which they wrote. Their subject matter and poetic forms came out of their roles as wives and mothers and their social class. Their use of form and diction was conventional but they believed, before Wordsworth, that poetry should be written in ordinary language. When they wrote about love, they tended to be satiric. In general, they adopted the male point of view and wrote about nature. They also wrote poems for children. Breen provides an extremely informative introduction; the poems themselves, however, lack head notes.

Kaplan, Cora, ed. *Salt and Bitter and Good: Three Centuries of British and American Women Poets.* New York: Paddington Press, 1975.
This anthology includes some poems from the eighteenth and nineteenth centuries. The editor explains that women poets were conscious of their inferior status and unconventional occupation; they were also handicapped by the culture, critical condescension, poor education, household duties, and a general guilt. Their situation did not improve until the twentieth century.

Kelly, A. A., ed. *Pillars of the House: An Anthology of Verse of Irish Women from 1690 to the Present.* Dublin: Wolfhound, 1988.
Irish women poets faced prejudice against them because of their ethnicity as well as their gender. According to Kelly, the women who did write were strong minded and had few children. Short biographical head notes to the poems are supplied.

Lonsdale, Roger, ed. *Eighteenth Century Women Poets: An Oxford Anthology*. New York: Oxford University Press, 1990.

This anthology supplies very complete head notes to the poems giving biographical information about the poets. The introduction traces the increase in numbers of women writers and readers during the eighteenth century. Lonsdale notes that earliest writers of the period wrote alone and in secret because they felt their lack of a classical education and society's disapproval. By the 1730's, however, more women wrote and found outlets for their poetry in the new periodicals and in publishing by subscription. He believes that possibly because Samuel Richardson had made the female consciousness important, women's poetry became very popular in the 1740's, becoming more formal. By the 1750's, critics had become aware of the importance of women readers, as women were becoming more educated. By the end of the century, women were writing much of the popular fiction and fashionable poetry. Their importance caused a backlash, and Wordsworth announced in *Lyrical Ballads* (1798) that poetry was a male activity. Women were not included in anthologies, and their poetry was forgotten. Lonsdale adds that he has included the best poetry by women of the time.

McGann, Jerome J. *The New Oxford Book of Romantic Period Verse*. Oxford: Oxford University Press. 1993.

The introduction to this anthology takes a more inclusive view of Romantic poetry than earlier anthologies have done. Besides defining Romanticism, McGann explains why women poets celebrated during the period were forgotten by the end of the century. He reprints selections from their poetry, as well as selections from the poetry of lesser-known male Romantics. The poetry is arranged chronologically rather than by poet.

Women's Poetry: History and Criticism

Edmond, Rod. *Affairs of the Hearth: Victorian Poetry and Domestic Narrative*. New York: Routledge, 1988.

According to Edmond, Victorians were obsessed with the ideology of the happy middle-class family possibly because of the strains caused by industrialization, urbanization, and secularism. They believed gender roles and parent-child relations were important. Few enduringly happy families are present in Victorian literature or art, however, possibly because the ideology was being eroded by new legal rights for women and because the ideology itself was changing. Experimentation with long verse narratives was also taking place. The author discusses *Aurora Leigh* and "Goblin Market" as examples.

Gilbert, Sandra M., and Susan Gubar, eds. *Shakespeare's Sisters: Feminist Essays on Women Poets.* Bloomington: Indiana University Press, 1979. The editors examine women's poetry in the light of a patriarchal tradition that denies women the right to be poets. While women novelists were tolerated, even the best-known nineteenth century women poets such as Elizabeth Barrett Browning were derided. These essays attempt to trace the outline of a feminine poetic tradition. Because the scope of the book is wide, its coverage of eighteenth and nineteenth century British women poets is limited to essays on Emily Brontë, Elizabeth Barrett Browning, and Christina Rossetti.

Hickock, Kathleen. *Representations of Women: Nineteenth Century British Women's Poetry.* Westport, Conn.: Greenwood Press, 1984. Hickock examines how nineteenth century women poets treat women, in the context of contemporary thought and in the context of male writers' treatment of women. The culture insisted that women were different from men in having no life of their own, existing only in relation to their families. Until late in the century, a woman who was not a wife was a failure, no matter what else she did. Women poets shared this view and also believed that poetry was essentially male. Although these conventions restricted women, they also provided a structure for their work. Women did protest subtly against cultural assumptions, showing, for example, that love produced sadness rather than fulfillment. Women's poetry was conventional not only because of their own beliefs but also because their audience, their publishers, and their critics demanded prudery and adherence to the patriarchal definition of the feminine ideal. Nevertheless, women poets often transcended the conventional. The poets discussed include Felicia Hemans, Letitia Elizabeth Landon, Caroline Norton, Eliza Cook, Adelaide Anne Proctor, Dora Greenwell, Jean Ingelow, Emily Pfeiffer, Mary Elizabeth Coleridge, and Michael Field. The author provides information on little-known poets and their work.

Leighton, Angela. *Victorian Women Poets: Writing Against the Heart.* New York: Harvester Wheatsheaf, 1992. The author believes that Victorian women's poetry has been neglected because it is self-consciously feminine. Beginning in the 1820's, however, many women wrote poetry because of the expansion of the

literary marketplace. The Victorians believed that women's imagina-
tions must conflict with social and sexual morality, so women writers
had to write despite their sensibility and allow the real world into their
writing. Leighton discusses the poetry of Felicia Hemans and Letitia
Elizabeth Landon in this context, using a biographical and historical
approach as well as a textual and aesthetic approach.

Montefiore, Jen. *Feminism and Poetry: Language, Experience, Identity
in Women's Writing.* New York: Pindar, 1987.
The author claims that women poets have been ignored or treated as
neurotics. They should be read in part to share their sufferings as
women, but readers should not be limited to the feminist implications
of their work. Montefiore believes that Romanticism injured women's
poetry by insisting poetry be written in the language of men about
universal topics. As part of her discussion of works by Christina
Rossetti, Elizabeth Barrett Browning, and other women poets, the
author examines how women treat poetic conventions established by
men.

Sitter, John, ed. *Eighteenth Century British Poets.* 2 vols. Detroit: Gale
Research, 1991.
This valuable two-volume survey is part of the *Dictionary of Literary
Biography*. The introductory material of each volume discusses the
hallmarks of the literature of the age. The first concentrates on the
exuberance of the age, the great diversity of its poetry, and the rediscovery of its women poets. The second volume mentions nostalgia for
the medieval, the folk traditions, the primitive, and the increasing
importance of the lyric. An article on each poet lists his or her works,
provides biographical and critical information, and lists further references.

DRAMA BY WOMEN

Carlson, Susan. *Women and Comedy: Rewriting the British Theatrical
Tradition.* Ann Arbor: University of Michigan Press, 1991.
The author, who writes from a feminist stance, believes that although
women heroines rarely gain power, women playwrights triumph by
writing comedy. She discusses Aphra Behn as a precursor of modern
feminists because Behn allowed her female characters to express
sexuality.

Cotton, Nancy. *Women Playwrights in England c. 1363-1758.* Lewisburg, Ohio: Bucknell University Press, 1980.

Cotton provides a biographical and critical survey of plays created by women during the period. It also contains a chronology of plays by women to 1750 and an analysis of the lives and works of Catherine Trotter, Delariviere Manley, and Mary Pix.

Davis, Gwenn. *Drama by Women to 1900: A Bibliography of American and British Writers.* London: Mansell, 1992.

The introduction to this useful source explains the problems peculiar to compiling a bibliography of dramatic works: Some were published, some not. Some were full-fledged plays, while others were recitations of various sorts. Women began writing plays after 1666. These included closet dramas, written by educated women for the upper classes. Such works were meant to be read not performed and were concerned with tragic or historical topics. Middle-class women also wrote for the professional theater and a wide audience. They specialized in comedy but also wrote in other genres. Other women wrote for amateur productions, which were very popular. Their orientation was conservative and often propagandized for abolition and temperance. From about 1700 to the middle of the nineteenth century, the stage was considered perfectly respectable. Many women who wrote in other genres also wrote plays. The book itself lists women playwrights and their works and identifies the type of plays they wrote.

Pearson, Jacqueline. *The Prostituted Muse: Images of Women and Women Dramatists 1642-1737.* New York: Harvester Wheatsheaf, 1988.

The author discusses women playwrights of the period and how the subject matter and themes of their work differs from those of male playwrights.

Schofield, Mary Anne, and Cecilia Macheski. *Curtain Calls: British and American Women and the Theater 1600-1820.* Athens: University of Ohio Press, 1991.

According to the authors, women of the seventeenth and eighteenth centuries played important, if often unacknowledged roles in the theater even though they faced insults, seduction, and even rape. They were involved in the business of the theater in addition to working as actresses and writers, but fewer women wrote plays than wrote in other genres. During this period, women's plays were more likely to be published than performed. The book provides statistics on the number of plays published or produced by women. It also lists the plays written by women during this time.

Tomalin, Claire. *Mrs. Jordan's Profession: The Actress and the Prince.* New York: Alfred A. Knopf, 1995.
Tomalin's work is a fascinating biography of Dora Jordan (1761-1816), a woman who was not only the most popular comic actress of her time but also the mistress of the man who eventually became King William IV. They lived together for twenty years and had ten children together until pressure from the royal family caused him to repudiate her. Tomalin provides a picture of theatrical life during the period and illuminates the role of women in the theater. She also provides a helpful bibliography.

Chapter 3

BRITISH WOMEN AUTHORS

JANE AUSTEN (1775-1817)

Jane Austen, the younger daughter of a clergyman was born in Steventon, a small community in Hampshire. Although her family was not wealthy, some of their relatives were, particularly on her mother's side. The family was literary, and her father kept a school. The children produced their own periodicals, put on plays, and read widely. Although she claimed to be uneducated and attended school for only a short time, her novels give evidence of a great deal of knowledge. She began to write at a very early age, but did not publish until she was older. Her life was uneventful. Although she received at least one proposal, she never married, but she and her sister were quite close. When her father retired, the family moved to Bath. At his death, they moved to Southampton, but they had no real home until 1809, when her brother, who had been adopted by wealthy relatives, gave them a house at Chawton. Here, she returned to writing, revised her early novels and finally saw them published. *Sense and Sensibility* appeared in 1811; *Pride and Prejudice* in 1813. These books were well received, and she could have moved in London literary circles. Instead, she chose to remain anonymous except to family members and close friends. *Mansfield Park* appeared in 1814. By this time, she was well enough known among connoisseurs of the novel that the Prince of Wales (the future George IV) asked that she dedicate her next book to him. That book was *Emma*. By the time she wrote *Persuasion*, which appeared after her death, she was already ill, probably with Addison's disease, an adrenal gland disorder. She died in Winchester at the age of forty-one. After her death, two novels appeared: *Persuasion* and *Northanger Abbey*, which was originally written in the 1790's. In 1870, a memoir of her life by J. E. Austen-Leigh appeared and the next year her juvenilia was published. Although critics of the novel had always been aware of her work, it became even more popular at this time. In the 1920's, her work began to be the subject of serious scholarship. Early criticism took her own self-deprecation at face value and considered her a miniaturist, someone who could dramatize the world she knew, but little else. Twentieth century critics were more apt to recognize her literary artistry as well as her gift for satire. Those critics writing in the 1980's and afterward recognize her feminism, which may have been somewhat covert, but which certainly existed. She remains an immensely popular writer both with scholars and with the general readers. Indeed, her novels have been made into successful Hollywood and made-for-television films. Modern editions of her work are readily available.

Anderson, Misty. "The Different Sorts of Friendship: Desire in *Mansfield Park.*" In *Jane Austen and Discourses of Feminism*, edited by Devoney Looser, pp. 167-184. New York: St. Martin's Press, 1995.
Anderson believes that Fanny Price and Mary Crawford in *Mansfield Park* achieve "an intimacy between them that can be called homo-erotic." This attachment cannot be sublimated as is Fanny's semi-in-cestuous attachment to her brother William, when she marries Ed-mund. Anderson's reading of the novel is an interesting, but not entirely convincing attempt to demonstrate this.

Auerbach, Nina. *Communities of Women: An Idea in Fiction.* Cambridge, Mass.: Harvard University Press, 1978.
The author discusses *Pride and Prejudice* as a description of a female community. She wonders whether the female community in which Jane Austen actually lived at Chawton was stultifying or enabling to Austen as a writer and she notes that Austen portrays powerful women unfa-vorably. She asserts that women can only exercise their power benevo-lently when it is transferred to the hero; this occurs in *Pride and Prejudice.*

Austen-Leigh, William, and Richard Arthur Austen-Leigh. *Jane Austen: A Family Record.* Revised and enlarged by Deirdre Le Fay. Boston: G. K. Hall, 1989.
Written by descendants of Jane Austen, this book provides a family history from 1600 to the early twentieth century and a detailed chro-nology of Austen's life. It is a readable, illustrated account of her life primarily based on letters.

Babb, Howard. *Jane Austen's Novels: The Fabric of Dialogue.* Columbus: Ohio State University Press, 1962.
In this slightly dated but still valuable reading of the novels, Babb argues that Austen reveals her characters through dialogues in which they attempt to judge others, or persuade others. Either they gain self-knowledge or descend into moral blindness.

Barker, Gerard. *Grandison's Heirs: The Paragon's Progress in the Late Eighteenth Century English Novel.* Newark: University of Delaware Press, 1985.
Barker maintains that Darcy, the hero of *Pride and Prejudice*, begins as an antihero, compared to Samuel Richardson's Sir Charles Grandison, but over the course of the novel develops into a Grandisonian paragon, only more realistic than Grandison himself. He discusses Austen's debt to Richardson and compares *Sir Charles Grandison* with *Pride and Prejudice.*

Barreca, Regina. *Untamed and Unabashed: Essays on Women and Humor in British Literature.* Detroit: Wayne State University Press, 1994.
Barreca argues that Austen never uses a conventional plot in which female characters accept male values; She cites the endings of *Sense and Sensibility* and *Mansfield Park* as proof of this. She discusses the plots of *Pride and Prejudice* and *Emma* to show that Jane Austen subverts authoritative discourse.

Booth, Wayne C. "Control of Distance in Jane Austen's *Emma*." In *The Rhetoric of Fiction.* 1961. Reprint. Chicago: University of Chicago Press, 1975.
In this classic study, first published in 1961, Booth explains the techniques used by Jane Austen to ensure that Emma retains the reader's sympathy despite her faults.

Bradbrook, Frank. *Jane Austen and Her Predecessors.* Cambridge, England: Cambridge University Press, 1966.
Bradbrook discusses the periodicals Jane Austen read and her debt to Samuel Johnson. He also notes her familiarity with the books explaining proper conduct both for men and for women, as well as her familiarity with the work of William Gilpin, who wrote on the picturesque landscape. He believes that her novels and letters show she was familiar with the novels of her predecessors.

Brown, Lloyd W. *Bits of Ivory: Narrative Techniques in Jane Austen's Fiction.* Baton Rouge: Louisiana State University Press, 1973.
Brown links Jane Austen to her eighteenth century predecessors and notes how the stylistic devices she uses: ironic diction, imagery, symbol, dialogue, and letter writing reveal character and illustrate the themes of her novels.

Burton, Antoinette. "Invention Is What Delights Me." In *Jane Austen and Discourses of Feminism*, edited by Devoney Looser, pp. 35-50. New York: St. Martin's Press, 1995.

Burton sees Austen as an early feminist because she protested the fact that histories written during her time paid no attention to women and were uninteresting to women. Burton discusses Austen's *The History of England from the Reign of Henry IV to the Death of Charles I*, part of the juvenilia, comparing it to Oliver Goldsmith's *History of England*.

Butler, Marilyn. *Jane Austen and the War of Ideas*. Oxford: Clarendon Press, 1975.

This highly influential study begins by discussing the history of the novel in the second half of the eighteenth century and the rise of sentimentalism and revolutionary feeling. After a discussion of novels influenced by revolutionary ideas, Butler locates Jane Austen ideologically as a conservative, allied to the landowning gentry, who believes the community is more important than the individual. She provides a reading of the novels that supports her thesis.

Castellanos, Gabriela. *Laughter, War and Feminism: Elements of Carnival in Three of Jane Austen's Novels*. New York: Peter Lang, 1994.

Castellanos discusses *Northanger Abbey*, *Pride and Prejudice*, and *Emma* in order to show that Austen's irony is typical of carnival in that it subverts orthodox values. Austen laughs at the notion of male superiority, adding, according to Castellanos, "carnivalesque laughter" to the sentimental novel. In *Northanger Abbey*, the heroine is not heroic and other typical novelistic "images, themes, episodes and sequences" are parodied. *Pride and Prejudice* shows "the universality of folly," even the hero and heroine err. *Emma*, whose heroine is appealing even when she errs, is an example of the upside down world of the carnival. Castellanos believes that laughter is Austen's response to the situation of women in a male-dominated society.

Castle, Terry. "The Austen Papers." *Lingua Franca: The Review of Academic Life* 5, no. 6 (September-October, 1995): 77-82.

Castle asserts that close relationships in Austen's novels often involve the heroine and the hero's sister. She notes that close same-sex relationships were common during Austen's time, and she maintains that Austen may have harbored unconscious incestuous feelings toward her sister Cassandra. Castle's argument, however, is not very convincing.

Evans, Mary. *Jane Austen and the State*. London: Tavistock, 1987.

Evans asserts that Austen's novels demonstrate the harmful effect of the market economy, particularly on women. This theme, she believes, places Austen in the tradition of European realism. She also notes that Austen was fully aware that self-interest often masquerades as morality and shows how her novels expose this self-interest. Finally, Evans maintains that Austen was aware of the political and economic changes occurring in her world and the increasing desire on the part of government for more control of the population.

Favret, Mary A. *Romantic Correspondence: Women, Politics, and the Fiction of Letters*. Cambridge, England: Cambridge University Press, 1993.

Jane Austen did not write revealing letters after the 1790's, and she does not make repeated reference to the physical appearance of her letters. Since she is aware that her letters will be read by people other than the person to whom they are addressed, they function as records of social life rather as than records of the inner life. Favret describes the importance of letters in *Mansfield Park*, *Lady Susan*, *Sense and Sensibility*, *Emma*, and *Persuasion*, maintaining that letters show the difficulty of maintaining privacy within a community.

Fergus, Jan. *Jane Austen: A Literary Life*. New York: St. Martin's Press, 1991.

Fergus discusses Austen's life, her juvenilia, and her novels in terms of the situation of the woman writer during her era. She is particularly informative about the economic aspect of publishing during the early nineteenth century and the immediate reception of the novels.

_____. "Tensions Between Security and Marginality." In *History, Gender and Eighteenth-Century Literature*, edited by Beth Fowkes Tobin, pp. 258-270. Athens: University of Georgia Press, 1994.

Fergus maintains that the Austen family was on the margin of the gentry class and it was further marginalized by its relative poverty. Jane Austen herself was marginalized even further as a woman. Fergus believes Austen's minor works, "Catherine: Or, The Bower" and *The Watsons*, concern highly marginalized young women. Her major novels, however, do not, except for minor figures. Fergus attributes this to Austen's need to maintain a balance between comedy and marginality.

Figes, Eva. *Sex and Subterfuge: Women Writers to 1850*. New York: Persea Books, 1982.

Figes analyzes "Love and Friendship" and "Lesley Castle" as literary parody.

Fleishman, Avrom. *A Reading of 'Mansfield Park': An Essay in Critical Synthesis*. Minneapolis: University of Minnesota Press, 1967.
A classic and still valuable study of *Mansfield Park*, as well as one of the first attempts to study one Jane Austen novel from many points of view. Its primary focus, however, is the relation of this novel to the history of its time and the issues of romanticism, the evangelical movement, and the slave trade. It also studies the critical reception of the novel, its place in the history of the novel, and its relation to myth and folklore.

Gard, Roger. *Jane Austen's Novels: The Art of Clarity*. New Haven, Conn.: Yale University Press, 1992.
Gard, who believes Jane Austen is one of the great European novelists as well as a moralist, notes her popularity with the general reader as well as with critics and attributes this to the graceful clarity of her writing. He traces the early development of her novels with particular attention to her characterization and her realism. He also devotes a full chapter to the second chapter of *Sense and Sensibility*. His discussion of *Pride and Prejudice* takes the form of a dialogue. He discusses *Mansfield Park* in terms of the critical attention now being paid to it. He also provides readings of *Emma* and *Persuasion*.

Gardiner, Ellen. "Privacy, Privilege and 'Poaching' in *Mansfield Park*." In *Jane Austen and Discourses of Feminism*, edited by Devoney Looser, pp. 151-166. New York: St. Martin's Press, 1995.
Gardiner believes *Mansfield Park* concerns the relationship between education and literary criticism. Fanny Price learns to use her reading to improve her society, demonstrating that moral authority is not merely the province of men, even of clergymen.

Grey, J. David, A. Walton Litz, and Brian Southam, eds. *The Jane Austen Companion with A Dictionary of Jane Austen's Life and Works*. New York: Macmillan, 1986.
An invaluable reference tool for any student of Jane Austen. This work contains brief articles on almost everything relating to the novelist from her relationship to consumerism to the games described in her novels, to the illustrations of her works. Outlines of her plots are included as are lists of characters.

Gillie, Christopher. *A Preface to Jane Austen*. London: Longman, 1974.
Gillie provides biographical facts and reads the juvenilia for clues to Jane Austen's beliefs. He also discusses her work in relation to that of her predecessors—Daniel Defoe, Jonathan Swift, Henry Fielding, and

Fanny Burney. He provides readings of the novels and comments on the situation of women during the period. One valuable chapter defines words used by Austen whose meanings ares now different than they were when she used them.

Halperin, John. *The Life of Jane Austen*. Baltimore: The John Hopkins University Press, 1984.
This biography caused a furor among some Austen critics because it attributed her ironic stance to her bitterness at being unmarried. Otherwise, it is an informative biography that contains intelligent analysis of Austen's work.

Harris, Jocelyn. "Jane Austen and the Burden of the (Male) Past: The Case Reexamined." In *Jane Austen and Discourses of Feminism*, edited by Devoney Looser, pp. 87-100. New York: St. Martin's Press, 1995.
Harris attempts to refute Gilbert and Gubar's belief that women writers were uncomfortable in the male literary tradition. She believes that the important literary influences on Austen were Geoffrey Chaucer, William Shakespeare, John Milton, and Samuel Richardson, pointing out the allusions to *Paradise Lost* in *Sense and Sensibility* and *Mansfield Park*, to Richardson in *Pride and Prejudice*, *Mansfield Park*, and *Sense and Sensibility*. She also sees allusions to *A Midsummer Night's Dream* in *Emma*, and allusions to many English writers, particularly Chaucer, in *Persuasion*. In addition, she finds evidence that Jane Austen was very much a Romantic author and she maintains that Austen revised Western culture's insistence that women were "vain, inconstant, necessarily mute, ignorant, and unequal."

_____. *Jane Austen's Art of Memory*. Cambridge, England: Cambridge University Press, 1989.
Harris links Jane Austen's novels with the considerable reading she must have done. In *Northanger Abbey*, she finds allusions to John Locke and Sir Philip Sydney. The narrative voice resembles the one used by Fielding in *Tom Jones*. She finds resemblances between Austen's novels and the novels of Samuel Richardson. She also sees connections between *Emma* and William Shakespeare's *A Midsummer Night's Dream*, and *Persuasion* and Geoffrey Chaucer's "The Wife of Bath's Tale."

Hoeveler, Diane. "Vindicating *Northanger Abbey*: Mary Wollstonecraft, Jane Austen and Gothic Feminism." In *Jane Austen and Discourses of Feminism*, edited by Devoney Looser, pp. 117-136. New York: St. Martin's Press, 1995.

Hoeveler maintains that Wollstonecraft and other women writers of Gothic fiction taught women that their suffering at the hands of men would be rewarded. In *Northanger Abbey*, on the other hand, Jane Austen satirized the suffering, passive, Gothic heroine as well as the sentimental heroine. She provides a reading of *Northanger Abbey* that demonstrates the connection between Wollstonecraft and Austen.

Honan, Park. *Jane Austen: Her Life*. New York: St. Martin's Press, 1987. Although it does not analyze Austen's novels, this readable biography thoroughly explores Austen's life. It goes into greater detail about Jane Austen's extremely brief engagement to Harris Bigg-Wither than other biographies and it provides detailed information about Austen's relatives.

Horwitz, Barbara. *Jane Austen and the Question of Women's Education*. New York: Peter Lang, 1991.
Horwitz outlines the positions taken by the writers on women's education who were Austen's predecessors and contemporaries. They agreed that the goal of women's education was to ensure that women would be good wives and mothers by training them to always exhibit good nature. Austen, however, believed the goal of education for both men and women must be self-knowledge. This ideal colors Austen's attitude toward marriage and toward conventional notions of masculinity and femininity. In addition, Austen pokes fun at characters who exhibit an overabundance of good nature. Horwitz provides readings of the most popular conduct books and Austen's novels to demonstrate this point.

Hudson, Glenda A. "Consolidated Communities: Masculine and Feminist Values in Jane Austen's Fiction." In *Jane Austen and Discourses of Feminism*, edited by Devoney Looser, pp. 100-116. New York: St. Martin's Press, 1995.
Hudson believes Austen focuses on brother-sister relationships and semi-incestuous marriages to advocate egalitarian marriage. She notes that marriages were forbidden between relatives by marriage and between blood relatives, and she shows that the danger of incest was an important component of many novels of the time. According to Hudson, Austen either satirized the dangers of incest or used its possibility as a vehicle to strengthen the family as in *Mansfield Park*. Hudson believes Jane Austen inadvertently promoted the idea that the family should be a safe haven and that a woman should be an "angel in the house."

Jane Austen Society. *Collected Reports of the Jane Austen Society 1976-1985*. Overton, Hampshire, England: Jane Austen Society, 1989.
This book contains the annual reports of the British Jane Austen Society, as well as interesting critical commentary on various aspects of her work.

Jerinic, Maria. "In Defense of the Gothic: Rereading *Northanger Abbey*." In *Jane Austen and Discourses of Feminism*, edited by Devoney Looser, pp. 137-150. New York: St. Martin's Press, 1995.
Jerinic believes *Northanger Abbey* is about the importance of the right of women to read and to read what they themselves choose. She also maintains that *Northanger Abbey* is more an imitation of a Gothic novel than a parody of one. She provides a reading of *Northanger Abbey* and compares it to Ann Radcliffe's *The Mysteries of Udolpho*.

Johnson, Claudia L. "Jane Austen." In *Equivocal Beings: Politics, Gender, and Sentimentality in the 1790's*, pp. 191-204. Chicago: University of Chicago Press, 1995.
Johnson reviews the history of criticism of *Emma* from the end of World War II to the present. She also notes that Emma is never condemned for her lack of conventional femininity. Johnson believes the novel is essentially about manliness. Knightley is seen as the "new man," not chivalrous in Edmund Burke's sense, but a throwback to the older tradition of a member of the gentry who does not bow to tyranny. Johnson believes this redefinition of masculinity makes conventional notions of femininity seem as undesirable as effeminate masculinity. Johnson believes Emma herself behaves like an effeminate man in her harmful behavior to Harriet Smith, the too-feminine woman, and to Jane Fairfax, a "gothicized" example of physical weakness and fortitude.

_____. *Jane Austen: Women, Politics and the Novel*. Chicago: University of Chicago Press, 1988.
This work constitutes one of the most important contributions to Jane Austen studies in the past decade. Johnson decries the critics who have seen Austen as a decorative emblem of English country life during the Regency, the critics who ally her with the aristocracy, and the critics who believe she is politically conservative. Johnson sees the times as particularly hostile to women writers who are not didactic or conservative and reads the novels as subversive attacks on patriarchal society, demonstrating that authority figures are satirized and shown to be

totally inadequate. Johnson establishes Jane Austen as a feminist author.

Kelly, Gary. "Jane Austen, Romantic Feminism and Civil Society." In *Jane Austen and Discourses of Feminism*, edited by Devoney Looser, pp. 19-35. New York: St. Martin's Press, 1995.
Kelly believes that Austen's novels show a feminized version of society and although he believes she is not a "romantic feminist," her novels are feminist in that she believes women can improve society. He also explains why her novels seem to belong to the late eighteenth century rather than the nineteenth century and why her novels remained popular while other novels by women authors were forgotten. He provides brief readings of the novels.

Koppel, Gene. *The Religious Dimension of Jane Austen's Novels*. Ann Arbor, Mich.: UMI Press, 1985.
Koppel not only demonstrates that Jane Austen was personally religious, he discusses her novels in terms of late twentieth century radical theology. He believes that *Emma* is concerned with spiritual perfection and that *Mansfield Park* proves that this world can never be perfect. He sees *Persuasion* as an exploration of the mystery of the human personality.

Lane, Maggie. *Jane Austen and Food*. London: The Hambledon Press, 1995.
Lane asserts that Jane Austen used food "to illustrate character and define moral worth." She also discusses the etiquette of meals, foods familiar to Jane Austen but no longer familiar to modern readers, housekeeping in Jane Austen's own home and in the novels, food in relation to gender, eating disorders, and the symbolic value of food. Lane even provides some recipes. She cites *Emma* to demonstrate her assertions.

Le Fay, Deirdre, ed. *Jane Austen's Letters*. New York: Oxford University Press, 1995.
This collection of letters supersedes previous collections in that it contains some new material and some of the letters are dated differently. Indices and annotations are supplied, as are physical descriptions of the manuscripts.

Lew, Joseph. "The Abominable Traffic: *Mansfield Park* and the Dynamics of Slavery." In *History, Gender and Eighteenth-Century Literature*, edited by Beth Fowkes Tobin, pp. 271-300. Athens: University of Georgia Press, 1994.

Lew discusses slavery in the Caribbean and antislavery agitation in England in the early nineteenth century and shows they are alluded to in *Mansfield Park*. He finds similarities between *Mansfield Park* and Elizabeth Inchbald's *A Simple Story*.

Looser, Devoney. Introduction to *Jane Austen and Discourses of Feminism*. New York: St. Martin's Press, 1995.

Looser describes how critics have questioned Jane Austen's feminism and in what senses Austen may be described as a feminist writer. Looser sees the novels as political and as explorations of gender issues.

McMaster, Juliet. *Jane Austen the Novelist*. New York: St. Martin's Press, 1995.

A fine collection of essays addressing Jane Austen's place in Western culture, her relation to feminist criticism, and her treatment of love. McMaster also provides readings of *The Watsons*, *Pride and Prejudice*, *Emma*, "Love and Friendship," and "The Beautifull Cassandra." Some of the essays appeared in an earlier collection and in *Persuasions*, the journal of the Jane Austen Society of North America.

Moler, Kenneth. *Jane Austen's Art of Allusion*. Lincoln: University of Nebraska Press, 1960.

Moler analyzes each of Austen's novels to show her use of the ideas of her predecessors and contemporaries, most of which she adapted to her own artistic ends. Like them, Austen was concerned with self-knowledge, the tension between art and nature, imagination and judgment, self and society, and the difficulty involved in judging others.

Mooneyham, Laura G. *Romance, Language and Education in Jane Austen' Novels*. New York: St. Martin's Press, 1988.

Mooneyham sees the correct use of language as central to the development of Jane Austen's plots. The lively heroines—Marianne, Elizabeth, and Emma—need to discipline themselves to avoid substituting wit for wisdom. Catherine has to learn to discern the true meaning of words. The quiet heroines—Elinor, Fanny, and Anne—need to use language to express themselves rather than remaining silent.

Morris, Ivor. *Mr. Collins Considered: Approaches to Jane Austen*. London: Routledge & Kegan Paul, 1987.

The author takes a different approach to one of Jane Austen's famous fools, Mr. Collins, the silly, obsequious clergyman in *Pride and Preju-*

dice. Morris sees him as an exemplar of the faults of his age, but no worse a human being than Darcy, her hero. Morris believes that Jane Austen herself was motivated by religious principles.

Mukherjee, Meenakshi. *Jane Austen*. New York: St. Martin's Press, 1991.
According to the author, Jane Austen subverted the limitations placed upon women by her society as well as their denigration by that society. Her comedy helps reconcile the tensions between conformity and rebellion present in the novels. Mukherjee discusses Austen's novels in the context of the writing of her predecessors and contemporaries, noting particularly the controversy over women's physical strength. She surveys Jane Austen criticism briefly, and she discusses the pictures of marriage and the class system in the novels as well as Jane Austen's interest in the world outside England. She also notes that Austen is concerned with the maintenance of privacy in a tightly closed world. Mukherjee believes their ambiguity makes the novels great.

Nardin, Jane. *Those Elegant Decorums: The Concept of Propriety in Jane Austen's Novels*. Albany: State University of New York Press, 1973.
Nardin discusses the novels as they illustrate Jane Austen's idea of propriety as it involves the idea that correct social behavior is an indication of moral worth, as well as a form of protection of the individual. She notes that Jane Austen uses levels of irony in her writing, and she defines some of the abstract terms used by Austen. The word "elegance," she points out, lacks a moral connotation, while other words, such as "propriety," have a moral and a social meaning.

Nicholson, Nigel. *The World of Jane Austen*. London: Weidenfeld & Nicolson, 1991.
A beautifully illustrated book that discusses places Jane Austen saw or may have seen. The portrayal of her life and personality may be unduly sunny, and there is much conjecture about how her life may have affected her novels and about how her novels may have reflected her life, but this book provides a readable account of her world.

Paris, Bernard J. *Character and Conflict in Jane Austen's Novels: A Psychological Approach*. Detroit: Wayne State University Press, 1979.
Paris gives an interesting reading of the novels, focusing on *Emma*, *Mansfield Park*, *Persuasion*, and *Pride and Prejudice*. He believes that certain tensions in the novels can best be resolved by looking at them with insights derived from Northrop Frye, who discussed the myths underlying comedy, and Karen Horney, whose ideas, Paris believes, shed light on both the characters in the novel and Jane Austen herself.

Poovey, Mary. *The Proper Lady and the Woman Writer*. Chicago: University of Chicago Press, 1984.

Poovey argues that Austen solved the contradiction between being a proper lady, which involves avoiding notice, and being a writer, which involves courting attention, by her choice of subject and by her literary style. Her reading of *Lady Susan* suggests to Poovey that Austen believed that women's unregulated desire is harmful, but so is society's attempt to control the individual. She traces this motif convincingly through all of Austen's novels, asserting that the tension between social duty and individual desire is resolved symbolically by focusing on romance rather than on social or psychological reality. In doing so, according to Poovey, Austen perpetuates the myth that romantic love will empower women permanently.

Roberts, Warren. *Jane Austen and the French Revolution*. New York: St. Martin's Press, 1979.

One of the first studies to demonstrate that Jane Austen was fully aware of the momentous events of her time and used them as background for her novels even when they were not specifically mentioned. In addition, Austen conveys the experience of living through great social change. Roberts not only discusses the effects of the French Revolution on Austen's writing but also her feminism, her attitude toward religion, and her treatment of the slave trade.

Ruderman, Anne Crippen. *The Pleasures of Virtue: Political Thought in the Novels of Jane Austen*. Lanham, Md.: Rowman & Littlefield, 1995.

According to Ruderman, Jane Austen's novels show that Austen believed that virtue ensures happiness and that the people with the deepest feelings and highest intelligence enjoy life the most. Ruderman also discusses Austen's views on education, sensibility, prudence, justice, pride, modesty, and religion. An extensive bibliography is included.

Ruoff, Gene. *Jane Austen's 'Sense and Sensibility.'* New York: St. Martin's Press, 1992.

Ruoff approaches this novel using feminist and new historical critical theory. He has chosen to write about *Sense and Sensibility* because he believes it crystallizes the most important aesthetic and social issues in her novels. According to Ruoff, *Sense and Sensibility* reflects the historic issues of the 1790's, although it was revised later. Because of this, he believes the novel is covertly revolutionary. Ruoff also discusses its critical reception, the legal issues involved in inheritance during Austen's time, the importance of birth order, and the tensions the novel illustrates between two codes of behavior—one based on passion, the other on reason. Ruoff asserts that Jane Austen had to remake the literary tradition in order to tell women's stories.

Said, Edward. "Jane Austen and Empire." In *Romanticism: An Anthology*, edited by Duncan Wu, pp. 417-433. Oxford: Blackwell, 1995.
Said reads *Mansfield Park* as evidence of the rise of imperialism in England. Antigua and the slave trade are important to Mansfield Park as an estate and as a symbol of England. Sir Thomas Bertram resembles Robinson Crusoe as one who rules a realm alone and must keep it in order and restore it to order if he leaves it for a time. Said maintains that family ties alone will not assure the stability of *Mansfield Park*. Its continuity, and that of England, depends on exploitation and imperialism.

Scheuermann, Mona. *Her Bread to Earn: Women, Money and Society from Defoe to Austen*. Lexington: University Press of Kentucky, 1993.
Scheuermann argues that Austen assumes her readers are rational and her characters are normal. Financial considerations are an integral part of Austen's novels, and Scheuermann provides readings of the novels to demonstrate this.

Siskind, Clifford. "Jane Austen and the Engendering of Disciplinarity." In *Jane Austen and Discourses of Feminism*, edited by Devoney Looser, pp. 51-70. New York: St. Martin's Press, 1995.
Siskind maintains that Austen's novels represented a new departure for the novel and were therefore remembered when the novels of other women who remained in the tradition of Richardson and Fielding were excluded from what came to be known as the canon. Her novels were considered worthy because irony tempered their romanticism. He also discusses the increase in the number of novels written by women and the rise of the periodical.

Southam, B. C. *Jane Austen*. Harlow, Essex, England: Longman, 1975.
This brief introduction to Jane Austen discusses her popularity as well as the fact that she was misread for years by those who considered her a miniaturist. Southam believes her picture of the age was entirely realistic as she question its self-satisfaction. He sees her novels as moving from literary to social satire, and he discusses her language, her thoughts on love and marriage, and the inner life of her heroines.

_____. *Jane Austen: The Critical Heritage*. 2 vols. London: Routledge & Kegan Paul, 1987.

A lengthy introduction to the second volume describes the tenor of Jane Austen criticism until 1940. Particular attention is paid to sensitive and accurate criticism written from the beginning of the nineteenth century and to criticism by well-known authors. The second part of each volume is an anthology of criticism.

_____. *Jane Austen's Literary Manuscripts: A Study of the Novelist's Development Through the Surviving Papers.* London: Oxford University Press, 1964.

A classic study in which the juvenilia and other unpublished material by Jane Austen is studied on a textual and on a critical basis. *Lady Susan's* relation to Austen's other work is discussed and possible reasons are given as to why *The Watsons* was never finished. Southam also writes about the canceled chapters of *Persuasion* and *Sanditon*, Jane Austen's unfinished novel.

_____, ed. *Sanditon: An Unfinished Novel*, by Jane Austen. Oxford: Clarendon Press, 1975.

In the introduction, Southam discusses this fragment of Austen's last novel. A facsimile of the original manuscript as well as the text of the novel is provided.

Stewart, Maaja. *Domestic Realities and Imperial Fictions: Jane Austen's Novels in Eighteenth Century Contexts.* Athens: University of Georgia Press, 1993.

Stewart reads Jane Austen as a skillful novelist and one who responded to the currents of her time: revolution, trade wars, slavery, and imperialism. She sees the primary conflict in the novels, as a conflict between the disinherited younger son, who has had to emigrate in order to make a living and then returns, and his landed older brother. They struggle over the family estate and the women who live in it. Thus, Stewart focuses more strongly than other critics have on issues such as Colonel Brandon's adventures in India, Sir Thomas Bertram's trip to Antigua, and Captain Wentworth's naval victories. Women characters, such as Fanny Price, are disinherited and dependent yet unthreatening.

Tanner, Tony. *Jane Austen.* Cambridge, Mass.: Harvard University Press, 1986.

Tanner discusses the novels in relation to Austen ideas about society, education, and language. He notes Austen's affinities with John Locke and Hannah More. His readings of the individual novels are compelling, finding anger to be the hidden evil in *Northanger Abbey*. He finds secrecy to cause sickness in *Sense and Sensibility*. He sees *Pride and*

Prejudice in terms of the history of its age and notes its use of letters. He also notes its resemblance to plays. *Mansfield Park*, he asserts, is Jane Austen's most important novel because it has to do with who shall inherit England. He also believes the reader is meant to feel sorry for Emma, whose life is so limited. He notes tendencies in *Persuasion* that have come to be known as modernist. He also notes the importance of time in the novel as well as its various settings. To him, the fact that there is no reliable authority figure in the novel means that Jane Austen is seeking replacements for the older institutions and values that have lost their validity. He also reads *Sanditon* as a commentary on the loss of stability in Jane Austen's world.

Ten Harmsel, Henrietta. *Jane Austen: A Study in Fictional Conventions*. London: Mouton, 1964.
This valuable study illustrates how Jane Austen used the conventions of the eighteenth century novel, but transformed them to suit her own aesthetic ends.

Thompson, James. *Between Self and World: The Novels of Jane Austen*. University Park: Pennsylvania State University Press, 1988.
Thompson uses Marxist theory, psychoanalytic theory, and language theory to interpret Austen's novels. He sees a condemnation of capitalism in Jane Austen's lack of interest in material things and in her examination of the marriage market. Thompson argues that marriage is important to the novels because it restores the intimacy that capitalism has destroyed. He also believes that for Jane Austen, language has become untrustworthy. He sees the heroines as narcissists who move from euphoria to despair before they come to know themselves. His thought-provoking arguments create a stimulating if not totally convincing work.

Todd, Janet. *Gender, Art and Death*. New York: Continuum, 1993.
Todd provides a detailed review of critical discussions of Jane Austen's feminism. She believes that Jane Austen did not believe in human perfectibility, disapproved strongly of excessive sensibility, and refused to see women as victims. She maintains that both Fanny Price in *Mansfield Park* and Anne Elliot in *Persuasion* are punished for excessive sensibility.

Tucker, George Holbert. *Jane Austen the Woman: Some Biographical Insights*. New York: St. Martin's Press, 1994.
Tucker refutes notions that Austen's novels are limited because she led an uneventful life. He argues for the depth of her education, the breadth

of her reading, and her thorough knowledge of political affairs and international events.

Wallace, Tara Ghoshal. *Jane Austen and Narrative Authority.* New York: St. Martin's Press, 1995.
Wallace asserts that each of Austen's novels experiments with narrative authority. The narrators are always fallible, but the text helps the reader interpret their remarks. She maintains that Austen struggled over whether to be a modest woman or a powerful author, so the powerful woman is a feature of her novels. She believes that *Lady Susan* is a paradigm of the connection between gender, language, and authority in her novels. In *Northanger Abbey*, she sees a struggle between the reader and the narrator to control the text. She is convinced that *Sense and Sensibility* is about female authority. In *Pride and Prejudice*, she shows barriers to understanding. *Mansfield Park*, Wallace asserts, is about the horrors of family life. She notes that in *Emma*, the narrative voice is always being undermined, allowing multiple readings of the text. In *Persuasion*, Wallace believes that Austen undercuts her own authority by attacking her own certainties.

Warner, Sylvia Townsend. *Jane Austen.* Harlow, Essex, England: Longman House, 1970.
This brief biography of Austen also describes her novels. It is simplified but not inaccurate.

Watkins, Susan. *Jane Austen's Town and Country Style.* New York: Rizzoli, 1990.
This beautifully illustrated book is a brief biography of Jane Austen augmented by comments on historic events, such as the war with France and the trial of Warren Hastings. Watkins also discusses the daily life and activities of the English aristocracy. These chapters are illustrated by pictures of their homes, gardens, clothing, and furniture. Unfortunately, these illustrations may mislead the unwary reader to believe that Jane Austen was a member of the aristocracy, or was wealthy herself. She was not.

White, Laura Mooneyham. "Jane Austen and the Marriage Plot: Questions of Persistence." In *Jane Austen and Discourses of Feminism*, edited by Devoney Looser, pp. 71-86. New York: St. Martin's Press, 1995.
White uses structuralist and psychoanalytic critical techniques in order to explain the persistence of the marriage plot. In addition to providing a reading of *Sense and Sensibility* and explaining the dissatisfaction many readers have felt with it, she also gives readings of *Persuasion*

and *Sanditon*. She maintains that the marriage plot itself is not as antifeminist as some critics believe.

Wilks, Brian. *Jane Austen*. London: Hamlyn, 1978.
This readable biography of Jane Austen is generously illustrated. There is no literary comment, but there are ample quotations from the juvenilia and the letters, as well as from the writing of family members and contemporaries.

Williams, Michael. *Jane Austen: Six Novels and Their Methods*. New York: St. Martin's Press, 1986.
Williams uses the reader response critical method formulated by Wolfgang Iser to examine Austen's novelistic techniques. He believes that *Northanger Abbey* is a parody of novels in general, and he believes *Sense and Sensibility* is an argument about taste. Williams reads *Pride and Prejudice* as a search for stability and notes that readers are often unsure in their responses to *Mansfield Park*, which he considers a great work, because readers can imagine alternate endings to it. In *Emma*, he sees affinities between readers and Emma, who is also trying to read events—a situation which explains why readers are so fond of her. He believes *Persuasion* may be unfinished.

JOANNA BAILLIE (1762-1851)

Baillie was born in Glasgow, Scotland, in 1762, the daughter of a clergyman. She appears to have fairly well educated for the times. Six years after moving to England, she published her *Poems of Nature and Rustic Manners* (1790). In 1798, she published *A Series of Plays*, which contained an "Introductory Discourse" setting out her critical theories. Her *Miscellaneous Plays* were published in 1804. *The Family Legend* was produced in 1810; *Metrical Legends* was published in 1821. *Poetic Miscellanies*, a verse anthology which she edited, appeared in 1823. Her play *The Martyr* appeared in 1826, followed by *Fugitive Verses* in 1840, and *Ahalya Baee, A Poem* in 1849. Her *Works* appeared in 1851, the year of her death. Her extensive circle of friends included many of the important literary figures of the day.

Ashfield, Andrew, ed. "Joanna Baillie." In *Romantic Women Poets 1770-1838*, pp. 65-107. New York: St. Martin's Press, 1995.
Ashfield provides a selection of Baillie's works as well as a brief biographical headnote.

Burroughs, Catherine B. "English Romantic Women Writers and Theatre
Theory: Joanna Baillie's Prefaces to the 'Plays on the Passions.'" In
Re-Visioning Romanticism: British Women Writers, 1776-1837, edited
by Carol Shiner Wilson and Joel Haefner, pp. 274-296. Philadelphia:
University of Pennsylvania Press, 1994.

According to Burroughs, women writers of the late eighteenth century
were interested in role playing and in theater criticism, although they
did not always write about these topics for publication. Even successful
women dramatists had to struggle against social prohibitions against
women writing. They often described themselves as anxiety ridden
individuals who were urged to write for the stage by a man, often the
theater manager. Joanna Baillie uses this convention but she is fairly
self-confident. Baillie believes characters can best win the sympathy
of the audience when playwrights show them alone in their "closets."
Baillie also advocates a natural style of acting and speech, a smaller
stage, and lighting that would echo the character's psychological state.
Burroughs connects the term "closet drama" to plays about homosexu-
als and notes that modern lesbian writers about the theater agree with
Baillie.

_____. "'Out of the Pale of Social Kindred Cast': Conflicted
Performance Styles in Joanna Baillie's *De Montfort*." In *Romantic
Women Writers: Voices and Countervoices*, edited by Paula R. Feldman
and Theresa M. Kelley, pp. 223-235. Hanover, N.H.: University Press
of New England, 1995.

Burroughs argues that Baillie's attempt to show private emotions on a
public stage was analogous to the woman writer's wish for, yet fear of,
public display. In describing *De Montfort*, Burroughs explains that De
Montfort is a hero-villain of the type that became known as Byronic.
He murders Rezenvelt, who had spared his life in a duel, yet his sister
Jane, portrayed as a perfect woman, insists that despite this act he is
still noble. He cannot be hypocritical, Burroughs notes, as women,
particularly women writers, must be.

Cox, Jeffrey. "Joanna Baillie." In *Seven Gothic Dramas 1789-1825*, pp.
50-57. Athens: Ohio University Press, 1992.

According to Cox, Baillie was a very popular dramatist who wanted
to dramatize the "psychology of passion" like other romantic writers.
He considers her plays to have been influenced by Gothic novels in
their settings, their rationalized supernaturalism, and their use of the
Byronic hero-villain as well as their stress on the importance of women
characters. He provides readings of *De Montfort* and *Orra*. He is also

interested in the impact of fear on women and the impact of male expectations on women.

Mellor, Anne K., and Richard E. Matlak, eds. "Joanna Baillie." In *British Literature 1780-1830*, pp. 439-499. Fort Worth, Tex.: Harcourt Brace College Publishers, 1996.
The editors discuss Baillie's life and work and provide a selection of her poetry and prose.

Wordsworth, Jonathan. Introduction to *A Series of Plays*, by Joanna Baillie. New York: Woodstock Books, 1990.
This edition of Joanna Baillie's plays includes an "Introductory Discourse" by her as well as two tragedies, *Count Basil* and *De Monfort*, and *The Tryal: A Comedy*. In his introduction, Wordsworth compares Baillie's introduction to William Wordsworth's "Preface to Lyrical Ballads" and finds Baillie's work to be better written. He asserts that Wordsworth and Samuel Taylor Coleridge derived the philosophy on which their writing is based, particularly that it should be spontaneous and that it should concern itself with "the lower orders," from Baillie. He also discusses the plays, finding *The Tryal* "lively" but "unnatural" and *De Monfort* a major work.

ANNA LAETITIA BARBAULD (1743-1825)

A child prodigy who was encouraged by her schoolmaster father, Anna Laetitia Aiken was born in Leicestershire. Her father was a Dissenter whose friends included Joseph Priestley and Josiah Wedgwood. In 1773, she published her first book, *Poems*. With her brother, John Aiken, she produced *Miscellaneous Pieces in Prose*. The next year, she married Reverend Rochemont Barbauld and with him established a school. They also adopted a nephew. Her husband's worsening mental illness (he committed suicide in 1808) gave her the entire responsibility for the school. For her nephew, she wrote *Lessons for Children* (1778). In 1781, *Hymns in Prose for Children* appeared. After selling the school, she seems to have had more time to write. Her political pamphlets include *An Address to the Opposers of the Repeal of the Corporation and Test Acts* (1790), *An Epistle to William Wilberforce* (1791), *Civic Sermons to the People* (1792) and *Sins of the Government, Sins of the Nation* (1793). She wrote poetry and edited the poetry of Mark Akenside (1794) and William Collins (1797), as well as Samuel Richardson's *Letters* (1804). Barbauld also wrote a still useful critical biography and introduction to Richardson's works. Her history of the novel until Richardson and her discussion of his contemporaries is surprisingly cogent and alive. Her analysis of his novels is clear. She also wrote biographical and critical introductions for an multivolume edition of *The British Novelists* (1810). The next year, she published *The Female Speaker*, a book of prose and poetry for young ladies, as well as *1811*, an antiwar poem that was severely censured and proved to be Barbauld's last published work. An anti-woman backlash coupled with the Romantic reaction against the Enlightenment destroyed her reputation. Feminist scholarship in the twentieth century began to revive Barbauld's reputation, as shown by the scholarly edition of her poetry published in 1994.

Armstrong, Isobel. "The Gush of the Feminine: How Can We Read Women's Poetry of the Romantic Period?" In *Romantic Women Writers: Voices and Countervoices*, edited by Paula R. Feldman and Theresa M. Kelley, pp. 13-32. Hanover, N.H.: University Press of New England, 1995.
Armstrong provides a highly informative reading of Barbauld's "Inscription for an Ice-House," connecting her poetry to Edmund Burke's ideas concerning the beautiful and the sublime as well as the ideas of Adam Smith and Thomas Malthus.

Ashfield, Andrew, ed. "Anna Laetitia Barbauld." In *Romantic Women Poets 1770-1838*, pp. 9-26. New York: St. Martin's Press, 1995.
Ashfield provides a selection of Barbauld's works as well as a brief biographical headnote.

Ellison, Julie. "The Politics of Fancy in the Age of Sensibility." In *Re-Visioning Romanticism: British Women Writers, 1776-1837*, edited by Carol Shiner Wilson and Joel Haefner, pp. 228-256. Philadelphia: University of Pennsylvania Press, 1994.
Ellison defines the term "fancy," connecting it with sensibility and imperialism. She differentiates between male and female sensibility, and she demonstrates how Anna Barbauld and Phillis Wheatley used "the motions of fancy" to approach political issues. Ellison analyzes A Summer Evening's Meditation," "An Epistle to William Wilberforce, Esq. on the Rejection of the Bill for Abolishing the Slave Trade," and *1811*. The last poem was condemned as too political, and therefore on a subject unsuitable for a woman writer. Ellison believes that "fancy" demands confidence, but eventually exhausts it.

McCarthy, William. "We Hoped the *Woman* Was Going to Appear: Repression, Desire, and Gender in Anna Letitia Barbauld's Early Poems."

In *Romantic Women Writers: Voices and Countervoices*, edited by Paula R. Feldman and Theresa M. Kelley, pp. 113-137. Hanover, N.H.: University Press of New England, 1995.

McCarthy denies that Barbauld is either unfeminine or unfeminist by providing readings of her early poems, particularly "The Groans of the Tankard," "To Wisdom," and "Corsica." He notes that her poems demonstrate their author's anger and sorrow at being deprived of freedom and opportunity because of her sex, but because of cultural constraints, her emotions had to be "encoded," rather than directly expressed.

McCarthy, William, and Elizabeth Kraft. Introduction to *The Poems of Anna Letitia Barbauld*, edited by William McCarthy and Elizabeth Kraft. Athens: University of Georgia Press, 1994.

An excellent scholarly tool as well as a fine introduction to Barbauld's life and work. The editors outline her biography, discuss her popularity, and analyze the causes of her loss of poetic reputation. Her poetry is reprinted, and missing poems are described. A discussion of textual problems is included, as well as extensive commentary and notes.

Messenger, Ann. *His and Hers: Essays in Restoration and Eighteenth Century Literature.* Lexington: University Press of Kentucky, 1986.

Messenger discuss Barbauld's poetry, particularly "The Groans of the Tankard," (1773) a light, mock-heroic work. She asserts elements in the poem are reminiscent of John Milton, Alexander Pope, and the Gothic novel. Its light tone allowed Barbauld to criticize her world. She also notes that the comic tone in "Letter of John Bull" (1791) masks an attack on English overeagerness to fight France. "The Cure on the Banks of the Rhone" (1791) is another antiwar piece. Barbauld's satire on the follies of ladies is more open; here she is not afraid to speak her mind, nor is she afraid to attack Mary Wollstonecraft's work in "The Rights of Women" (1792). Barbauld also wrote literary criticism, and Messenger credits her with appreciating the early women writers and approving of their use of satire.

Rodgers, Betsy. *Georgian Chronicle: Mrs. Barbauld and Her Family.* London: Methuen, 1958.

The author discusses Barbauld's parents, her early life at the school her father ran, her work as a schoolteacher, and the reception of her poetry. Rodgers also discusses Barbauld's friends and acquaintances as well as her surviving nieces and nephews. A great many previously unpublished letters are included in an appendix to the book.

Ross, Marlon B. "Configurations of Feminine Reform: The Woman Writer and the Tradition of Dissent." In *Re-Visioning Romanticism: British Women Writers, 1776-1837*, edited by Carol Shiner Wilson and Joel Haefner, pp. 91-110. Philadelphia: University of Pennsylvania Press, 1994.

According to Ross, for women to engage in politics at all during the Romantic period, they had to dissent from conventional ideology, which excluded them from the political realm. Many of those who did engage in political controversy came from a tradition of religious dissent. Conservative women such as Hannah More disguised their political writing by using the form of the conduct book. Barbauld used the form of the occasional poem, which could be political but at that time was usually a vehicle for expounding morality. Ross compares Barbauld to More and finds Barbauld more democratic. Ross also notes that many of Barbauld's poems are both moral and political, using "The Mouse's Petition" as an example. Ross also provides a reading of Barbauld's *1811* and Lucy Aiken's "On Seeing Blenheim Castle."

Wilson, Carol Shiner. "Lost Needles, Tangled Threads: Stitchery, Domesticity, and the Artistic Enterprise in Barbauld, Edgeworth, Taylor, and Lamb." In *Re-Visioning Romanticism: British Women Writers, 1776-1837*, edited by Carol Shiner Wilson and Joel Haefner, pp. 167-190. Philadelphia: University of Pennsylvania Press, 1994.

Wilson points out how these authors often used their approval of needlework to subvert domesticity in their work. She quotes poetry and stories to show the importance of the mother, the value of female authors as educators, the use of sewing to teach orderliness, and these authors' disdain for using needlework merely to decorate. She connects Barbauld's acceptance of class boundaries with her stoicism. Wilson also discusses Barbauld's "Characters," "Washing Day," and "The Rights of Women."

THE BRONTËS

The following is a list of books written about the Brontë family. Individual biographies of Anne, Charlotte, and Emily, as well as a listing of works about them appear after these entries. Modern editions of the Brontës' works are readily available.

Barker, Juliet. *The Brontës*. New York: St. Martin's Press, 1995.

More than one thousand pages long, Barker's biography is a truly monumental work, much of which is based on previously unpublished material, including essays written by the sisters in French. Barker also provides a complete description of the children's writing about Gondal, Angria, and Glasstown, the imaginary worlds they created. Barker believes that the Brontës were not as eccentric as previous biographers made them out to be. She notes the great accomplishment of Patrick Brontë, who began life as a peasant and managed to become a respected clergyman.

Davies, Stevie. *The Brontë Sisters: Selected Poems*. Manchester, England: Fyfield Books, 1985.
The author believes the Brontës' poetry has been unfairly neglected, asserting that it is typical of Romantic poetry in that it assumes the primacy of the imagination and often includes personal confession. Although, according to Davies, its rhyme schemes, ideas, and vocabulary are often repetitive, the poetry shows great intensity. Davies further notes that the poetry and the novels share similar themes and that the poetry of each sister differs from that of the others. The selection of poetry in this book attempts to demonstrate the variety in the Brontë sisters' work.

Evans, Barbara, and Gareth Lloyd Evans. *The Scribner Companion to the Brontës*. New York: Charles Scribner's Sons, 1982.
This literary guide is a valuable source of information on the Brontës as it provides biographical information, complete with lists of friends and relatives of the family. A discussion of the juvenilia is provided as well as a synopsis of all published works. The initial reception of each work is described as well as the current commentary on it. The authors list and discuss all the characters and settings mentioned in the Brontës' work, as well as actual places associated with the family. Unfortunately, the volume is dated.

Gardiner, Juliet. *The Brontës at Haworth: The World Within*. New York: Clarkson N. Potter, 1992.
This extremely attractive book is full of pictures illustrating the daily life of the times and of the Brontës themselves. It includes pictures done by the Brontës, pictures of the Brontës and their relatives, and pictures of the scenery and houses in the vicinity of Haworth as well as of the area where Patrick Brontë was born. Biographical information and a list of the Brontës' connections are also provided.

Knapp, Bettina L. *The Brontës: Branwell, Anne, Emily, Charlotte.* New York: Continuum, 1991.

Knapp discusses the life and works of the Brontës and provides a chronology of events in their lives. She sees Anne as a feminist writer with a strong moral vision. Her poetry, according to Knapp, gives evidence of great religious anxiety. Knapp outlines the plot of *The Tenant of Wildfell Hall* and discusses its relationship to Gothic novels. Knapp believes that Emily's poetry is strongly influenced by her involvement with nature. She feels that *Wuthering Heights*, because it is based on myth, is not wholly fathomable. Knapp summarizes the plot and gives a reading of the novel. Knapp believes that Charlotte's poetry is a bridge between her inner life and the world around her. She discusses *The Professor* and *Jane Eyre* as providing evidence of Charlotte's concern with feminist issues. She discusses *Shirley* in terms of social realism and *Villette* as disguised biography. Knapp believes that the Brontës' contribution to the art of the novel involved their adding elements of the unconscious, such as dreams and signs, and the supernatural to the realism of the novel.

Taylor, Irene. *Holy Ghosts: The Male Muses of Emily and Charlotte Brontë.* New York: Columbia University Press, 1990.

Taylor believes that Emily and Charlotte created male muses for themselves in the same way that the male Romantics provided themselves with female muses. She asserts further that these male muses had religious aspects. Taylor is convinced that *Wuthering Heights* is about female creativity, and she believes that Heathcliff represents the male muse in his energy—particularly his insistence on "doing" rather than merely "being." Taylor also discusses Charlotte's early work and Emily's poetry. The author asserts that by reading Emily's poetry, Charlotte learned to reconcile her desire to be feminine ("to be") and to enjoy fame ("to do").

Anne Brontë (1820-1849)

The youngest Brontë, Anne was brought up by her clergyman father and her aunt after the death of her mother. She began writing with her sister Emily at a very young age. With her sisters, she went to boarding school at Roe Head, but left when she became ill. Later, she became a governess, a position that provided her with materials for her novels. She had to leave her second job when her brother, a tutor in the same household, became romantically involved with the lady of the house.

Anne's first novel, *Agnes Grey* (1847), described the plight of a governess; the second, *The Tenant of Wildfell Hall* (1848), describes the plight of a young woman married to an alcoholic. Brontë also wrote poetry, most of which was published after her death. She published under the name Acton Bell. New editions of her novels are available in paperback in The World's Classics series from Oxford University Press.

Bell, Arnold Craig. *The Novels of Anne Brontë: A Study and Reappraisal.* Braunton, Devon, England: Merlin Books, 1992.
Bell is personally enraged that Anne Brontë's work has been devalued, primarily because of her sister Charlotte's comments. This perspective gives his criticism a slightly different flavor than that of other scholars. He supplies a brief biography and discusses *Agnes Grey*'s composition, sources, style, structure, and characterization. He asserts that *The Tenant of Wildfell Hall* is even better than *Agnes Grey* and goes on to discuss its similarities to *Wuthering Heights* and *Jane Eyre*. He refuses to believe that Branwell is the inspiration for Arthur Huntingdon, disagreeing with many other scholars. Indeed, he asserts that the debauched society Anne describes in *The Tenant of Wildfell Hall* could have been known to her only through her reading. He provides a highly detailed reading of the novel as well as a defense of it.

Berry, Elizabeth Hollis. *Anne Brontë's Radical Vision: Structures of Consciousness.* Victoria: English Literary Studies, 1994.
Berry examines patterns of imagery in Anne Brontë's poetry and fiction in order to investigate dichotomies she believes to be inherent in social structures. She maintains that Brontë represents social problems such as inequality, isolation, abuse, and alcoholism through images that connect the external setting with inner feelings. She further asserts that contrasting images of place add structure to Brontë's texts. She provides readings of Brontë's early poetry and discusses its reception by critics. She also provides a detailed reading of *Agnes Grey*, asserting that it joins moral purpose with complex imagery and poetic language. Her analysis of *The Tenant of Wildfell Hall* demonstrates the novel's complexity and broad scope.

Chitham, Edward. *A Life of Anne Brontë.* Oxford: Blackwell, 1991.
Chitham explains how difficult it is to write a biography of Anne Brontë, who saved no letters and kept no journals. He gleans information about her from her novels and the writing of those who knew her so as to produce a convincing discussion of her life and work.

Figes, Eva. *Sex and Subterfuge: Women Writers to 1850*. New York: Persea Books, 1982.
According to Figes, the Brontës wrote about spoiled sons because of their experience with Branwell, their severely troubled brother. Figes outlines the plot of *The Tenant of Wildfell Hall* and sees it as an excellent picture of the dangers of marriage to an alcoholic, as well as a demonstration of the dangers of spoiling sons. Figes also believes Anne Brontë is critical of the clergy.

Langland, Elizabeth. *Anne Brontë: The Other One*. London: Macmillan, 1989.
Langland discusses Brontë's life and work, both her novels and her poetry. She also comments on the influences on her work and her literary reputation, particularly the conventional view of her as "a literary Cinderella."

Marsdan, Hilda, and Robert Inglesfield, eds. *Agnes Grey*, by Anne Brontë. Oxford: Clarendon Press, 1988.
The introduction to this edition discusses the circumstances of its publication in so far as they are known, and what the editors consider the unfair treatment of the author by her publisher, Thomas Newby. The editors also discuss the textual history of the novel and list its early editions. They briefly describe what they consider to be the autobiographical components of the novel. Explanatory notes are included.

Masefield, Muriel. *Women Novelists from Fanny Burney to George Eliot*. Freeport, N.Y.: Books for Libraries Press, 1934.
Masefield discusses Brontë's novels as autobiographical. She believes the spoiled children in *Agnes Grey* are based on Brontë's young charges and that the alcoholic husband in *The Tenant of Wildfell Hall* is a portrait of Brontë's brother Branwell.

Charlotte Brontë (1816-1855)

Charlotte Brontë seems to have been the member of the Brontë family most attuned to the outside world. She was born in 1816 to a father who had the ability to become a clergyman and a gentleman although he was born a peasant, and his highly literate wife. Maria Branwell Brontë died in 1821, and her sister, Elizabeth Branwell, came to raise the children. Charlotte and her sisters suffered at their first school, a school for the daughters of clergymen at Cowan Bridge. Charlotte later described the abusive conditions there, including semistarvation, in *Jane Eyre*. Later, she was happy at Miss Wooler's school at Roe Head, where she, unlike her sisters, made lifelong friends. She taught at the school and later became a governess. In order to begin a school of their own, she and Emily went to a school in Brussels to improve their French. Emily hated it, but Charlotte enjoyed it at least until she fell in love with the owner's husband, Professor Constantine Héger, who was only interested in her intellectual development. She returned home to find her brother's alcoholism worsening. To earn money, she paid for the publication of the sisters' poetry. Only two copies of the book were sold, but *Jane Eyre* was published under the pseudonym Currer Bell in 1847, and became a best-seller. She and Anne went to London to identify themselves to their publisher and he introduced them to London's literary society. Charlotte spent some time in London, met other literary figures, including Elizabeth Gaskell who became her first biographer, and may have fallen in love with her publisher. Her brother and sisters died, but she continued to publish. *Shirley* appeared in 1849, *Villette* in 1853. After much soul searching, she accepted a marriage proposal from Arthur Nicholls, her father's curate. The brief marriage appeared to be quite happy, although she did no more writing. She died during her pregnancy, in 1855. Her novels are readily available in paperback editions.

Alexander, Christine. *The Early Writings of Charlotte Brontë*. Buffalo, N.Y.: Prometheus Books, 1983.
This valuable study provides biographical information and lists the location of the Brontë manuscripts. The early works are analyzed in terms of Charlotte's anxieties over whether women should write at all and her anti-Romanticism. The early work is also discussed in relation to Brontë's later, published writing.

Ashfield, Andrew, ed. "Charlotte Brontë." In *Romantic Women Poets 1770-1838*, pp. 261-266. New York: St. Martin's Press, 1995.
Ashfield provides a selection of her works as well as a brief biographical headnote.

Blom, Margaret Howard. *Charlotte Brontë*. Boston: Twayne, 1977.
Blom provides biographical information and a reading of the juvenilia and the novels that should be helpful to students. The relationships between the novels as well as the novels' depiction of the position of women is stressed. An annotated bibliography is provided too, but it is outdated.

Figes, Eva. *Sex and Subterfuge: Women Writers to 1850*. New York: Persea Books, 1982.
According to Figes, Charlotte Brontë used myth to resolve the conflict between anger and piety and to disguise her own unlawful passions. She used passionate imagery and unrestrained writing to cope with her love for a married man, Constantine Héger. She discusses the plot of *Villette*, its use of religion, and its imagery. Figes also discusses *Jane Eyre*, seeing it as wish fulfilling and as an exposition of the conflict arising when women both love men and see them as oppressors. She describes elements of the plot in terms of female repression and castration.

Fraiman, Susan. "Jane Eyre's Fall from Grace." In *Jane Eyre: Complete, Authoritative Text with Biographical and Historical Contexts, Critical History, and Essays from Five Contemporary Critical Perspectives*, edited by Beth Newman, pp. 614-632. New York: Bedford Books of St. Martin's Press, 1996.
In this Marxist analysis of *Jane Eyre*, Fraiman focuses on Grace Poole as a working woman and shows how Jane identifies with the exploited members of the working class throughout the novel. Fraiman sees the novel as a "narrative of rebellion and self-respect as a working woman."

Fraser, Rebecca. *The Brontës: Charlotte Brontë and Her Family*. New York: Crown, 1988.
Fraser's work is a readable biography, with interesting illustrations, but it does not analyze the works of Charlotte Brontë or her sisters.

Gezari, Janet. *Charlotte Brontë and Defensive Conduct: The Author and the Body at Risk*. Philadelphia: University of Pennsylvania Press, 1992.
Gezari asserts that Brontë believed she needed to defend herself and her writing and that Brontë created characters who also needed to defend themselves. She asserts further that the method Brontë used involved "the body—its organs, senses, and appendages—as the site of social conflict and restraint." To demonstrate this, Gezari offers readings of *The Professor*, *Jane Eyre*, *Shirley*, and *Villette*.

Gilbert, Sandra M. "Plain Jane's Progress." In *Jane Eyre: Complete, Authoritative Text with Biographical and Historical Contexts, Critical History, and Essays from Five Contemporary Critical Perspectives*, edited by Beth Newman, pp. 475-501. New York: Bedford Books of St. Martin's Press, 1996.

Gilbert provides a feminist reading of *Jane Eyre* in which the novel is seen as Jane's pilgrimage from Gateshead, the unhappy home in which she is oppressed, to Lowood, where Mr. Brocklehurst, "the large bad wolf," oppresses her further, to Thornfield, where all the women are oppressed to some degree. Gilbert sees Bertha Mason as seen as Jane's double. Jane's return to Rochester, after realizing she cannot marry St. John, and her acceptance of Rochester's proposal of marriage signal the attainment of Jane's selfhood.

Homans, Margaret. *Bearing the Word: Language and Female Experience in Nineteenth-Century Women's Writing.* Chicago: University of Chicago Press, 1986.

Homans discusses Jane Eyre's fear of being made an object and the relationship of the novel to the Gothic and to Romantic writing. Dreams of children and suggestions of childbirth are traced through the novel. The novelist maintains that replacing the absent mother with "mother nature" is an acceptance of death.

Kooman-Van Middendorp, Gerarda Maria. *The Hero in the Feminine Novel.* New York: Haskell House, 1966.

The author discusses Charlotte Brontë's life and describes William Crimsworth, hero of *The Professor.* She notes he was drawn from Professor Héger, Brontë's schoolmaster in Belgium, but she believes Crimsworth, whom she calls "a stick," is far inferior to Héger. She also notes that Héger is the original of Paul Emanuel, the hero of *Villette* also, and she considers him to be Brontë's best-drawn hero, noting, however, that he also attempts to subjugate the heroine. She gives a detailed description of Rochester, the hero of *Jane Eyre*, maintaining that Brontë intended him to be a basically good person who needed to suffer so that his goodness could become apparent. Kooman-Van Middendorp, however, believes him to be an "inferior being." She also discusses the novel's critical reception and the possible sources for Rochester. She also describes Robert Moore, the hero of *Shirley*, whom she considers "harsh," and compares him to the hero of Elizabeth Gaskell's *North and South.* Kooman-Van Middendorp agrees with Brontë herself that she does not create wholly plausible male characters.

Michie, Elsie. "White Chimpanzees and Oriental Despots: Racial Stereotyping and Edward Rochester." In *Jane Eyre: Complete, Authoritative Text with Biographical and Historical Contexts, Critical History, and Essays from Five Contemporary Critical Perspectives*, edited by Beth

Newman, pp. 584-598. New York: Bedford Books of St. Martin's Press, 1996.

Michie sees Rochester as a colonizer because he acquired wealth in Jamaica and is the master of an estate in England. She points out, however, that he is described as darker than the average Englishman, resembling an Irishman or a "white chimpanzee," and an "oriental despot" as well. She traces the history of both stereotypes in England and also discusses Thornfield as a harem. Michie maintains that Jane civilizes Rochester, the despot, but St. John goes off to attempt to rule India, thus satisfying the ambiguous attitudes of the English toward their role as colonizers.

Moglin, Helen. *Charlotte Brontë: The Self-Conceived*. New York: W. W. Norton, 1976.

This biography is based primarily on the Brontës' letters and diaries. It also provides readings of the novels, blaming their "faults" on Charlotte's insecurities. That women are doomed to powerlessness is the message of *The Professor*, Moglin asserts. The heroine of *Jane Eyre* gains power because Charlotte has made Jane a representation of herself and an example of the new, independent woman. In *Shirley*, she sees the workers as placed in the powerless position of women. She explains the ending of *Villette* by saying that Paul could not return because in real life, Héger was unavailable to Charlotte. Her analysis of the novels is interesting, but not always convincing.

Newman, Beth, ed. *Jane Eyre: Complete, Authoritative Text with Biographical and Historical Contexts, Critical History, and Essays from Five Contemporary Critical Perspectives*. New York: Bedford Books of St. Martin's Press, 1996.

This book contains the text of *Jane Eyre*, essays about Charlotte Brontë and her time, and essays about the novel from several critical points of view.

Peters, Margot. *Charlotte Brontë: Style in the Novel*. Madison: University of Wisconsin Press, 1973.

Peters focuses on Brontë's technique, discussing her use of adverbs as intensifiers often indicating timelessness, and the multifacetedness of experience. She also mentions her use of syntactic inversion as contributing to the strength of her prose as does her use of negatives, certain kinds of punctuation, and inconsistencies. Peters believes, too, that Brontë uses contrasts between antitheses to establish her themes as well as to control her use of language. She also discusses Brontë's use of figurative language, literary language, and allusion. She argues that *Jane Eyre* derives much of its power through its use of courtroom language.

Plasa, Carl. "Silent Revolt: Slavery and the Politics of Metaphor in *Jane Eyre*." In *The Discourse of Slavery*, edited by Carl Plasa and Betty J. King, pp. 64-93. London: Routledge, 1994.
Plasa reads *Jane Eyre* as a commentary both on society and on the aspirations of nineteenth century middle-class women. He sees Bertha as "the uncertain figure of otherness," and he believes Brontë's use of slavery as a metaphor to criticize class and gender ideology weakened the fight against genuine slavery.

Sadoff, Dianne F. "The Father, Castration, and Female Fantasy in *Jane Eyre*." In *Jane Eyre: Complete, Authoritative Text with Biographical and Historical Contexts, Critical History, and Essays from Five Contemporary Critical Perspectives*, edited by Beth Newman, pp. 518-536. New York: Bedford Books of St. Martin's Press, 1996.
In this psychoanalytic reading of *Jane Eyre*, Sadoff reads the relationship between Jane and Rochester as a masochistic one, but one that is culturally produced rather than natural.

Schwartz, Nina. "No Place Like Home: The Logic of the Supplement in *Jane Eyre*." In *Jane Eyre: Complete, Authoritative Text with Biographical and Historical Contexts, Critical History, and Essays from Five Contemporary Critical Perspectives*, edited by Beth Newman, pp. 549-564. New York: Bedford Books of St. Martin's Press, 1996.
According to Schwartz in her deconstructive reading of *Jane Eyre*, Jane wishes to see herself as good and deserving of success because of her own efforts, while on the other hand, she identifies herself as part of the aristocracy and is therefore automatically deserving of success. Schwartz believes this ambiguity was typical of the age.

Showalter, Elaine. *A Literature of Their Own: British Women Novelists from Brontë*. Princeton, N.J.: Princeton University Press, 1970.
In this classic study, Showalter discusses the plight of women in *Jane Eyre* noting that they are likely to be starved, beaten, and imprisoned. She asserts that these things are done in order to control them, particularly their sexuality.

Smith, Margaret, ed. *The Letters of Charlotte Brontë: With a Selection of Letters by Family and Friends. Vol. 1: 1829-1847*. Oxford: Clarendon Press, 1995.

This extensive collection of letters includes a history of the letters themselves and a discussion of textual problems, as well as a chronology of Charlotte Brontë's life. Also included is Ellen Nussey's "Reminiscences of Charlotte Brontë by a Schoolfellow," which attempts to portray Brontë as a Christian heroine. The introduction discusses Brontë's relationship with Nussey and with her father, her moods as reflected in the letters, the satiric tone of some of them, her reaction to her life in Brussels and to Professor Héger, her relationship with Branwell, and her work. Extensive, highly informative notes are provided.

Stowall, H. E. *Quill Pens and Petticoats: A Portrait of Women of Letters.* London: Wayland, 1970.
This work discusses Brontë's life and quotes copiously from her letters and novels and those of her friends. Stowall credits the Brontës with adding "intensity" and "atmosphere" to the novel.

Williams, Judith. *Perception and Expression in the Novels of Charlotte Brontë.* Ann Arbor, Mich.: UMI Research Press, 1988.
Williams discusses *The Professor, Jane Eyre, Shirley,* and *Villette,* in terms of the struggle to perceive the world outside oneself, to understand it, and "to express the experience in a work of art." She sees most of the imagery in these novels as expressive of the inner, female world, or the outer, masculine world. These views of the world must be harmonized in an androgynous way to achieve androgynous perception. Full perception, however, may never be achieved, but the struggle, according to Williams, is the important thing.

Winnifrith, Tom. *Charlotte Brontë: Unfinished Novels.* Dover, N.H.: Alan Sutton, 1993.
Winnifrith discusses the provenance of these novels and differentiates them from the juvenilia. He also discusses their links with the published novels. He provides the text of "The Story of Willie Ellin," "Ashwood," "The Moores," and "Emma."

_____, ed. *The Poems of Charlotte Brontë: A New Annotated and Enlarged Edition of the Shakespeare Head Brontë.* Oxford: Basil Blackwell, 1984.
In the introduction, Winnifrith explains the textual problems involved in editing Charlotte's poetry. He also provides biographical data, discusses the Angrian stories, and gives the text of her poetry.

Emily Brontë (1818-1848)

Emily Brontë was born in 1818. Shortly afterward, the Reverend Patrick Brontë, his wife Maria, and their children moved to Yorkshire, where another child was born before Maria's death in 1821. The children were cared for by their father, and a rather cold aunt, but they amused themselves by making up stories and creating books. Emily went to a boarding school for the daughters of poor clergymen in 1824. It was the prototype for the Lowood School in *Jane Eyre*. She left because of ill health. In 1835, she attended school again, at Miss Wooler's school at Roe Head, where Charlotte taught, but she was very unhappy and came home. She was only happy at home, where she did the housekeeping, collected animals, and roamed the moors. Charlotte prevailed on Emily to publish her poetry in 1846, but the book was unsuccessful. *Wuthering Heights*, on the other hand, published in 1847, created a sensation, although many readers disapproved of it. Her brother Branwell, an alcoholic, died in 1848. Emily died, at the age of thirty, three months later. Paperback editions of *Wuthering Heights* are widely available.

Armstrong, Nancy. "Imperialist Nostalgia and *Wuthering Heights*." In *Wuthering Heights: Complete, Authoritative Text with Biographical and Historical Contexts, Critical History, and Essays from Five Contemporary Critical Perspectives*, edited by Linda H. Peterson, pp. 428-450. Boston: Bedford Books of St. Martin's Press, 1992.
Armstrong believes Lockwood's study of the inhabitants of Wuthering Heights is similar to that of tourists, photographers, and folklorists who were interested in the inhabitants of rural Great Britain. This essay is illustrated with interesting old photographs.

Ashfield, Andrew, ed. "Emily Brontë." In *Romantic Women Poets 1770-1838*, pp. 260-266. New York: St. Martin's Press, 1995.
Ashfield provides a selection of her works as well as a brief biographical headnote.

Bloom, Harold, ed. *Emily Brontë's 'Wuthering Heights.'* New York: Chelsea House, 1987.
A collection of illuminating articles on *Wuthering Heights*. In the introduction, Bloom discusses the book's debt to Lord Byron's *Manfred* and notes that the relationship between Catherine and Heathcliff is beyond morality, gender, or religion.

Chitham, Edward. *A Life of Emily Brontë*. Oxford: Basil Blackwell, 1987.

Because there is a lack of reliable information on Emily Brontë's life, Chitham attempts to reconstruct it from her work and the work of her sisters, particularly Charlotte Brontë's *Shirley*. He discusses her experience at the schools she attended, Cowan Bridge and Roe Head, and at the Hégers' establishment at Brussels. He also discusses her relationship with the Heaton family at Ponder Hall. Chitham believes that Brontë could write only when she lived at home. He also discusses important themes of *Wuthering Heights*, which he identifies as orality, the close connection between life and death, the reconciliation of opposites, and separation and reunion. He also discusses features of the Gondal stories: infidelity, mysterious children, a haunted landscape. In addition, he writes about Brontë's relationship to nature, the reception of *Wuthering Heights*, and Brontë's final illness and death.

Davies, Stevie. "Baby-Work: The Myth of Rebirth in *Wuthering Heights*." In *Emily Brontë's 'Wuthering Heights*,' edited by Harold Bloom, pp. 119-136. New York: Chelsea House, 1987.
Davies traces the bird imagery in the novel, from the nest full of dead lapwings to the feathers in the pillow pulled apart by Catherine. The author asserts that Heathcliff is seen in relation to birds, which represent freedom, thus making him the unwitting agent of the restoration of the Earnshaws.

_____. *Emily Brontë*. Bloomington: Indiana University Press, 1988.
Davies provides a compelling analysis of Emily Brontë's poetry and *Wuthering Heights*, believing that Brontë is both familiar and unknowable. The author notes that early readers were unaware of Brontë's gender, and he believes that despite its relationship to gossip, lullaby, and fairy tale, the novel is ungendered. He also finds connections between *Wuthering Heights* and works by William Shakespeare, John Milton, and Sir Walter Scott as well as the Bible. He also discusses Brontë's relationship to Protestant Dissent and her belief in nature. In addition, he discusses her poetry and its relation to the landscape. He notes that both Emily Brontë and her heroines refuse to adapt to conditions they dislike.

Eagleton, Terry. "Myths of Power: A Marxist Study on *Wuthering Heights*." In *Wuthering Heights: Complete, Authoritative Text with Biographical and Historical Contexts, Critical History, and Essays from Five Contemporary Critical Perspectives*, edited by Linda H.

Peterson, pp. 399-414. Boston: Bedford Books of St. Martin's Press, 1992.

Eagleton sees Catherine's decision to marry Edgar Linton for social advantage rather than Heathcliff as the crucial event of the book. The author maintains that this novel is more unified than those of Charlotte Brontë because *Wuthering Heights* does not attempt to unify its realistic and the romantic aspects.

Figes, Eva. *Sex and Subterfuge: Women Writers to 1850.* New York: Persea Books, 1982.

According to Figes, *Wuthering Heights* reflects the author's consciousness of the importance of nature, which makes any conflict between men and women seem petty. She sees Heathcliff as representing nature. She also discusses the author's use of multiple narrators and language. She feels the crucial element in the story is Catherine's marriage for class advantage.

Frank, Katherine. *A Chainless Soul: A Life of Emily Brontë.* Boston: Houghton Mifflin, 1990.

Frank provides a highly readable life of the entire Brontë family and an excellent introduction to Emily's poetry. The book provides lucid readings of the poetry and attempts to explain her attachment to home, to images of food, and to the Yorkshire countryside. Frank brings to life the richness of Emily's imagination as well as her originality as a poet and novelist. The works of the rest of the family are also discussed in an extremely useful fashion.

Gilbert, Sandra M. "Looking Appositely: Catherine Earnshaw's Fall." In *Emily Brontë's 'Wuthering Heights,'* edited by Harold Bloom, pp. 79-98. New York: Chelsea House, 1987.

Gilbert gives a feminist reading of *Wuthering Heights*, asserting that Catherine and Heathcliff were originally androgynous until Catherine was captured by the Lintons and turned into a young lady, which was her fall into hell. Her education gave her no choice but to marry Linton, a decision that led to her death.

Ghnassia, Jill Dix. *Metaphysical Rebellion in the Works of Emily Brontë.* New York: St. Martin's Press, 1994.

In this examination of Brontë's poetry, essays in French and *Wuthering Heights*, Ghnassia finds that Brontë was expressing her rebellion against the condition of not only of women, but of the entire cosmos. As a rebel against God, rejecting conventional notions of salvation, she is related to the Romantics, particularly Byron. This book focuses primarily on the poetry, discussing it in the order in which it was written.

Homans, Margaret. *Bearing the Word: Language and Female Experience in Nineteenth-Century Women's Writing*. Chicago: University of Chicago Press, 1986.

Homans provides a convincing reading of *Wuthering Heights* centering on the use of male and female narrators and the inability of the male narrator, Lockwood, to read nature. Homans also asserts that unlike her mother, the second Cathy accepts patriarchy. She believes that Heathcliff's cruelty, particularly his tendency to separate parents and children, is a result of his early separation from his own family. She insists that Brontë had to identify with Lockwood and with patriarchy in order to write this novel.

——————. "The Name of the Mother in *Wuthering Heights*." In *Wuthering Heights: Complete, Authoritative Text with Biographical and Historical Contexts, Critical History, and Essays from Five Contemporary Critical Perspectives*, edited by Linda H. Peterson, pp. 341-358. Boston: Bedford Books of St. Martin's Press, 1992.

Homans explains Lacan's view of the genesis of symbolic language as compensation for the male baby's loss of complete identification with the mother and attempts to harmonize it with Nancy Chodorow's theory that women speak both the figurative language of the male and the presymbolic language of the female. She sees the male characters in the novel using symbolic language and the female characters using presymbolic language. The first Cathy refuses to use symbolic language and renounce her bond with nature, but her daughter accepts patriarchy and survives, as does Brontë herself.

——————. "Repression and Sublimation of Nature." In *Emily Brontë's 'Wuthering Heights*,' edited by Harold Bloom, pp. 61-78. New York: Chelsea House, 1987.

Homans believes nature is too important in this novel to be imprisoned in language. The first Catherine tries to repress her love for nature, but it bursts out. Homans reads the novel in terms of repression, noting that Catherine represses her knowledge of Heathcliff's cruelty which is, by her own admission, her own.

Jacobs, Carol. "*Wuthering Heights*: At the Threshold of Interpretation." In *Emily Brontë's 'Wuthering Heights*,' edited by Harold Bloom, pp. 99-118. New York: Chelsea House, 1987.

Jacobs sees Lockwood's dream as a losing struggle with a text that resists interpretation, much as this novel does. She also believes that the themes of the novel include: naming, usurpation, homelessness, and passion.

Knoepflmacher, U. C. *Emily Brontë, Wuthering Heights*. Cambridge, England: Cambridge University Press, 1989.

The author provides a helpful chronology, matching events from Emily's life with other literary events and with world events. As far as the novel itself is concerned, he discusses Lockwood's role as surrogate for the reader, Brontë's relationship to other Romantic authors, the narrative structure of the novel, and the various interpretations of the novel, which he believes have to do with power, sex, and class. He also discusses the critical reception of the novel and its influence. A guide to further reading is provided.

Kooman-Van Middendorp, Gerarda Maria. *The Hero in the Feminine Novel*. New York: Haskell House, 1966.

The author describes Heathcliff, whom she finds "savage, brutish" and "unique," as a projection of Emily Brontë's own "perversity," whose source is probably Bluebeard or some other folktale.

Levy, Anita. *Other Women: The Writing of Class, Race, and Gender, 1832-1898*. Princeton, N.J.: Princeton University Press, 1991.

Levy discusses how the nineteenth century saw women, as well as members of other races and members of the lower classes, as different from "rational," white, upper-class Englishmen. She examines *Wuthering Heights* in the light of nineteenth century anthropology and sociology. Catherine becomes a domesticated version of her mother, who is identified with nature and sexuality and is ultimately damaged. Heathcliff's dark skin makes him a demon. Levy believes the novel prepares the ground for the new rhetoric of psychology. Finally, she asserts the novel dramatizes the process of change in middle-class culture and the domestication of women.

Michie, Elsie B. *Outside the Pale: Cultural Exclusion, Gender Difference and the Victorian Woman Writer*. Ithaca, N.Y.: Cornell University Press, 1993.

In view of the fact that Patrick Brontë came from Ireland and that Ireland was very much in the news when *Wuthering Heights* was written, Michie believes that Heathcliff was meant to reflect Irish origins. She further believes that colonialism caused the English to dehumanize natives of the countries they controlled.

Miller, J. Hillis. *"Wuthering Heights*: Repetition and the Uncanny." In *Wuthering Heights: Complete, Authoritative Text with Biographical and Historical Contexts, Critical History, and Essays from Five Contemporary Critical Perspectives*, edited by Linda H. Peterson, pp. 371-384. Boston: Bedford Books of St. Martin's Press, 1992.

Miller asserts that the reader is drawn to interpret the events in *Wuthering Heights* just as Lockwood and the other narrators do. He believes that interpretation itself is the key activity in the novel.

Peterson, Linda H., ed. *Wuthering Heights: Complete, Authoritative Text with Biographical and Historical Contexts, Critical History, and Essays from Five Contemporary Critical Perspectives*. Boston: Bedford Books of St. Martin's Press, 1992.

This scholarly edition contains the text of *Wuthering Heights* as well the "Biographical Notice of Ellis and Acton Bell," the earliest "biographies" of the Brontës, essays describing various critical methodologies, essays about the novel, using that methodology, and a useful bibliography.

Roper, Derek, and Edward Chitham, eds. *The Poems of Emily Brontë*. Oxford: Clarendon Press, 1995.

This volume contains all the poetry by Emily Brontë that is known to exist, including the undated poems and fragments. The editors discuss Brontë's poetry and the Gondal stories and poems in the introduction. They also discuss the manuscript versions and early editions of her work. Commentary on the poetry is also provided.

Sonstroem, David. *"Wuthering Heights* and the Limits of Vision." In *Emily Brontë's 'Wuthering Heights,'* edited by Harold Bloom, pp. 27-46. New York: Chelsea House, 1987.

Sonstroem believes readers may find this novel puzzling because none of the characters understands what is happening. They all refuse to see or they deny what they do see. Even religion is powerless here.

Van Ghent, Dorothy. "On *Wuthering Heights*." In *The English Novel: Form and Function*. New York: Harper & Row, 1953.

Van Ghent points out that the main characters in this novel are too intense and elemental to be realistic. The novel's realism, then, must come from the narrators. The complex narrative form of the novel expresses the tension between nature and society, myth and domesticity. Catherine and Heathcliff cannot live together; they can regain the unity they experienced in childhood only through death. This novel is also discussed in relation to Emily Brontë's poetry.

Wion, Philip K. "The Absent Mother in *Wuthering Heights*." In *Wuthering Heights: Complete, Authoritative Text with Biographical and Historical Contexts, Critical History, and Essays from Five Contemporary Critical Perspectives*, edited by Linda H. Peterson, pp. 315-329. Boston: Bedford Books of St. Martin's Press, 1992.

Wion asserts that Emily Brontë's loss of her mother, when Emily was only three years old, explains much of her psychological development. Furthermore, he believes that the events in *Wuthering Heights* can be explained by Catherine's inability to separate herself psychologically from Heathcliff and forge her own identity.

FRANCES BROOKE (1724-1789)

The daughter of a clergyman, Frances Brooke was orphaned at an early age. She moved to London where she edited a periodical, the *Old Maid* (1755-1756). She also wrote *Virgina* (1756), a tragedy in verse. She married in 1756, and had a son the next year. In 1760, she translated a French novel, *Letters from Juliet, Lady Catesby*, into English. Three years later, she wrote *The History of Lady Julia Mandeville*, a sentimental novel in epistolary form which was a huge success. She spent the years 1763-1768 in Canada. That experience led her to write another epistolary novel, *History of Emily Montague*. It appeared in 1769, and became known as the first Canadian novel. After producing other translations she wrote *The Excursion*, also an epistolary novel. The novel Charles Mandeville (1790) may have been written by her. Among her theatrical writings, she created *Sinope*, a tragedy, as well as *Rosina* and *Marian*, which were very successful musicals. In addition, she helped managed the Haymarket opera house.

McMullen, Lorraine. *An Odd Attempt in a Woman: The Literary Life of Frances Brooke*. Vancouver: University of British Columbia Press, 1983.

McMullen discusses the life and times of Frances Brooke, who not only wrote the first novel set in North America but also wrote plays and essays. McMullen quotes extensively from diaries, letters, and other works of the period as well as from Brooke's works. There are full discussions of *The History of Lady Juliet Mandeville* and *History of Emily Montague* as well as *All's Right at Last*, and *Charles Mandeville*, which may have been written by Brooke. Her dramas and other writing are also discussed. McMullen evaluates Brooke's work and explains in what ways she upheld the mores of her world and how she transcended them, becoming a link between the Neoclassic and the Romantic eras. The book is illustrated.

Messenger, Ann. *His and Hers: Essays in Restoration and Eighteenth Century Literature*. Lexington: University Press of Kentucky, 1986.
Messenger describes the plot of the *History of Emily Montague*, She believes it is a highly conventional sentimental novel except for the character of Arabella Fermor, a clever comic figure who looks back to William Shakespeare's Beatrice and Rosalind and forward to Jane Austen's sharper heroines. She also compares Arabella to Alexander Pope's Belinda in his "Rape of the Lock," maintaining that Brooke's Arabella is the more developed character. She also discusses Brooke's use of irony and digression.

Todd, Janet. *The Sign of Angellica: Women, Writing and Fiction 1600-1800*. New York: Columbia University Press, 1989.
Todd summarizes the plot of *The History of Lady Julia Mandeville*, noting the absence of villains as well as the absence of a happy ending. The extreme sensibility of the hero and heroine are important. Todd demonstrates that sentimental values flourish in a patriarchal community isolated from trade and the city. Female sensibility is valued to such an extent that even the heroes are feminized. Todd also notes that while originality of neither sentiment or language is important to this type of novel, its fantasies of female importance despite passivity provide a form of escapism important in popular writing to this day.

ELIZABETH BARRETT BROWNING (1806-1861)

The oldest of eleven children, Elizabeth Barrett was encouraged to read by her father, who provided her with a tutor in the classics. She began to write poetry when she was thirteen; her health deteriorated when she was in her teens. The cost of publishing her first book *The Battle of Marathon* (1820) was paid by her father. She also wrote for the Annuals, compilations of verse and fiction that were much enjoyed by the Victorians. Her first major work, *Poems* (1844), won the admiration of Robert Browning, whom she eventually married after a dramatic elopement. They lived in Florence from 1846 on, where they had a son. While in Florence, she wrote *Casa Guidi Windows* (1851) and *Poems Before Congress* (1860) about contemporary Italian politics. Her most popular works are *Sonnets from the Portuguese* (1850) and *Aurora Leigh* (1857). The first inverts the sonnet tradition by having a female poet write about a male. The second is concerned with poetic theory and the position of women in society. After her death, *Last Poems* (1862) was published. She was a highly regarded poet during her lifetime, and many hoped she would be named Poet Laureate in 1850. A paperback edition of *Aurora Leigh* is available in The World's Classics series of Oxford University Press.

Anderson, Amanda. "Reproduced in Finer Motions: Encountering the Fallen in Barrett Browning's *Aurora Leigh.*" In *Tainted Souls and Painted Faces: The Rhetoric of Fallenness in Victorian Culture*, pp. 167-197. Ithaca, N.Y.: Cornell University Press, 1993.
Anderson notes that the involvement of the heroine, Aurora Leigh, with Marion Erle, a prostitute, has important consequences for the heroine as an artist. She believes that Aurora attempts to blend art and philanthropy just as Barrett Browning has joined epic poetry and realist fiction in a formal synthesis. In Anderson's reading of the poem, Barrett Browning is attempting to change the depiction of all women in art.

Ashfield, Andrew, ed. "Elizabeth Barrett Browning," *Romantic Women Poets 1770-1838*, pp. 267-286. New York: St. Martin's Press, 1995.
Ashfield provides a selection of her works as well as a brief biographical headnote.

Cooper, Helen. *Elizabeth Barrett Browning, Woman and Artist.* Chapel Hill: University of North Carolina Press, 1988.
Cooper reads Browning as a female poet in the tradition of female poets, and she believes familiarity with Barrett Browning's work can reshape modern knowledge of Victorian poetry. Cooper bases her reading on feminist critical theory and believes the central issue to be "how a woman poet empowers herself to speak." Cooper asserts that Barrett Browning is also indebted to the male poetic tradition and even to her illness, which gave her the leisure to read and to write. Cooper asserts that in *Casa Guidi Windows* Barrett Browning examines her place in the poetic tradition and criticizes men in their public and political roles. *Aurora Leigh* explains the development of the female artist. Cooper discusses Barrett Browning's poems in chronological order and concludes that her work offers a paradigm for the study of female poets in general.

David, Deirdre. *Intellectual Women and Victorian Patriarchy: Harriet Martineau, Elizabeth Barrett Browning, George Eliot.* Ithaca, N.Y.: Cornell University Press, 1987.
David believes that Barrett Browning allied herself with patriarchy because she identified with male poets, "male modes of political

thought," and male aesthetics. She bases her argument on *Aurora Leigh*, which David believes states Barrett Browning's conservative views on gender and politics. David also discusses Barrett Browning's reading, insisting that it is important because it, rather than real life, generated Barrett Browning's poetry. David considers Barrett Browning's reading masculine because she read Latin and Greek like her poetic forebears and because she chose to write *Aurora Leigh* in a "male" genre, the epic. David discusses the poem and its reception, and she demonstrates by quoting from Barrett Browning's work that the poet was a conservative critic of "materialism, mercantilism, and aggressive individualism."

Donaldson, Sandra. *Elizabeth Barrett Browning: An Annotated Bibliography of the History and Criticism 1826-1990*. New York: G. K. Hall, 1993.
Donaldson compiled this bibliography in order to show the range of response to Barrett Browning's poetry as well as to increase access to the critical material. Selections include writings on her life, work, and thought in French and Italian as well as in English. Material on the Barrett and Browning families and on the Browning Library and the Browning Society are also included. Most citations are books and articles, but newspaper reviews are included as well. This material is indexed by works in addition to the general index. Donaldson's comprehensive work supersedes other bibliographies.

Dow, Miroslava Wein. *A Variorum Edition of Elizabeth Barrett Browning's 'Sonnets from the Portuguese.'* Troy, N.Y.: Whitston, 1980.
Dow's introduction explains how Barrett Browning's life influenced her work. She describes the early poetry and demonstrates its connections to the poet's letters. In addition, she provides a detailed reading of Sonnet Five. She also discusses the textual history of the work.

Forster, Margaret. *Elizabeth Barrett Browning: A Biography*. New York: Doubleday, 1989.
This biography is based on hundreds of newly discovered letters that shed light on Barrett Browning's childhood and on her life before her marriage. Forster discusses the lives of the poet's parents as well as Barrett Browning's own life. Although this illustrated and readable book summarizes Barrett Browning's poetry, it does not offer readings of it.

Karlin, David, ed. *Robert Browning and Elizabeth Barrett: The Courtship Correspondence 1845-1846*. Oxford: Clarendon Press, 1989.

Karlin has provided a selection of letters from the 573 letters that the
two poets exchanged. Karlin believes these letters provide a more
satisfying view of their courtship than any of the fiction about it
because of their awareness of rhetoric. He also believes these letters
dramatize the interplay of powerful minds. The letters he has selected
are about love, but he gives a complete calendar of the other letters the
couple exchanged. Biographical information and complete notes are
provided.

Leighton, Angela. *Elizabeth Barrett Browning*. Bloomington: Indiana
University Press, 1986.
Leighton lucidly relates Barrett Browning's poetry to feminist literary
theory. She explains why it was so difficult for a Victorian women to
be taken seriously as writer of poetry at all, and she asserts that Barrett
Browning's search for a muse led her first to her father and then to a
symbolic sister. She provides readings of some early poems, some of
the *Sonnets from the Portuguese* and *Aurora Leigh*. Leighton also
attempts to explain the decline in Barrett Brown's reputation after her
death.

_____. *Victorian Women Poets: Writing Against the Heart*. Char-
lottesville: University Press of Virginia, 1992.
Leighton sees Barrett Browning as an heir of the poetry of female
sensibility written by Felicia Hemans and Letitia Elizabeth Landon and
as going beyond them to examine society's role in the development of
the woman poet. She provides a reading of "The Romaunt of the Page"
that examines the fate of women in society and notes that "Lord
Walter's Wife" is actually about sexual politics. She examines the
influence of George Sand on Barrett Browning, as well as discussing
Barrett Browning's writing on slavery (which reminded her of the
condition of women) and child labor. Leighton also discusses the
meaning of Italy in Barrett Browning's life and work and provides
readings for parts of *Aurora Leigh*.

McSweeney, Kerry, ed. *Aurora Leigh*, by Elizabeth Barrett Browning.
Oxford: Oxford University Press, 1993.
McSweeney discusses Barrett Browning's life and the fact that her
early poetry was formed by her reading. He considers *Aurora Leigh* to
be a convincing psychological portrait and a vivid portrait of the age.
He also discusses the genesis of the work in her own experiences as a
woman artist and in her reading. In addition, he outlines the critical
reputation of the book and supplies a bibliography.

Mermin, Dorothy. *Elizabeth Barrett Browning: The Origin of a New Poetry*. Chicago: University of Chicago Press, 1989.

Mermin argues that Elizabeth Barrett Browning saw herself as the inheritor of a male poetic tradition, not as a "poetess." She began writing from a male point of view, but adopted the female point of view as her writing developed, not finding her true voice until she was forty. Mermin maintains that Barrett Browning kept on developing as a poet until her death. She provides a biography and readings of *The Seraphim and Other Poems*, *Sonnets from the Portuguese*, *Poems*, *Casa Guidi Windows*, *Aurora Leigh*, *Poems Before Congress* and *Last Poems*. A bibliography is included.

Radley, Virginia. *Elizabeth Barrett Browning*. Boston: Twayne, 1972.

Radley describes Barrett Browning's life, mostly through quoting her letters. She also summarizes her works, explaining her poetry. A chronology of her life and a bibliography are provided. The latter, however, is outdated.

Reynolds, Margaret, ed. *Aurora Leigh*, by Elizabeth Barrett Browning. Athens: Ohio University Press, 1992.

An excellent critical introduction to the poem discusses the problems of women poets as well as Barrett Browning's thought. There is a chapter on textual and editorial difficulties and another on the poem's publishing history. There is also a description of the manuscripts. The text of the poem is given as well as a bibliography.

Simons, Judy. *Diaries and Journals of Literary Women from Fanny Burney to Virginia Woolf*. Iowa City: University of Iowa Press, 1990.

Simons discusses the diary Barrett Browning kept for one year which, according to Simons, gave evidence of the poet's "passionate nature" and sheds light on her work as a female poet. It was written at a time when her father was away from home, a situation that allowed her to make certain discoveries about herself. The poet believed she suffered from a lack of intellectual stimulation which caused her to concentrate too strongly on her emotions and, according to Simons, decided to learn more about political affairs and to read more serious material. Simons believed Barrett Browning stopped keeping her diary because she had achieved the beginnings of independence.

Stephenson, Glennis. *Elizabeth Barrett Browning and the Poetry of Love*. Ann Arbor, Mich.: UMI Research Press, 1989.

Stephenson notes that late nineteenth century critics focused on Barrett Browning as merely a character in a love story while recent critics have ignored her love poetry to focus on *Aurora Leigh* and its position in feminist literary history. Stephenson believes Barrett Browning's love poetry is worthy of interest because it is not sentimental and because it resists patriarchy in its conceptions of "women's role in love relationships" and "the questions of woman's voice in love poetry." Stephenson provides detailed readings of the early ballads and lyrics, "Lady Geraldine's Courtship," *Sonnets from the Portuguese*, *Aurora Leigh*, and *Last Poems*. An extensive bibliography is also provided.

Stone, Marjorie. *Elizabeth Barrett Browning*. New York: St. Martin's Press, 1995.
Stone notes that Barrett Browning was considered a major English poet from the 1840's through the 1890's, but, like other women writers, was then excluded from the canon. She discusses both nineteenth century and contemporary readings of Barrett Browning's work. Stone considers Barrett Browning a Romantic because, like the male Romantic poets, she is interested in consciousness, meditation, and Promethean themes. Her works show the influence of Dante and John Milton. Stone also finds similarities between Barrett Browning's works and those of Thomas Carlyle and John Ruskin. She considers her a feminist writer because she gives a voice to heretofore silent women, and "decenters masculine metaphors and myths." In addition, she shows how some women can avoid being objects of exchange in a male economy. Stone believes that Barrett Browning has been devalued as a poet, partly because her life has been so thoroughly dramatized and because she is often ironic.

Stowall, H. E. *Quill Pens and Petticoats: A Portrait of Women of Letters*. London: Wayland, 1970.
Stowall notes that Barrett Browning read Greek, Latin, Hebrew, French, and Italian. She attributes the poet's invalidism to a pony accident and says she was particularly shy, but notes her friendship with Mary Russell Mitford, by 1836 a well-known poet twenty years older than Barrett Browning. Stowall quotes from their correspondence and a poem about her dog, Flush. She also discusses "A Dream of Exile" (1844) and "The Seraphim" (1844). She describes Barrett Browning's relationship and elopement with Robert Browning and her best-known poetry. She notes Barrett Browning's ambivalence about Napoleon, her sympathy with the poor, and her hatred of American slavery. Stowall describes Barrett Browning's meeting with George Sand and her reconciliation with her family. She discusses *Aurora*

Leigh as "an interesting experiment" and describes its reception. Some Victorians were upset at its author's sympathy for fallen women.

FANNY BURNEY (1752-1840)

Although she never received a formal education, Fanny Burney read widely and began to write when she was quite young. After her stepmother persuaded her that writing was unfeminine, she burned her early work on her fifteenth birthday. She resumed writing, however, and published her first work, *Evelina* (1778), anonymously. Her father was a well-known musician and historian of music whose circle of friends was wide and influential. These friends approved of the book and it became very popular, as did her next book, *Cecilia* (1782). That novel helped secure a position for Burney as a member of Queen Charlotte's court. She found this position extremely difficult and confining, but she kept a wonderful *Diary* (published 1842-1846), describing not only her own life at court but also the troubles caused by the apparent insanity of George III. She left the court in 1791, married General Alexandre D'Arblay, a French émigré, in 1793, and had a son in 1794. Needing money, she wrote a play entitled *Edwy and Elgiva* (1795). Burney wrote a satire, *The Witlings*, which she withdrew at the urging of her father, probably on the grounds that satire was unfeminine. Her subsequent novels included *Camilla* (1796) and *The Wanderer* (1814). After surviving breast cancer and the deaths of her husband and her son, she died at the age of eighty-seven. Paperback editions of her novels are available.

Adelstein, Michael E. *Fanny Burney*. New York: Twayne, 1968.
    Burney's work is discussed in relation to her life. Adelstein believes that her work reflects her own social and economic problems and that it was strongly affected by her father's negative reaction to *The Witlings*, her satiric play. He maintains that although only one of her novels (*Evelina*) was important, she influenced the development of the novel by initiating the novel of manners. He maintains further that her journals provide an excellent picture of the age. This book is somewhat dated in that it never takes into account her status as a woman writer.

Baldwin, Louis. *One Woman's Liberation: The Story of Fanny Burney*. Wakefield, N.H.: Longwood Academic, 1990.
    Baldwin provides the reader with a simplified, dramatized version of Burney's life and excerpts from *Evelina*. Unlike most recent scholars, he believes she was unconcerned with the issues of her day.

Barker, Gerard. *Grandison's Heirs: The Paragon's Progress in the Late Eighteenth Century English Novel.* Newark: University of Delaware Press, 1985.

Barker points out the resemblances between Sir Charles Grandison, the perfect hero of Samuel Richardson's *The History of Sir Charles Grandison*, and the even more perfect hero of *Evelina*, Lord Orville. Since the focus of the novel is on Evelina, the heroine, Orville's role is merely to instruct the heroine and represent the perfect man. Barker also asserts that Orville's lack of sexuality is a result of Evelina's and Burney's fear of sexuality.

Bloom, Edward A., and Lillian D. Bloom, eds. *Camilla*, by Fanny Burney. New York: Oxford University Press, 1983.

In their introduction, the editors describe the genesis of *Camilla* and the events of Burney's life during its production. They also discuss its characters, its themes, and its reception, as well as the later edition of the novel. The Blooms include a bibliography and a chronology of Burney's life as well as the text of *Camilla*.

_____, eds. *Evelina*, by Fanny Burney. New York: Oxford University Press, 1983.

The editors in their introduction to the novel, discuss Burney's wish to remain anonymous, the publishing history of the book, and the effect its success had on her life. They also discuss the plot and themes of the novel, stressing the importance of Villars' letters to the structure of the novel and its focus on the importance of prudence. The Blooms also discuss character, setting, and the influence of the novel on later writers. They include information about the novel's publishing history as well as a bibliography and a chronology of Burney's life.

Brophy, Elizabeth. *Women's Lives and the Eighteenth Century Novel.* Tampa: University of South Florida Press, 1991.

Brophy discusses Burney's concern for young women and their happiness. She believes that Burney is ambivalent about the proper role for her heroines. They must be intelligent, but not overly learned. *Cecilia* concerns strong female characters who are entirely competent, but the female characters in *Evelina* and *Camilla* need the guidance of men. Brophy outlines the plots of these novels and discusses Burney's use of satire. In general, she sees tensions between the independent role of the professional woman writer and the conservative insistence on the subordination of women reflected in these three novels.

Craft-Fairchild, Catherine. *Masquerade and Gender: Disguise and Female Identity in Eighteenth-Century Fictions by Women.* University Park: Pennsylvania State University Press, 1993.

Craft-Fairchild discusses whether attending masquerades limited or increased the power of women. She reads Burney's *The Wanderer* to show that Burney wrote it to undermine patriarchy, pointing out that in the world of the novel, women have no work, no identity, and no freedom. All the male characters are cruel. Feminist ideology is put into the mouths of undesirable and outspoken women, but the "good" women suffer as much as the outspoken women. She attributes the poor reception of the novel to its feminist stance.

Cutting-Gray, Joanne. *Woman as Nobody and the Novels of Fanny Burney.* Gainesville: University of Florida Press, 1992.

Cutting-Gray offers a feminist reading of Burney's work. The author argues that Burney may use the vocabulary of patriarchy but she is not determined by it. Instead, her subject is the victimization of women by the patriarchy. She is concerned with namelessness and female identity. Evelina conceals her powers from others and herself. Cecilia and Camilla retreat into hysteria and madness to escape a society that silences them. *The Wanderer* is also concerned with female namelessness. Cutting-Gray also discusses Burney's journals and compares her views with those of contemporary feminist theoreticians such as Julia Kristeva, Jean-François Lyotard, Hannah Arendt, and Luce Irigaray. She provides an extensive bibliography.

Devlin, D. D. *The Novels and Journals of Fanny Burney.* New York: St. Martin's Press, 1987.

Devlin provides biographical information and maintains that Burney's life, rather than her reading, influenced the development of her novels. Devlin also stresses the didactic function of her novels and compares them to the works of Hannah More and Mary Wollstonecraft, believing that all three writers disapprove of the indulgence of sensibility but sense that society may be oppressive. *Evelina, Camilla,* and *The Wanderer* are discussed fully.

Doody, Margaret Anne. *Frances Burney: The Life in the Works.* New Brunswick, N.J.: Rutgers University Press, 1993.

In this scholarly biography, which discusses Burney's work thoroughly, Doody shows that Burney was an ambitious novelist who examined her society carefully. Her novels are both comic and violent, and their form expresses tension and anxiety. Doody argues compellingly that Burney's reputation deserves rehabilitation. This book should be considered the definitive analysis of Burney's life and works.

_____. Introduction to *Cecilia: Or, Memoirs of an Heiress*, by Fanny Burney. Edited by Margaret Anne Doody and Peter Sabor. New York: Oxford University Press, 1988.
Doody discusses the circumstances under which *Cecilia* was written, particularly its relation to *The Witlings*, Burney's then unpublished play. She also discusses the characters in relation to the theme of the novel, the misuse of riches. She also notes Burney's criticism of society's treatment of women and the poor, as well as her treating middle-aged female characters as worthy of respect. She notes that Burney's readers were not entirely comfortable with the work but it did influence other novelists, such as Mary Wollstonecraft and William Godwin. The editors supply a publishing history of the text, a bibliography, a chronology of Burney's life and an appendix that includes Dr. Charles Burney's draft introduction to *Cecilia*, a glossary of French terms, and a discussion of London, finance, and "fashionable amusements."

_____. Introduction to *The Wanderer: Or, Female Difficulties*, by Fanny Burney. Edited by Margaret Anne Doody, Robert L. Mack, and Peter Sabor. New York: Oxford University Press, 1991.
Doody considers *The Wanderer* to be a Romantic novel, illustrating the darker side of Burney's thought. She discusses how it came to be written, its relation to the French Revolution and to the Gothic novel. She sees its theme as the tyranny of society, particularly over women and the poor. Doody examines the plot and the relationship of the novel to the works of Mary Hays, Mary Wollstonecraft, and Elizabeth Hamilton. She also discusses its savaging by the reviewers. Finally, she asserts that the novel means to prove "we are not at home in the universe." The editors provide a bibliography and a chronology of Burney's life.

Epstein, Julia. *The Iron Pen: Frances Burney and the Politics of Women's Writing*. Madison: University of Wisconsin Press, 1989.
Epstein sees Burney as a conflicted, angry social reformer. She reviews recent criticism stressing feminist aspects of Burney's work, and she analyzes passages from Burney's journals about crises in her life to show that writing represented a means of overcoming the pressures her society placed on women. She also offers readings of *Evelina*, *Camilla*, *Cecilia*, and *The Wanderer*.

Figes, Eva. *Sex and Subterfuge: Women Writers to 1850*. New York: Persea Books, 1982.

Figes says Burney claimed she began writing as a lark and joked about the influence of her first novel, *Evelina*. Ten years later, when she wrote *Camilla*, she was much more apologetic about writing at all. She insisted on eliminating anything political from her novels because politics might be considered unfeminine and because she was afraid her father and her connections would disapprove. Figes summarizes the novels and provides readings of them.

Hufstader, Alice. *Sisters of the Quill*. New York: Dodd, Mead, 1978.

Hufstader discusses Burney's early life and her time at court, quoting liberally from Hester Thrale's diary, as well as from Burney's diary. She feels that Burney was much too intimidated by her elders, and she stresses the danger George III may have posed to the women of his court while he was insane.

Johnson, Claudia L. "Frances Burney." In *Equivocal Beings: Politics, Gender, and Sentimentality in the 1790's*, pp. 141-190. Chicago: University of Chicago Press, 1995.

Johnson points out that Burney's early novels, *Evelina* and *Cecilia*, are fairly conservative but manage to indict patriarchy in general and the heroines' fathers in particular for not taking proper care of their daughters. Her later novels, however, insist on filial and institutional veneration no matter what the sins of the authority figures. Johnson attributes this to the fact that the later novels were written during a period of intense political conservatism. She believes that *Camilla* was written to refute Wollstonecraft, whom Burney misread, and that *The Wanderer* is an "anti-Udolpho." Both novels are summarized.

Kooman-Van Middendorp, Gerarda Maria. *The Hero in the Feminine Novel*. New York: Haskell House, 1966.

This book briefly discusses Burney's life and evaluates her achievement. Kooman-Van Middendorp also describes Lord Orville, the hero of *Evelina*, and Mortimer Delville, the hero of *Cecilia*, calling the first a "prig" and the second an egotist. She asserts, however, that Burney invented the domestic hero, a character perfected by Jane Austen.

Kowaleski-Wallace, Beth. "A Night at the Opera: The Body, Class and Art in *Evelina* and Fanny Burney's *Early Diaries*." In *History, Gender and Eighteenth Century Literature*, edited by Beth Fowkes Tobin, pp. 141-158. Athens: University of Georgia Press, 1994.

Noting that Fanny Burney loved opera, Kowaleski-Wallace reads the scene in *Evelina* in which Evelina is forced to accompany the lower class, ill-bred Branghtons to the opera and suffers because they behave improperly. Evelina is frightened because if her father continues to disown her she could fall to the status of the Branghtons. Burney is anxious because just as the audience may not pay attention to the opera, readers may not pay attention to her novels.

Manley, Seon, and Susan Belcher. *O, Those Extraordinary Women!* Philadelphia: Chilton Book Company, 1972.
The authors discuss Burney's early connections with Samuel Johnson and his circle and the financial success of her novels.

Masefield, Muriel. *Women Novelists from Fanny Burney to George Eliot.* Freeport, N.Y.: Books for Libraries Press, 1934.
Masefield provides a dated but entertaining view of Burney's early life, retelling anecdotes about Samuel Johnson and her father's circle and quoting humorous anecdotes about court life from Burney's journal. She also discusses the novels, which she believes deteriorate after *Evelina*, although she admires Burney as a satirist of sensibility.

Rogers, Katherine M. *Fanny Burney: The World of 'Female Difficulties.'* New York: Harvester Wheatsheaf, 1990.
Rogers maintains that although Fanny Burney protested woman's victimization by society, she accepted notions of female passivity and the importance of avoiding indelicacy. Only her marriage and her journals show independence. Rogers also asserts that Burney's contribution to the novel was the dramatization of women's psychological problems. She discusses Burney's life and work and the tension between intelligence and conformity that affect the structure of her novels.

Simons, Judy. *Diaries and Journals of Literary Women from Fanny Burney to Virginia Woolf.* Iowa City: University of Iowa Press, 1990.
Simons maintains that early women writers wrote both to express themselves and as family historians. She feels that Burney's early diaries were tentative and satirical, while those written while Burney was at court show evidence of depression and those written during her later life record her daily life from a historical perspective. Simons finds Burney's authorial technique in her diaries to be similar to those in her published work and she sees tension between her need to write and her need to fill what she considered her proper domestic role. In addition, Simons believes that Burney did not want to reveal this

tension, nor the need for emotional release writing afforded her. According to Simons, the decorous surface of Burney's writing, both in her novels and in her diaries, is meant to conceal nonconformity and emotional pain.

_____. *Fanny Burney*. Totowa, N.J.: Barnes & Noble, 1987.
Simons discusses Burney's life and her heroines. She also summarizes and discusses her novels, journals, and plays, believing that Burney's writing deteriorated with age because of her timidity, but she credits her with beginning a tradition of writing by women.

Stowall, H. E. *Quill Pens and Petticoats: A Portrait of Women of Letters*. London: Wayland, 1970.
Stowall discusses Burney's early life, by describing her appearance and quoting from her *Diary*. She also describes the reception of *Evelina* and *Cecilia*.

Straub, Kristina. *Divided Fictions: Fanny Burney and Feminine Strategy*. Lexington: University Press of Kentucky, 1987.
Straub sees Burney's fiction as lacking both philosophical and aesthetic unity because Burney's reading taught her to expect little from life as a woman, but much from life as a human being. She asserts that Burney's "ability to sustain and express contradiction is both a response to ideological conflicts in the culture and a strategy for female psychic survival in mid-eighteenth century life." *Evelina* is discussed in the greatest detail because it shows how Burney tried to harmonize her commitment to patriarchal modes of thought with a young woman's control of her own destiny. *Cecilia* shows her awareness that this is too painful a process. The readings of her last two novels, *Camilla* and *The Wanderer*, are less detailed but show "the cultural paradoxes" involved when women seek power. Straub also refers to Burney's journals to demonstrate Burney's insecurities.

Todd, Janet. *The Sign of Angellica: Women, Writing and Fiction 1600-1800*. New York: Columbia University Press, 1989.
Todd believes that Burney was horrified at the self-indulgence of sensibility and attacked it. Todd also believes that Burney was ambivalent about becoming known. She wrote not only to earn money but also to inculcate correct behavior, and when her later novels were unpopular, she worried about her culture. Her novels are concerned with patriarchy, of which she approved, according to Todd, and respectability. Burney insists that money and duty are important; disguise is wrong. Education for women is problematic. Witty older women are

disapproved of but utter truths. Marriage leads to control by the husband. Todd maintains that Burney became a teacher inculcating the truths of patriarchy.

CHARLOTTE CHARKE (C.1713-1760)

Charke was the youngest of Colley Cibber's twelve children. Her father was an actor, dramatist, and eventually the Poet Laureate of England whom Henry Fielding mocked in *Joseph Andrews*. At school, Charlotte studied Latin as well as Italian and French. She married Richard Charke, who also worked in the theater; she had a daughter with him, but they soon separated. She acted at the Drury Lane and Haymarket Theaters and wrote her own comedy, *The Carnival: Or, Harlequin Brunderer* (1735). She also wrote *The Art of Management: Or, Tragedy Expelled* (1735). She may have also written *Tit for Tat: Or, Comedy and Tragedy at War* (1743). Her major work is the *Narrative of the Life of Mrs. Charlotte Charke, Youngest Daughter of Colley Cibber* (1755), in which she describes the theater of the time as well as her own life. She also wrote several prose narratives, including *The History of Henry Dumont and Mrs. Charlotte Evelyn* (1756), *The Mercer: Or, Fatal Extravagance* (1755), *The Lover's Treat: Or, Unnatural Hatred* (c.1758), and *The History of Charles and Patty* (n.d.). The first book concerns itself with slavery and mocks a homosexual. She died in poverty in London in 1760.

Ferguson, Moira. *British Woman Writers 1578-1799*. Old Westbury, N.Y.: Feminist Press, 1985.
Ferguson discusses Charke's childhood and short-lived marriage, and notes that Charke became a puppeteer in 1737. Ferguson praises her autobiography for its "zesty self-confidence," but notes that it might not be entirely authentic.

Morgan, Fidelis, with Charlotte Charke. *The Well-known Troublemaker: A Life of Charlotte Charke*. London: Faber, 1988.
Charke's memoirs are supplemented with illustrations and an epilogue concerned with reviving her reputation. Morgan believes Charke exaggerated incidents in her life and discusses her acting in masculine roles. Her need for money is stressed.

MARY DELANY (1700-1788)

Delany was born in 1700, a member of a family interested in politics, but without influence after the death of Queen Anne. Forced by her family to marry a much older man who died eight years later, she was left with only a small income. In 1741, she married an Irish clergyman, Patrick Delany, a friend of Jonathan Swift. After Patrick Delany's death, she continued her interest in literature, which may have begun when she met Swift, and became a central member of the Bluestocking Circle, a group of women who held conversations about literature. The royal family granted her a pension and a house. At court, she befriended the much younger Fanny Burney. She created collages of flowers, and she wrote poetry, a libretto for George Frideric Handel (1744), and an unpublished romance, *Marianna* (1759). Her most important works, however, were her autobiography and her letters. Her letters to Swift were published in 1766. She died in 1788. An early edition of her letters was published in 1820. A later edition was published in 1861-1862.

Hufstader, Alice. *Sisters of the Quill.* New York: Dodd, Mead, 1978.
    Hufstader describes Delany's life and times as well as her circle of famous acquaintances, including nearly all the well-known figures of her time. Hufstader also explains how Delany's autobiographies were edited and how her descendants attempted to create an image of her appropriate to their own age.

Thaddeus, Janice Farrar. "Mary Delany, Model to the Age." In *History, Gender and Eighteenth Century Literature*, edited by Beth Fowkes Tobin, pp. 113-140. Athens: University of Georgia Press, 1994.
    Thaddeus wishes to define Delany's character and investigate "the sources of her power by analyzing her life." She describes Delany's life and her letters and autobiography, asserting that the autobiography is unreliable because Lady Augusta Llanover, Delany's great-grand-niece and the work's editor, excised anything she thought improper. According to Thaddeus, elements of Delany's life were used by Sarah Scott in her novel *A Description of Millenium Hall.*

MARIA EDGEWORTH (1767-1849)

Edgeworth was one of twenty-two children. Her father, a writer who was much interested in education, was married four times. She went to school in England, but returned to Ireland in 1782 to help run the estate and teach her younger brothers and sisters. She translated Mme de Genlis' *Adèle et Théodore* (1782) as *Adelaide and Theodore* (1783) and wrote *Letters for Literary Ladies* (1795). In that work, Edgeworth defended women's education and their right to publish. *The Parent's Assistant* (1795) was a collection of children's stories, and *Practical Education* (1798), written with her father, was a manual of instruction for teaching children at home. *Castle Rackrent*, her first and arguably her best novel, appeared in 1800. Her other fiction includes *Belinda* (1801), *Leonora* (1806), *Ennui* (1809), *Tales of Fashionable Life* (1812), *Patronage* (1814), and *Helen* (1834). She also wrote children's stories and edited her father's memoirs. After her father's death, she remained on his estate, except for visits abroad, during one of which she rejected a proposal of marriage. She corresponded with many famous literary figures. She died at the age of eighty-two. *The Absentee*, *Belinda*, and *Castle Rackrent* are available in paperback in The World's Classics editions of Oxford University Press.

Barry, F. V. *Maria Edgeworth: Chosen Letters*. New York: AMS Press, 1979.
Barry declares that Edgeworth's letters were never merely personal. She saw herself as a teacher and used them to teach. She discusses Edgeworth's writing and her life and maintains that Edgeworth's letters show her enjoyment of life and her interest in science, nature, art, children, and people in general.

Colvin, Christina, ed. *Maria Edgeworth in France and Switzerland: Selections from the Edgeworth Family Letters*. Oxford: Clarendon Press, 1979.
These letters were exchanged during two trips. The first, in 1802, she took with her father and stepmother, who hoped to find her a suitor. During the later trip, in 1820, Maria was in charge because her father had died. Colvin provides a biography of Richard Lovell Edgeworth and his fourth wife, Frances Anne Edgeworth; a stepsister, Charlotte, is also described. The introduction describes their friends and acquaintances and the political situation in 1820. Extensive notes are supplied.

Figes, Eva. *Sex and Subterfuge: Women Writers to 1850*. New York: Persea Books, 1982.
Figes discusses *Castle Rackrent*, describing its use of irony, characterization, and narrative technique, as well as its plot. She believes that Edgeworth's father made her write her later fiction much more conventionally. According to Figes, *Belinda* has a conventional heroine

who learns to be sensible, but the book's best character is the Lady Delacour, who does not behave properly yet is most readers' favorite character. Another character, Mrs. Freke, is a cruel caricature of a feminist. In *Belinda*, Edgeworth has written a conventionally didactic novel about the dangers both sensibility and "unfeminine behavior" pose to a young woman. In *The Absentee* (1812), according to Figes, Edgeworth comes close to social criticism by blaming absentee English landlords for poor economic conditions in Ireland. Figes describes *Patronage* (1814) as a didactic novel describing the perfect wife. According to Figes, the perfect young woman is modeled after Hannah More's character in *Coelebs in Search of a Wife*. She is English, educated, but less so than her husband; she is also modest, although beautiful, and enjoys domesticity, although she is accomplished. She is, of course, a rational person, rather than a romantic. Figes notes that Edgeworth condemns political corruption, but she remains politically conservative.

Harden, O. Elizabeth McWhorter. *Maria Edgeworth's Art of Prose Fiction*. The Hague: Mouton, 1971.
Admitting that Edgeworth's aim was primarily didactic, Harden argues that her work is artful and should be valued more highly than it is. She discusses the children's stories and the works written with her father as well as the novels, tales, and minor works, quoting from them generously. She notes that Edgeworth valued reason over emotion and used contrasting characters to dramatize this. Harden also finds Edgeworth's characterizations vivid and her narrative techniques skilled. Harden provides a reading of *Castle Rackrent*, Edgeworth's best-known work, which she considers an accurate picture of an irresponsible gentry and a poverty-stricken peasantry. Harden also summarizes *Belinda*, which she considers an excellent work despite its poorly constructed plot.

Hawthorne, Mark D. *Doubt and Dogma in Maria Edgeworth*. Gainesville: University of Florida Press, 1967.
Hawthorne compares the works on education written under the influence of Edgeworth's father with her fiction in order to examine the direction of her thought as it developed. He considers her a didactic novelist, but also a writer skilled in psychology and philosophy. He believes her doubts about dogma are identifiable in her use of structure, symbol, and irony. He concentrates his discussion on her lesser-known works, and he does not discuss *Helen*. He does discuss her life, *Letters for Literary Ladies*, *Practical Education*, and her literature for chil-

dren, maintaining that her father's rationality is reflected in the explicit "morals" of her stories, but not in her plots or characters. He argues that *Belinda* is about the moral education of Lady Delacour, not the marriage of Belinda. He argues further that, in *Tales of Fashionable Life*, she tries to reconcile her ideas with her father's rationalism. He believes that *Patronage* also represents her ideas about the reconciliation of rationality and the imagination, as does *Ormond*. Hawthorne maintains that Edgeworth's reconciliation of rationalism with emotion and imagination was a forerunner of Victorianism.

Hurst, Michael. *Maria Edgeworth and the Public Scene: Intellect, Fine Feeling and Landlordism in the Age of Reform*. Coral Gables, Fla.: University of Miami Press, 1969.
A thoughtful discussion of Edgeworth's place in Irish political and economic history from the 1820's through the 1840's. Hurst believes that Edgeworth was a penetrating and articulate observer whose comments on Irish affairs and the Irish way of life illuminate the time. He does not discuss her literary work.

Kirkpatrick, Kathryn J. Introduction to *Castle Rackrent*, by Maria Edgeworth. Edited by George Watson. New York: Oxford University Press, 1995.
Kirkpatrick discusses *Castle Rackrent* as the first "socio-historical novel, the first Irish novel, the first Big House novel, the first saga novel," its popularity in its own day, and its later rediscovery. Kirkpatrick also notes its relationship to Irish history and to Edgeworth family history and outlines its plot. She also discusses *Ennui*, Edgeworth's second Irish novel. The publishing history, a chronology of Edgeworth's life, and a bibliography are also provided. Appendices include a glossary, commentary, and a discussion of Edgeworth's relationship to Ivan Turgenev.

Kooman-Van Middendorp, Gerarda Maria. *The Hero in the Feminine Novel*. New York: Haskell House, 1966.
The author describes Lord Colambre, the hero of *The Absentee*, as an example of Edgeworth's father's influence on her characterization of men. Lord Colambre is morally superior and he will not marry a heroine with a flawed education, but, Kooman-Van Middendorp maintains, he is not boring despite the fact he is made to voice Maria Edgeworth's theories on the causes of Irish poverty. Kooman-Van Middendorp believes the hero of *Helen*, written after Richard Edge-

worth's death, is more natural and notes that he insists on marrying the heroine despite the fact that her descent is clouded.

Kowaleski-Wallace, Elizabeth. *Their Fathers' Daughters: Hannah More, Maria Edgeworth, and Patriarchal Complicity.* New York: Oxford University Press, 1991.

Kowaleski-Wallace examines the works of Maria Edgeworth because she believes she represents a case of female complicity with patriarchy. This psychoanalytic reading attempts to see what Edgeworth obtained from her complicity and how it ultimately failed her. Kowaleski-Wallace maintains that Richard Edgeworth metaphorically seduced his daughter and that she gained maternal authority by her concern for the Irish poor. Edgeworth insisted that women behave rationally because she feared irrationality. Kowaleski-Wallace provides readings of *Belinda* and *The Absentee*.

McCormack, W. J., and Kim Walker, eds. *The Absentee*, by Maria Edgeworth. New York: Oxford University Press, 1988.

In their introduction, the editors see *The Absentee* as a celebration of difference and as an injunction to fulfill one's function in society. The editors discuss the origins of the book and its relationship to the Old Testament story of Esther as well as its other allusions that make interpretation problematic. They see this as a precursor of Irish modernism. A bibliography and a chronology of the life of Edgeworth are included. Appendices contain the publishing history of the novel, a chapter on "The Tradition of Grace Nugent," which is an Irish ballad, and Edgeworth's notes for an essay on Edmund Burke.

Mack, Robert, ed. *Oriental Tales.* New York: Oxford University Press, 1992.

In his introduction to this collection, which includes Maria Edgeworth's "Murad the Unlucky," Mack notes the revival of interest in Edgeworth's writing. He describes this story as one calculated to instill moral principles in children, particularly the idea that good judgment rather than mere luck determines happiness. The world the tale describes is not romantically exotic but poor, urban, and crowded. Mack considers Edgeworth's explanations attempts to "deconstruct" earlier glamorizations of the East, such as *The Arabian Nights*, in order to understand the East.

Masefield, Muriel. *Women Novelists from Fanny Burney to George Eliot.* Freeport, N.Y.: Books for Libraries Press, 1934.

This brief account of Edgeworth's life is dated but charming; Masefield points out that Edgeworth is the first novelist of Irish life. Masefield also outlines the plots of *Castle Rackrent*, *Ormond*, and *Ennui*. She considers Edgeworth a novelist of manners whose novels would be better if they were shorter.

Mellor, Anne K., and Richard E. Matlak, eds. "Maria Edgeworth." In *British Literature 1780-1830*, pp. 535-555. Fort Worth, Tex.: Harcourt Brace College Publishers, 1996.
The editors discuss Edgeworth's life and work and provide a selection of her writing.

Myers, Mitzi. "De-Romanticising the Subject: Maria Edgeworth's 'The Bracelets,' Mythologies of Origin, and the Daughter's Coming to Writing." In *Romantic Women Writers: Voices and Countervoices*, edited by Paula R. Feldman and Theresa M. Kelley, pp. 88-112. Hanover, N.H.: University Press of New England, 1995.
Myers provides a reading of "The Bracelets," contending that Edgeworth counters the conventional romantic view of childhood established by William Blake and William Wordsworth, which entirely ignores the experiences of girls. Myers also demonstrates how Edgeworth's own childhood experiences prepared her to be a writer.

Newcomer, James. *Maria Edgeworth*. Lewisburg, Ohio: Bucknell University Press, 1973.
Newcomer provides biographical information and a chronology of Edgeworth's life. He describes her books and her friendships with important English intellectuals, such as Erasmus Darwin and Sir Humphrey Davy, as well as her friendships with businessmen and European intellectuals. He also discusses her writings on education and her stories for children as well as her moral tales. *Belinda* and *Helen* are considered by Newcomer to be novels of manners, and he argues that *Castle Rackrent* is highly original and was highly influential. He summarizes the plot and comments on Edgeworth's irony and humor. Newcomer also describes Edgeworth's *Three Tales of Fashionable Life*, which he concedes are didactic, but he believes that they are also imaginative and humorous. Characterization is the most important feature of *Patronage*, he maintains, as is the treatment of anti-Semitism in *Harrington*. He believes that *Ormond*, which he describes as a realistic, moral romance of manners, is Edgeworth's second best novel.

Teets, Bruce. Introduction to *Castle Rackrent*, by Maria Edgeworth. Coral Gables, Fla.: University of Miami Press, 1964.

In his introduction to the novel, Teets describes the historical situation in Ireland in the late eighteenth and early nineteenth centuries. He also discusses Edgeworth's other novels and the narrative techniques she uses in *Castle Rackrent*, which he believes is not only a charming novel but an influential one.

SUSAN FERRIER (1782-1854)

Born in Edinburgh the youngest of ten children, Susan Ferrier never married, but she did lead an active social life in both England and Scotland. Her novel *Marriage* (1818) compares marriages based on rational affection with those based on lust, or a desire for economic or social advancement. It contains some humor and Scots local color, but it is also extremely didactic. Despite this, it was extremely popular. *The Inheritance* (1824) and *Destiny* (1831) resemble it. *Marriage* and *The Inheritance* are available in modern editions.

Doyle, John A., ed. *Memoirs and Correspondence of Susan Ferrier 1782-1854*. London: John Murray, 1898.
This is a discussion of Ferrier's life and work based on her letters.

Foltinek, Herbert, ed. *Marriage*, by Susan Ferrier. New York: Oxford University Press, 1986.
Foltinek discusses Ferrier's work, the evolution of her thought and the textual changes she made in the second edition of *Marriage*. He sees her novels as influenced by the late eighteenth century vogue for novels of education in which the fate of the spoiled child is contrasted with the fate of the well-brought up child.

Johnson, R. Brimley. *Balls and Assemblies from Fanny Burney, Jane Austen, Maria Edgeworth, Susan Ferrier, and Mary Russell Mitford*. London: John Lane, 1928.
Johnson discusses Ferrier's life briefly, maintaining that she was modest and recognized her own limitations, attitudes which explain why she published so little. He believes *Destiny* is technically superior to *Marriage*, and that clever dialogue and apt characterization are more important than her plots. He outlines the typical plot of her novels and presents an excerpt from *Marriage*.

Parker, W. M. *Susan Ferrier and John Galt*. London: Longmans, Green, 1965.

Parker considers Ferrier the originator of the Scottish novel of manners. This book contains biographical information, a summary of the
plots of her novels, and a critical evaluation of them. The author
believes that *The Inheritance* shows the influence of Jane Austen. The
reception of *The Inheritance* is discussed, as is that of *Destiny*, which
Parker argues is fine satire. Parker asserts that although Ferrier's novels
are overly didactic, they demonstrate her love for Scotland.

SARAH FIELDING (1710-1768)

One of six children of an army officer, Sarah Fielding was brought up
by her maternal grandmother and sent to boarding school. On her own,
she studied Greek and Latin and read deeply in English literature. During
the 1740's, she lived with her brother Henry, the playwright and later
novelist, or her sisters in London. She said in the preface to her first novel,
The Adventures of David Simple (1744), that she wrote out of economic
necessity. *The Adventures of David Simple* concerns David Simple, a man
engaged on a search for a man as good as he is himself. Henry Fielding
revised the second edition of the work and was accused of writing it, an
accusation which he denied. Sarah Fielding also wrote *Familiar Letters
Between the Characters in David Simple* (1747) and *David Simple:
Volume the Last* (1753), a sequel. Her other well-known work is *The
Governess: Or, Little Female Academy* (1749) a book of educational
advice for mothers and stories for their daughters. She also wrote *The
History of the Countess of Dellwyn* (1759), *The History of Ophelia* (1760),
The Lives of Cleopatra and Octavia (1757) and *Memoirs of Socrates*
(1762), a translation. She died in 1768, comparatively poor. *The Adven-
tures of David Simple* is available in paperback in The World's Classics
edition of Oxford University Press.

Brophy, Elizabeth. *Women's Lives and the Eighteenth Century English
Novel*. Tampa: University of South Florida Press, 1991.
  Brophy discusses Sarah Fielding's very conventional view of a happy
  marriage in the David Simple novels where the husband is a benevolent
  ruler. In *The History of the Countess of Dellwyn*, Fielding insists a good
  wife honors even a cad. Brophy points out that Fielding's heroines are
  intelligent, but their mental ability does not prove to be of much
  practical benefit. Mrs. Teachum in *The Governess* teaches that obedi-
  ence, not intelligence, is important and that women should defer to
  men, accepting their protection. According to Brophy, Fielding be-

lieves that women are important, but except in *The History of Ophelia*, feels their best chance for happiness remains marriage.

Cadogan, Mary. Introduction to *The Governess: Or, Little Female Academy*, by Sarah Fielding. London: Pandora, 1987.
Cadogan points out that this book is the first of a long line of school stories in English literature. She considers it a realistic account of children's ordinary experience and a celebration of female friendship. Cadogan also discusses Mrs. Teachum and her philosophy of education. She notes, too, that the book is entertaining as well as didactic, and she believes it influenced other writers, including Maria Edgeworth.

Carey, Meredith. *Different Drummers: A Study of Cultural Alternatives in Fiction*. Metuchen, N.J.: Scarecrow Press, 1984.
Carey provides a reading of *The Adventures of David Simple*, which she believes redefines friendship.

Grey, Jill. Introduction to *The Governess: Or, Little Female Academy*, by Sarah Fielding. London: Oxford University Press, 1968.
In her introduction to this book, Grey discusses the influences on Sarah Fielding, her influence on other writers, and Fielding's beliefs about education, as well as the significance of this particular work. The text of *The Governess* is provided as well as a thorough bibliography of Fielding's work, the work about her, the publishing history of *The Governess*, and its place in the history of literature for children.

Johnson, R. Brimley. Introduction to *The Lives of Cleopatra and Octavia*, by Sarah Fielding. London: Scholartis Press, 1928.
Although this work is dated, it provides a bibliography of Fielding's work with some annotation. Johnson sees Fielding as a bluestocking and a pioneer. He believes that *The Adventures of David Simple* is a Richardsonian, albeit fairly realistic, picture of middle-class life. He admits it is a didactic, picaresque work, but he insists it is also a vigorous, humorous satire. Johnson also discusses *The Governess*, *The Cry: A New Dramatic Fable*, *History of the Countess of Delwyn*, and *The History of Ophelia*. He sees *The Lives of Cleopatra and Octavia* as fictional biography, maintaining that Fielding portrays Cleopatra as utterly without romance or passion, wanting only power. He compares this with descriptions of Cleopatra by other writers and finds Fielding's version extremely dark, noting, too, that Henry Fielding disliked the work.

Kelsall, Malcolm. Introduction to *The Adventures of David Simple*, by Sarah Fielding. London: Oxford University Press, 1994.

In his introduction, Kelsall provides a biography of Sarah Fielding, discussing her relationship with her brother Henry, her friends, and her education. He describes the publishing history of her book and evaluates her as a novelist, believing her to be more interested in the general than the particular. He maintains the world she creates is too dark, but he approves of her concern with moral issues, asserting that the last volume of the David Simple series is its best. He provides notes to the work and a chronology of Sarah Fielding's life as well as a newly updated bibliography.

Todd, Janet. *Women, Writing and Fiction, 1660-1800.* New York: Columbia University Press, 1989.

Todd considers Sarah Fielding a sentimental novelist who weighed the claims of individual fulfillment against moral imperatives. She notes that with the help of her brother she constructed a "feminine" image of herself. Partly because later ages distrusted this in an artist and partly because her work was not in the tradition of literary realism that had become the norm for the novel, according to Todd, her novel decreased in popularity. The plot of *The Adventures of David Simple* is constructed of incidents which are meant to induce empathy in the reader, and throughout the novel, happiness is the precursor of misery, wealth of poverty. Tears are always a sign of the proper sympathy. One woman, Cynthia, is allowed feminist ideas, but she is not exemplary. Todd goes on to explain that while in the first part of the novel, a valid human society is established, in the second part it is lost.

ELIZABETH GASKELL (1810-1865)

The daughter of a clergyman, who was also a farmer and then a civil servant, Elizabeth Stevenson was brought up in a country town like the one she wrote about in *Cranford* and was fairly well educated for the time. In 1832, she married William Gaskell, a Unitarian minister; the couple had four daughters and a son who died young. She first published a poem, "Sketches Among the Poor" (1837), in *Blackwood's Magazine*. Her first novel, *Mary Barton* (1848), concerned relations between management and labor in the industrial north of England. She published in various periodicals, most important in *Household Words*. *Cranford* appeared in 1851-1853. Her novel, *Ruth* (1853), was sympathetic to the plight of the "fallen woman." *North and South* (1854-1855) also concerned industrial relations and the differences between the agricultural South and the industrial North. Her other works include the *The Life of Charlotte Brontë* (1857), *Round the Sofa* (1859), *Sylvia's Lovers* (1863), *Cousin Phillis* (1864), *A Dark Night's Work* (1863), and the posthumously published *Wives and Daughters* (1865). Her novels and many of her short stories are available in paperback in The World's Classics editions of Oxford University Press.

Anderson, Amanda. "Melodrama, Morbidity, and Unthinking Sympathy: Gaskell's *Mary Barton* and *Ruth*." In *Tainted Souls and Painted Faces: The Rhetoric of Fallenness in Victorian Culture*, pp. 108-140. Ithaca, N.Y.: Cornell University Press, 1993.
Anderson asserts that the prostitute Esther in *Mary Barton* reflects Gaskell's fear that fiction will hinder rather than help the process of reform. Gaskell, Anderson asserts, believes romance and melodrama are the most appropriate genres in which to represent the fallen woman because these genres elicit the sympathy of the reader. She believes *Ruth* is particularly interesting because it illustrates the relationship between fallenness as a religious concept and as a secular idea. For Gaskell, materialism and rationality indicate fallenness. Redemption can come only through unthinking sympathy. Ruth's redemption is rooted in maternity. Anderson's readings of the novels are compelling.

Berke, Jacqueline, and Laura Berke. "Mothers and Daughters in Mrs. Gaskell's *Wives and Daughters*." In *The Lost Tradition: Mothers and Daughters in Literature*, edited by Cathy N. Davidson and E. M. Broner, pp. 95-109. New York: Frederick Ungar, 1980.
The authors discuss Gaskell's comparison of the effects of two kinds of upbringing and the ways in which mothers influence the character of their daughters.

Brodetsky, Tessa. *Elizabeth Gaskell*. Leamington Spa, England: Berg, 1986.
Brodetsky provides a biography of Gaskell as well as an analysis of her novels, her short stories, and her biography of Charlotte Brontë. To Brodetsky, Gaskell represents the model mid-Victorian middle-class woman, a religious wife and mother knowledgeable about both rural and industrial England. Brodetsky concludes that although Gaskell's ideas were conventional and her novels didactic, she was an accomplished storyteller.

Bonaparte, Felicia. *The Gypsy Bachelor of Manchester: The Life of Mrs. Gaskell's Demon*. Charlottesville: University Press of Virginia, 1992.

Bonaparte analyzes Gaskell's work to "read" her mind and finds she rebelled inwardly against the Victorian conventionality she seemed to typify and endorse. The works and her letters are quoted to attempt to prove that Gaskell's characters reflected her own secret identity. The book is interesting, but not entirely convincing.

Chappie, J. A. *Elizabeth Gaskell: A Portrait in Letters*. Manchester, England: Manchester University Press, 1980.

This readable biography is a collection of Gaskell's letters describing her life with interpolations of relevant material by Chappie connecting the letters. The book also includes attractive illustrations.

Chappie, J. A., and Arthur Pillard, eds. *The Letters of Mrs. Gaskell*. Cambridge, Mass.: Harvard University Press, 1967.

These letters span the time from just before Gaskell's marriage to her death. Chappie discusses Gaskell's relationship with her husband and daughters, her social life, her travels, Manchester as she knew it, and her attitude toward her own work and writing in general. The editors also explain how they collected and dated the letters. They provide indices of family members and literary figures as well as a general index.

Craik, W. A. *Elizabeth Gaskell and the English Provincial Novel*. London: Methuen, 1975.

Craik discusses *Mary Barton*, *Ruth*, *North and South*, *Sylvia's Lovers*, and *Wives and Daughters* in order to trace the development of Gaskell's art, her debt to other writers, her influence on other novelists, and her relationship to her contemporaries. He asserts that *Mary Barton* is highly original, and that *Ruth* contains some of Gaskell's best writing. Craik praises the broad range of characters in *North and South* and asserts that *Sylvia's Lovers* is one of the great English novels. He finds resemblances between *North and South* and Jane Austen's novels as well as George Eliot's *The Mill on the Floss*, Anne Brontë's *Agnes Grey*, and Charlotte Brontë's *Jane Eyre*.

Easson, Angus, ed. *Cousin Phillis and Other Tales*, by Elizabeth Gaskell. New York: Oxford University Press, 1981.

In his introduction, Easson discusses Gaskell as a natural storyteller who wrote short fiction for practical reasons as well as artistic ones. The stories earned money and did not require much time to write. He discusses her stories in terms of romance and imagination. A bibliography and a chronology of Gaskell's life are provided as well as notes explaining the text of the stories.

_____. *Elizabeth Gaskell*. London: Routledge & Kegan Paul, 1979.

This authoritative study provides biographical information and a discussion of the influence of Unitarianism on Gaskell. Easson also discusses her education, her reading, her love of music and drawing, her knowledge of science, her travels, and her family. He provides information on the reception of the novels as well as readings of her novels and her other writing.

_____, ed. *North and South*, by Elizabeth Gaskell. New York: Oxford University Press, 1982.

In his introduction, Easson describes the circumstances surrounding the writing of *North and South* and Gaskell's relationship to Charles Dickens. He also discusses the novel as a psychological drama, and he discusses its reputation. He outlines its publishing history and provides a bibliography and explanatory notes.

Figes, Eva. *Sex and Subterfuge: Women Writers to 1850*. New York: Persea Books, 1982.

Figes sees Gaskell's life as normal, since Gaskell was happily married to a Unitarian clergyman. According to Figes, Gaskell's charity work with the poor of Manchester opened her eyes to their plight. She believed the rich did not know how the poor suffered, and she believed it was women's duty to mediate between the working man and his employer. According to Figes, *Mary Barton* is about the failure of communication between employers and employees, a failure which women can remedy. Gaskell also discusses prostitution and the temptation to marry for social advancement.

Ganz, Margaret. *Elizabeth Gaskell: The Artist in Conflict*. New York: Twayne, 1969.

Ganz provides biographical information and discusses Gaskell's writing thematically. She classifies *Mary Barton*, *Ruth*, and *North and South* as social criticism and "Mr. Harrison's Confessions," *Cranford*, and *Wives and Daughters* as humor. She also discusses *The Life of Charlotte Brontë*, *Sylvia's Lovers*, and the short stories.

Homans, Margaret. *Bearing the Word: Language and Female Experience in Nineteenth-Century Women's Writing*. Chicago: University of Chicago Press, 1986.

Homans relates Gaskell's records of her daughter's infancy to Homans' own theory of language. She further believes Gaskell justified her writing by thinking of it as a duty whose performance involves passing on the father's words, which convey ideas acceptable to the patriarchy, just as the mother passes on the father's seed. Homans does believe, however, that Gaskell often covertly criticizes patriarchy. Homans discusses the circumstances which produced *Mary Barton* and provides a reading of that novel. She also discusses "Lizzie Lee" as an example of the conflict between mother-daughter love and paternal domination. "Lois the Witch" and *The Life of Charlotte Brontë* are also discussed in terms of Homan's theory of language. In her extensive analysis of *Wives and Daughters*, Homans repeats her point: Gaskell believed it was permissible for women to write only if they transmitted the laws of patriarchy.

Hopkins, A. B. *Elizabeth Gaskell: Her Life and Work.* New York: Octagon Books, 1971.
Hopkin's work is a complete, if slightly dated biography that analyzes Gaskell's novels, stories, and letters.

Kooman-Van Middendorp, Gerarda Maria. *The Hero in the Feminine Novel.* New York: Haskell House, 1966.
The author mentions that Gaskell was the first woman novelist to write on social problems involving labor relations. She describes John Barton, the hero of *Mary Barton*, as a very good man, if not a typical laborer. She believes Thornton, the hero of *North and South* was meant to be an example of a good, if not typical, employer. According to Kooman-Van Middendorp, Gaskell wanted to improve industrial relations in England by having labor and management understand each other's problems. She also describes the hero of *Sylvia's Lovers*; the theme of that novel, she maintains, concerns the sad consequences of immoral actions even when they are committed by basically good people. Kooman-Van Middendorp concludes that Gaskell's heroes are more realistic than those of the Brontës, and they represent a return to heroes who are meant to be morally better than the average man, as described by the early women novelists.

Kucich, John. *The Power of Lies: Transgression in Victorian Fiction.* Ithaca, N.Y.: Cornell University Press, 1994.
Kucich asserts that Gaskell shared the views of gender traits held by conventional Victorians, disapproving of masculine women and effeminate men. He also believes Gaskell considers lying to be a vice "normal" in women, but indicative of effeminacy in men. He further asserts that constancy and compassion are female rather than male traits, as impulsiveness is a male trait. Those who display the traits

appropriate to members of the opposite sex must learn to give them up in order to be happy. Those who do not threaten class stability. His reading of *Cranford* stresses the fact that the ladies of Cranford are deceitful and socially ambitious in order to gain power.

Lansbury, Coral. *Elizabeth Gaskell*. Boston: Twayne, 1984.
Lansbury provides a chronology of Gaskell's life as well as biographical information as she explains the role Unitarianism played in Gaskell's life. Lansbury summarizes and analyzes the novels and many of the short stories, as well as *The Life of Charlotte Brontë*. She believes that Gaskell speaks to modern problems, including labor relations, the place of women in society, and the problems of an industrial society. She asserts that Gaskell was innovative in her use of reverie to achieve psychological subtlety in her characters.

Lewis, Suzanne, ed. *A Dark Night's Work and Other Stories*. New York: Oxford University Press, 1992.
In her introduction, Lewis describes Gaskell as a talented storyteller who was interested in women's place "in a patriarchal society," and who felt it was important for women to work. She is concerned with Gaskell's relationship with Charles Dickens and the effect of serialization on Gaskell's work. She discusses the plots of "A Dark Night's Work," "Libbie Marsh's Three Eras," "Six Weeks at Heppenheim," "Cumberland Sheep Shearers," "Clopton Hall," and "The Grey Woman." A bibliography, a chronology of Gaskell's life, and explanatory notes are also provided.

McVeigh, John. *Elizabeth Gaskell*. New York: Humanities Press, 1970.
McVeigh maintains that Gaskell used her fiction to explain the social effects of the Industrial Revolution. He separates her work into three categories: novels of social criticism, the biography of Charlotte Brontë, and novels of country life. He examines the themes of her works and quotes extensively from them. His work is somewhat dated.

Michie, Elsie B. *Outside the Pale: Cultural Exclusion, Gender Difference, and the Victorian Woman Writer*. Ithaca, N.Y.: Cornell University Press, 1993.
Michie believes that Gaskell identified with prostitutes because, as a writer, she also displayed herself before the public. Certainly, she wrote about prostitutes and worked to reform them, believing that the influence of a good family life could save them. In *Ruth*, she denies the conventional dichotomy between "pure" and "impure" women. In general, Michie believes, Gaskell tries to redefine the feminine rather

than protest women's exclusion from "masculine" realms. Michie also provides a reading of *North and South* in which she connects prostitution with the economic exploitation of the working classes.

Moers, Ellen. *Literary Women*. Garden City, N.Y.: Doubleday, 1976.
Moers discusses *Mary Barton* as the first industrial novel and John Barton as a portrait of the first radical working man.

Sabiston, Elizabeth Jean. "Anglo-American Connections: Elizabeth Gaskell, Harriet Beecher Stowe and the 'Iron of Slavery.'" In *The Discourse of Slavery*, edited by Carl Plasa and Betty J. King, pp. 94-117. London: Routledge, 1994.
Sabiston enumerates the many similarities between the lives of Elizabeth Gaskell and Harriet Beecher Stowe. She believes *Uncle Tom's Cabin* resembles *Mary Barton*, because slavery is analogous to capitalist exploitation. Sabiston also points out the connection between power and the possibility of sexual abuse. She asserts both these writers were more concerned with the exploration of ideas rather than with aesthetics, stressing the need for strong social ties and the need for the individual to become more virtuous before society could be improved.

Sanders, Andrew, ed. *Sylvia's Lovers*, by Elizabeth Gaskell. New York: Oxford University Press, 1982.
Sanders introduces this novel, which he considers Gaskell's gravest and most profound, by explaining its connection to the town of Whitby and to the works of Charlotte Brontë, George Eliot, Charles Dickens, and William Thackeray. Sanders sees the novel's theme as the changes wrought by the passage of time. He outlines the plot briefly as well as the unhappy ending of the novel. A bibliography, a chronology of Gaskell's life, and the words of songs referred to in the novel are included, as are explanatory notes.

Schor, Hilary M. *Scheherezade in the Marketplace: Elizabeth Gaskell and the Victorian Novel*. New York: Oxford University Press, 1992.
Schor notes that Gaskell was involved with major changes in English society, writing about industrialization, the working classes, and prostitution. She was intelligent and sophisticated, yet she wrote conventional fiction extolling the domestic virtues. According to Schor, Gaskell herself was unconventional for wanting to publish and to change women's lives. Schor is interested in the relationship of ideology to narrative in Gaskell's work, and she focuses on this theme in her analysis of the novels.

Sharps, John Geoffrey. *Mrs. Gaskell's Observation and Invention: A Study of her Non-Biographical Works*. Fontwell, Sussex, England: Linden Press, 1970.
   The author sees Gaskell primarily as a social reformer. He summarizes her works and discusses their literary and biographical significance. His critical opinions tend to be outdated.

Shelston, Alan, ed. *Ruth*, by Elizabeth Gaskell. New York: Oxford University Press, 1985.
   Shelston, in his introduction, discusses the background of this novel and its relationship to *Mary Barton* and to *Cranford*. The theme of her novel, unwed motherhood, caused Gaskell some anxiety, but Shelston asserts that most reviewers were sympathetic. He notes that her anxiety may have caused her to confuse both the time period and the geographic setting of the novel and, more important, her own feelings about the guilt or innocence of the unwed mother. He also mentions the influence of Protestant Dissent on the novel. A bibliography, a chronology of Gaskell's life, and explanatory notes are provided.

Spencer, Jane. *Elizabeth Gaskell*. New York: St. Martin's Press, 1995.
   Spencer discusses Gaskell's life and believes Gaskell saw writing not only as a form of escape from life but also as her religious duty. She discusses Gaskell's novels, her relationship with Charles Dickens, and the change in the position of women that occurred in the nineteenth century. Spencer alludes to feminist revisions of Jacques Lacan's theories of language to explain aspects of Gaskell's work, particularly her reconciliation of masculine language and feminine cultural authority. Spencer believes Gaskell's position was somewhat ambiguous. Although she was a confident spokeswoman for society, she was marginalized as a woman and a Unitarian. She provides readings of the novels, the biography of Charlotte Brontë, and "Cousin Phillis."

Stoneman, Patsy. *Elizabeth Gaskell*. Bloomington: Indiana University Press, 1987.
   Stoneman discusses Gaskell's work from both a feminist and a psychoanalytic point of view. She sees Gaskell as a working woman whose men and women friends nurtured her. She notes that Gaskell discussed gender separation and class separation in her work. She also provides a history of Gaskell's reputation among critics and reviews the feminist criticism of her work.

Swindells, Julia. *Victorian Writing and Working Women: The Other Side of Silence*. Minneapolis: University of Minnesota Press, 1985.

Swindells discusses how professionalization shut women out of medicine and out of literature. She notes, however, that a few women—Gaskell, George Eliot, and Elizabeth Barrett Browning—did become known as professional authors. She explores what these women had in common that permitted them to do this. Her discussion of Gaskell centers on the author's fears that her novels would be considered "unfeminine," realizing her attacks on class norms as well as gender norms were potentially dangerous to her literary reputation. Swindells discusses evidence of the tension she finds in Gaskell's work because Gaskell is a woman.

Watson, Elizabeth Porges, ed. *Cranford*, by Elizabeth Gaskell. New York: Oxford University Press, 1980.
In her introduction, Watson discusses Gaskell's love for this book and for country life. She also discusses the book's origin as a series of short stories and how this affected the structure of the novel. A bibliography, a chronology of Gaskell's life, and explanatory notes are included.

Welch, Jeffrey. *Elizabeth Gaskell: An Annotated Bibliography 1929-1975*. New York: Garland, 1977.
Welch provides a chronology of Gaskell's life and works and lists the editions of her works. He also lists and summarizes critical books and articles concerning her writing.

Weyant, Nancy S. *Elizabeth Gaskell: An Annotated Bibliography of English Language Sources*. Metuchen, N.J.: Scarecrow Press, 1994.
Weyant notes a new interest in Gaskell's short fiction and in her biography of Charlotte Brontë on the part of feminist critics. She also notes the existence of the Gaskell Society, devoted to the study of Gaskell's works. Weyant lists earlier bibliographies and lists and evaluates books and articles about Gaskell up to 1991. In addition, she includes a list of master's and honors theses about Gaskell.

Wright, Edgar. Introduction to *Mary Barton*, by Elizabeth Gaskell. New York: Oxford University Press, 1987.
In his introduction, Wright notes that *Mary Barton* was received with interest when it was published because its subject, the condition of England, was a matter of great concern. In the novel, Gaskell describes the horrific living conditions of the poor in order to encourage the alleviation of these conditions. Wright outlines the plot and analyzes the characters. He also notes Gaskell's concern for working women, her use of humor, and her narrative methods. He also points out the relationship of this novel to her other works. A bibliography, a chro-

nology of Gaskell's life, and explanatory notes are included. An appendix includes the original rough sketch for the novel, notes for an epilogue, and the poem "Sketches Among the Poor," Gaskell's first published work.

_____. *Mrs. Gaskell: The Basis for Reassessment.* London: Oxford University Press, 1965.
Wright discusses Gaskell's era and describes her treatment of religion, family, tradition, Manchester, the countryside, and industrialization. He believes her work should be reassessed. To do so, he analyzes her themes and techniques, concentrating on her novels and long stories.

_____, ed. *My Lady Ludlow and Other Stories,* by Elizabeth Gaskell. London: Oxford University Press, 1989.
In his introduction, Wright maintains that Gaskell was a natural story-teller. He also discusses her life and her friendship with Charlotte Brontë. These stories, he maintains, share as common elements a belief in the importance of tolerance and forgiveness, as well as a country setting. Her subject is the reaction to social change, and her approach is comic. He points out autobiographical elements in the stories, as well as Gothic elements. A bibliography, a chronology of Gaskell's life, and explanatory notes are included. An appendix includes "Round the Sofa," the machinery she used in the first edition of the stories to tie them together.

SUSANNAH GUNNING (C.1740-1800)

The daughter of a clergyman, Gunning wrote conventional novels about love in collaboration with her sister. They included *Histories of Lady Frances S... and Lady Caroline S,,,* (1763), *Family Pictures* (1764), *The Picture* (1766), and *The Hermit* (1770). Family scandals over her sister's marriage and her father's illicit liaisons interrupted her writing, but she then used them as material in *Anecdotes of the Delborough Family* (1792) and *Memoirs of Mary* (1793). She also wrote *Delves* (1796), *Love at First Sight* (1797), and *Fashionable Involvements* (1800), as well as the poem *Virginius and Virginia* (1792).

Todd, Janet. *Gender, Art and Death.* New York: Continuum, 1993.
Todd argues that Gunning used Gothic elements in her narratives about her family, stressing her own role as wronged mother who needed to

earn money to support her children. Todd describes Gunning's life, marriage, and literary works.

_____. *The Sign of Angellica: Women, Writing and Fiction 1600-1800*. New York: Columbia University Press, 1989.

Todd discusses *Coombe Wood* (1783), which may been written by Gunning or her sister, Elizabeth. It idealizes aristocratic wealth, but not aristocratic immorality. Todd notes that novels of sensibility denigrated both the aristocracy and the commercial classes. In these novels, the heroine has become a passive sufferer, totally saintly. Her death is not only beautiful but also elevating to those who witness it. Clichés abound and femininity is all powerful. Todd also discusses the connections between the Gunning family's problems and their fiction.

ELIZABETH HAMILTON (1758-1816)

Hamilton was born in Belfast and was brought up by an aunt and uncle in an upper-middle-class home that had adopted Rousseau's philosophy of education. She was fairly well educated and well read, but she regretted her lack of a classical education. She became a writer as an alternative to marriage. Her brother had lived and worked in India and was an orientalist. When he died, she wished to continue his work, but she feared it was unfeminine. In 1790, she did publish her *Translation of the Letters of a Hindoo Rajah; Written Previous to, and During the Period of His Residence in England; To Which is Prefixed a Preliminary Dissertation of the History, Religion, and Manners of the Hindoos*. In 1800, she published the satirical *Memoirs of Modern Philosophers: A Novel*. The next year, she published *Letters on Education*. She turned to history in *Memoirs of the Life of Agrippina, the Wife of Germanicus* (1804), which is part fiction. She was asked to educate a young noblewoman, but left that position when she found it compromised her independence. She then wrote *Letters, Addressed to the Daughter of a Nobleman, on the Formation of Religious and Moral Principle* (1806), a theological and philosophical work. She also wrote *The Cottagers of Glen Burnie* (1808) to advocate class reconciliation under the supervision of middle-class women. *Exercises in Religious Knowledge; for the Instruction of Young Persons* (1809), is another theological work. *A Series of Popular Essays, Illustrative of Principles Essentially Connected with the Improvement of the Understanding, the Imagination, and the Heart* (1813) concerns epistemology. It was followed by *Hints Addressed to the Patrons and Directors of Schools* (1815), which was meant to show middle-class women how to run schools for the poor. Hamilton died the following year, but much of her work, particularly *The Cottagers of Glen Burnie*, remained popular long after her death.

Kelly, Gary. *Women, Writing and Revolution: 1790-1827*. Oxford: Clarendon Press, 1993.
Kelly discusses Hamilton's life and work in great detail, describing each of her books and the reactions to them. He sees her as a writer who managed to discuss subjects the times thought unfeminine, in a feminine way. She saw her works as "translations," or as popularizations, in other words, as extensions of women's domestic, charitable, and educational duties.

Luria, Gina. Introduction to *Letters Addressed to the Daughter of a Nobleman on the Formation of the Religious and the Moral Principle*, by Elizabeth Hamilton. 2 vols. New York: Garland, 1974.
Luria provides information on the life of Hamilton and discusses her correspondence with her brother as well as her relationship with her mentor, George Gregory. She describes *Letters of a Hindoo Rajah* and its reception. Luria also tells how Hamilton came to write the very popular satire, *Memoirs of Modern Philosophers: A Novel* after meeting Godwin and his circle. Luria notes that *The Cottagers of Glen Burnie* was Hamilton's most popular work.

_____. Introduction to *Memoirs of Modern Philosophers: A Novel*, by Elizabeth Hamilton. New York: Garland, 1974.
Luria provides a biography of Hamilton, describes her relationship with William Godwin, and discusses her work and its reception. She notes that Hamilton was interested in helping the poor and spent time as a governess. Her most popular work was *The Cottagers of Glen Burnie*. According to Luria, both Jane Austen and Maria Edgeworth valued Hamilton's books.

MARY HAYS (1760-1843)

Mary Hays was a member of a Dissenting family. Dissenters were Protestants who did not belong to the Anglican church. She received her education at a Dissenting academy. She published *Cursory Remarks* (1792) defending public prayer, and this work caused her to be noticed by the radicals of the day, including William Godwin and Mary Wollstonecraft. She also wrote *Letters and Essays, Moral and Miscellaneous* (1793).

Her novel *Memoirs of Emma Courtney* (1796) concerned a heroine who tells her beloved of her feelings before he has declared his own. For this, Hays was attacked as immoral. *The Victim of Prejudice* (1799) argued for sexual equality. In an article in the *Monthly Magazine* and in the *Annual Necrology for 1797-98*, Hays defended Mary Wollstonecraft after her death. Perhaps Hays's best-known work is *Appeal to the Men of Great Britain in Behalf of Women* (1798), which appeared anonymously. In it, she argued for more independence for women and for vocational training for them. The six-volume *Female Biography: Or, Memoirs of Illustrious and Celebrated Women* (1803) discusses well-known women. Hays also wrote didactic short stores, *The Brothers: Or, Consequences* (1815), and *Family Annuals: Or, The Sisters* (1817). She died at the age of eighty-three.

Adams, M. Ray. "Mary Hays, Disciple of William Godwin." In *Studies in the Literary Backgrounds of English Radicalism*, pp. 83-103. New York: Greenwood Press, 1968.
Adams discussion Hays's relationship with the Godwin circle, using *Memoirs of Emma Courtney* for biographical information. Adams notes that Hays's early writings were well-received, but after 1800 she became a figure of ridicule even though her views were no more radical than those of others. Although she was an antimonarchist and a materialist, she was never an atheist. Adams provides a reading of *Memoirs of Emma Courtney*, asserting it is much more readable than most of the novels of the time. Adams believes some of the ridicule it received was the result of its being misunderstood.

Ashfield, Andrew, ed. "Mary Hays." In *Romantic Women Poets 1770-1838*, pp. 29-33. New York: St. Martin's Press, 1995.
Ashfield provides a selection of Hays's works as well as a brief biographical headnote.

Kelly, Gary. *Women, Writing and Revolution: 1790-1827*. Oxford: Clarendon Press, 1993.
Kelly discusses the revolutionary events of the 1790's, asserting that the times enabled women to write. Even during the post-revolutionary period, women were still enabled to write as popularizers. He places Mary Hays within the revolution in taste and feeling that produced sentimentalism and that particularly affected middle-class professionals, discussing her life, her work, and the response to it. The readings of her works are quite complete. He notes Hays's feminism, her

attempts to feminize philosophy and history, and, despite this, her approval of domesticity and capitalism.

Luria, Gina. Introduction to *Letters and Essays, Moral and Miscellaneous*, by Mary Hays. New York: Garland, 1974.
In her introduction to this facsimile edition of Hays's work, Luria discusses Hays's life, her friendship with William Godwin, her connection with Romanticism, and, briefly, her work.

——————. Introduction to *Memoirs of Emma Courtney*, by Mary Hays. New York: Garland, 1974.
Luria provides a brief biography of Mary Hays and discusses her reading, her relationship with well-known Dissenters, such as Joseph Priestley, and her relationship with the Godwin circle. Luria notes that Hays introduced Mary Wollstonecraft to William Godwin. Luria also explains that Hays's unpopularity was caused by the late eighteenth century antirevolutionary backlash. Luria believes that *Memoirs of Emma Courtney* is partially autobiographical. She also discusses Hays's later novels, noting her love of knowledge and virtue and her belief in progress and reform. A bibliography is supplied.

McDonald, Lynn. *Women Founders of the Social Sciences*. Ottawa: Carleton University Press, 1994.
McDonald supplies a brief biography of Hays and a brief list of sources for further reading. She sees Hays as an "unmitigated radical" whose writing was too often ignored. She describes Hays's "Thoughts on Civil Liberty" as relating female liberation to liberty in general. She discusses Hays's reaction to the French Revolution and to Mary Wollstonecraft's writings. She sees Hays's *The Victim of Prejudice* as melodramatic, but daring in its treatment of issues such as illegitimacy, sexual harassment, prostitution, crime, and capital punishment. She notes that Hays's *Appeal to the Men of Great Britain in Behalf of Women* uses materialist and utilitarian arguments for women's equality. She also notes that Hays's six-volume *Female Biography: Or, Memoirs of Illustrious and Celebrated Women* is a major accomplishment, because Hays writes entertainingly and informatively of women of accomplishment as far back as the fifth century B.C.

Todd, Janet. *The Sign of Angellica: Women, Writing and Fiction 1600-1800*. New York: Columbia University Press, 1989.
Todd summarizes the plot of *Memoirs of Emma Courtney*, in which the heroine pursues the man she loves, who turns out to be married. He dies, and the man she later marries dies, leaving her to be the comfort

of her daughter and her true love's son, who finally marry. According to Todd, although Hays says she is warning against the dangers of indulging in sensibility, the book actually glorifies it.

Tompkins, J. M. S. "Mary Hays, Philosophess." In *The Polite Marriage*, pp. 150-190. Reprint. Freeport, N.Y.: Books for Libraries Press, 1969.
In this work, which was first published in 1938, Tompkins discusses Hays's life, her connection with the Godwin circle and the Romantics, her feminism, and her writing. Tompkins maintains that *Letters and Essays, Moral and Miscellaneous* is autobiographical. She notes that *Cursory Remarks* was well-received but egotistic, and that Mary Wollstonecraft's *Vindication of the Rights of Woman* influenced Hays's life profoundly, causing her to be more independent. The plot of *Memoirs of Emma Courtney* is discussed, as is its reception and its relation to Elizabeth Hamilton's *Memoirs of Modern Philosophers: A Novel*. Tompkins briefly discusses Hays's later life and later works.

Ty, Eleanor. *Unsex'd Revolutionaries: Five Women Novelists of the 1790's*. Toronto: University of Toronto Press, 1993.
According to Ty, Hays uses the conventions of the sentimental novel, its stress on sensibility and pathos, and a vulnerable heroine to show the devastating effects of patriarchy's oppression of women. Ty also describes how Hays uses the language of political revolution in order to effect a revolution in the status and treatment of women. Ty demonstrates how Hays uses emotional situations in *Memoirs of Emma Courtney* and *The Victim of Prejudice* to dramatize the appeals she made to reason in her *Appeal to the Men of Great Britain in Behalf of Women*. Ty believes that when Hays wrote the earlier novel, *Memoirs of Emma Courtney*, she believed that the French Revolution would improve the status of women in England, but by the time she wrote *The Victim of Prejudice*, she was less optimistic. The heroine of that novel, Mary Raymond, is a victim of society who writes her story in her prison cell. The villain is the antithesis of that Burkean ideal, a benevolent and paternal squire. Sir Peter Osborne is a rapist and an oppressor who eventually destroys the heroine. Hays hoped that the portrayal of such victimization would lead to an improvement in the position of women.

FELICIA HEMANS (1793-1835)

Born in Liverpool as Felicia Browne, she grew up in Wales where she studied modern languages and Latin. Her first book, *Poems*, was published when she was only fourteen. *England and Spain: Or, Valour and Patriotism* appeared in 1808. *Domestic Affections* appeared in 1812. She married Captain Alfred Hemans and had five children, but she and her husband were separated when she was twenty-six years old. She supported her children by her writing, which included *Modern Greece* (1817), *Translations from Camoens and Other Poets* (1818), *Tales and Historic Scenes* (1819), and *Wallace's Invocation to Bruce* (1819). *The Skeptic* (1820) was a religious poem, as was *Superstition and Error* (1822). *Lays of Many Lands* (1825) was based on her extensive knowledge of European languages. She also wrote for the *Edinburgh Review* and wrote three plays, one of which, *The Vespers of Palermo* (1823) was performed. *The Forest Sanctuary* (1825) contained her most famous poem, "Casablanca." Her other works include *Records of Woman* (1828), *Songs of the Affections* (1830), *Hymns on the Works of Nature* (1833), and *Hymns for Childhood* (1834). She also wrote *National Lyrics and Songs for Music* (1834) and *Scenes and Hymns of Life* (1834). Her poetry was widely admired both in England and in the United States, but was ignored after the first decades of the twentieth century.

Armstrong, Isobel. "The Gush of the Feminine: How Can We Read Women's Poetry of the Romantic Period?" In *Romantic Women Writers: Voices and Countervoices*, edited by Paula R. Feldman and Theresa M. Kelley, pp. 13-32. Hanover, N.H.: University Press of New England, 1995.
Armstrong discusses "Arabella Stuart" and "Casablanca," noting that they join the discourse of the law with language related to the senses.

Clarke, Norma. *Ambitious Heights: Writing, Friendship, Love—The Jewsbury Sisters, Felicia Hemans and Jane Carlyle*. London: Routledge, 1990.
Clarke provides a readable book about the relationship between the ability to be a professional writer, like the Jewsbury sisters and Felicia Hemans, and the ability to sustain a marriage. Clarke believes that Hemans' encouragement helped Maria Jane Jewsbury, just as the encouragement of other women writers, such as Mary Russell Mitford, nourished Hemans. Readings of Hemans' poetry are provided.

Harding, Anthony John. "Felicia Hemans and the Effacement of Women." In *Romantic Women Writers: Voices and Countervoices*, edited by Paula R. Feldman and Theresa M. Kelley, pp. 138-149. Hanover, N.H.: University Press of New England, 1995.

Harding notes that Hemans locates the transcendence sought for by the Romantic poets in death and the total loss of individuality. He provides a reading of "Madeline: A Domestic Tale," and "A Spirit's Return," as well as love poetry from her 1830 collection. He maintains that she insists that death alone validates a woman's love by making it either heroic or eternal. He also provides readings of *The Forest Sanctuary* and "The Rock of Cader Idris." Harding denies the poems are feminist in the modern sense of the term, but he considers them to be "always competent and sometimes brilliant."

Hemans, Felicia. *Records of Woman, 1828*. Oxford: Woodstock Books, 1991.

The introduction, written by J. W. (Jonathan Wordsworth), describes Hemans as a popular poet who uses fiction to explore her values as a woman and a writer. He provides readings of several poems, which concern her feelings of loss and the relationship of an artist to art. He believes that Hemans is afraid that devotion to art disrupts a woman's life.

Leighton, Angela. *Victorian Women Poets: Writing Against the Heart*. New York: Harvester Wheatsheaf, 1992.

Leighton points out that Hemans was both famous and respectable because the public perceived her as forced to write poetry, not out of a desire for fame, but because she was not supported by her father or her husband. She wrote for the Annuals, which were highly popular periodicals that appeared at Christmas, and her writing exhibited great variety. Some of her poems are melancholy, others jocular. Most, according to Leighton, urge weary endurance. Her verse is technically confident and was quite influential. Leighton compares her work to that of Letitia Elizabeth Landon.

McGann, Jerome J., Anne Mack, J. J. Rome, and George Mannejc. "Literary History, Romanticism, and Felicia Hemans." In *Re-Visioning Romanticism: British Women Writers, 1776-1837*, edited by Carol Shiner Wilson and Joel Haefner, pp. 210-227. Philadelphia: University of Pennsylvania Press, 1994.

McGann defends Hemans' poetry from the charge of sentimentality by showing how her poetry stresses the evanescence of the material and the stability of the ideal. He use "The Stately Homes of England" as an example. Anne Mack considers Hemans "the poet of all that is admirable, exquisite and celebrated." Rome and Mannejc believe her poetry is merely sentimental and current interest in it will soon fade.

Mellor, Anne K., and Richard E. Matlak, eds. "Felicia Dorothea Browne Hemans." In *British Literature 1780-1830*, pp. 1179-1247. Fort Worth, Tex.: Harcourt Brace College Publishers, 1996.
The authors discuss Heman's life and work and provide a selection of her poetry.

Reiman, Donald. Introduction to *Records of Woman*, by Felicia Dorothea Hemans. New York: Garland, 1978.
Reiman writes that Hemans was the most popular woman poet in England, probably because she wrote about ordinary concerns without attempting to plumb philosophical or psychological depths. He notes that her literary contemporaries admired her personally but did not take her work seriously, possibly because in its polish, neatness, and clarity were closer to eighteenth century poetry than to nineteenth century poetry. Also, her work differed from that of the Romantics, since it did not involve itself with any tortuous route to self-discovery. This edition is a facsimile of her original book.

_____. Introduction to *Tales, Historic Scenes, and Other Poems*, by Felicia Dorothea Hemans. New York: Garland, 1978.
This facsimile edition contains the same introduction as *Records of Woman*.

Trinder, Peter W. *Mrs. Hemans*. Cardiff: University of Wales Press, 1984.
In this discussion of Hemans' life and work, Trinder analyzes her poetry and discusses her reading in relation to her work. He also discusses the failure of her marriage and the reception of her work. Finally, he discusses her influence. He gives readings of "An Old Church in an English Park," "The Restoration," "Modern Greece," "Tales of Historic Scenes," and *The Vespers of Paloma* (a play).

Wolfson, Susan. "'Domestic Affections' and 'The Spear of Minerva': Felicia Hemans and the 'Dilemma of Gender." In *Re-Visioning Romanticism: British Women Writers, 1776-1837*, edited by Carol Shiner Wilson and Joel Haefner, pp. 128-166. Philadelphia: University of Pennsylvania Press, 1994.
Wolfson quotes critics' opinions of Hemans as a very feminine poet and then goes on to show she cast doubts on the idealization of

domesticity that pervaded acceptable women's writing during the nineteenth century. Wolfson notes, too, that Hemans' situation, living in her mother's house with her children but without her husband, relieved her of domestic chores. Hemans was crushed, however, when her mother died. Wolfson notes further that Hemans wrote about different kinds of women but when she wrote about women artists, she focused on their suffering. Wolfson quotes from *Domestic Affections* and *Records of Woman*. The latter, according to Wolfson, demonstrates that a domestic life is unfulfilling for women. Wolfson asserts that Hemans' dilemma is that she finds both domesticity and writing poetry bring suffering.

_____. "Gendering the Soul." In *Romantic Women Writers: Voices and Countervoices*, edited by Paula R. Feldman and Theresa M. Kelley, pp. 33-68. Hanover, N.H.: University Press of New England, 1995.
Wolfson provides readings of "Domestic Affections," "Evening Prayer: At a Girl's School," and "The Indian City," in which Hemans undercuts the apparent approval of the domestic role for women over artistic endeavors she demonstrates in "Properzia Rossi."

ELIZABETH INCHBALD (1752-1821)

Elizabeth Inchbald was born to a rural Catholic family who provided her with little formal education, but she did have some connections in the theater. She ran off to London to make her career there, married an actor, and became an actress and a prolific playwright. She wrote twenty-one plays, of which eighteen were published, and wrote novels and criticism. She also wrote biographical information and drama criticism for what eventually became an anthology of 125 plays from the time of William Shakespeare to her own time. Her best-known play is *Lovers' Vows* (1798), because it is used in Jane Austen's *Mansfield Park*. Her novels are *A Simple Story*, written in 1777 and published in 1791, and *Nature and Art* (1796). Inchbald was acquainted with the great theatrical figures of the day as well as the political radicals. She lived frugally and quietly toward the end of her life. *A Simple Story* is available in paperback in The World's Classics edition of Oxford University Press.

Barker, Gerard. *Grandison's Heirs: The Paragon's Progress in the Late Eighteenth Century English Novel*. Newark: University of Delaware Press, 1985.

Although Barker admits that Dorriforth, the hero of *A Simple Story*, is generally thought to be modeled on John Kemble, an actor to whom Inchbald was strongly attracted, he also shares some characteristics of Sir Charles Grandison, the perfect hero of Richardson's novel. Barker describes the novel, commenting on its psychological realism and its popularity. He notes that the second half of the novel is inferior to the first because the characters are either wholly good or wholly evil.

Craft-Fairchild, Catherine. *Masquerade and Gender: Disguise and Female Identity in Eighteenth Century Fictions by Women*. University Park: Pennsylvania State University Press, 1993.
Craft-Fairchild is interested in whether masquerades limited or increased the power of women. She reads *A Simple Story* to demonstrate that Inchbald questions the psychology of patriarchy while allowing it to triumph. Craft-Fairchild believes that Miss Milner's love for a Roman Catholic priest causes her downfall, making her part of the patriarchal system and allowing Dorriforth to control her. Craft-Fairchild maintains that *A Simple Story* is actually quite subtle in the way it undermines patriarchy.

Jenkins, Elizabeth. "Elizabeth Inchbald." In *Ten Fascinating Women*, pp. 99-117. New York: Coward-McCann, 1960.
In this romanticized biography, Jenkins summarizes *A Simple Story* and the plots of Inchbald's plays. Jenkins maintains that the crucial event in Inchbald's life was her love for the actor John Kemble.

Kelly, Gary. *The English Jacobin Novel 1780-1805*. Oxford: Clarendon Press, 1976.
Kelly discusses Inchbald as a novelist who was interested in the effects of education on women's experience. He believes her work avoided the excesses of sensibility and didacticism and notes that it was well received and influential. He describes the structure of *A Simple Story* as based on contrast and the accumulation of detail, and he notes its use of dramatic unity. He describes *Nature and Art* as a satire on liberals and intellectuals. He summarizes the novel, which focuses on the importance of education and the belief that virtue will ultimately triumph. Kelly maintains that Inchbald was satirizing the ideas of Hannah More and was much more sincere in her desire to help the poor than More was. Like Hannah More, she showed how women could enter public life by means of religion and philanthropy, including antislavery agitation. Kelly considers Inchbald the founder of the Jacobin novel.

Littlewood, S. R. *Elizabeth Inchbald and Her Circle: The Life Story of a Charming Woman (1753-1821)*. Reprint. Folcroft, Pa.: Folcroft Library Editions, 1973.

First published in 1921, this biography is very old-fashioned, but it does describe Inchbald's life in the theater, her plays, her novels, and her critical works. Littlewood succeeds in describing the age as well.

Manvell, Roger. *Elizabeth Inchbald: England's Principle Woman Dramatist and Woman of Letters in Eighteenth Century London: A Biographical Study*. Lanham, Md.: University Press of America, 1987.

Manvell provides a complete picture of Inchbald's life and her family, friends, and acquaintances. He also describes the plots of Inchbald's novels, provides synopses of her plays, and quotes extensively from her criticism.

_____, ed. Introduction to *Selected Comedies*, by Elizabeth Inchbald. Lanham, Md.: University Press of America, 1987.

In his introduction to Inchbald's work, Manvell discusses her life and the work of playwrights who were her contemporaries. He describes her plays as "comedies of manners, humours and intrigues." He also describes the influences on the collection of plays, which mostly concern marriage and the relationship between British colonialism. These plays include *I'll Tell You What*, *Such Things Are*, *Everyone Has Her Fault*, *The Wedding Day*, *Wives As They Were*, and *Maids As They Are*.

Scheuermann, Mona. *Her Bread to Earn: Women, Money and Society from Defoe to Austen*. Lexington: University Press of Kentucky, 1993.

Scheuermann discusses *Nature and Art* to prove that Inchbald believed that poor women were victimized.

Spencer, Jane. Introduction to *A Simple Story*, by Elizabeth Inchbald. Edited by J. M. S. Tompkins. New York: Oxford University Press, 1988.

Spencer discusses Inchbald's life and work. She also discusses *A Simple Story* as a novel about "desire and its prohibition." She notes its autobiographical significance as well as its treatment of themes widely discussed at the time, especially the rights of women and the importance of female education. She also points out the novel's eroticism and its treatment of the hero and heroine. She maintains that the heroine in the second half of the novel represents a repudiation of the first half of the novel. A chronology of Inchbald's life, a bibliography, and explanatory notes from the 1969 edition of this novel are included in this volume.

Tompkins, J. M. S., ed. *A Simple Story*, by Elizabeth Inchbald. Oxford: Oxford University Press, 1967.
Tompkins outlines the publishing history of this book as well as its relation to other novels written by women. commenting on its didacticism. According to Tompkins, the most original features of the novel are its treatment of the Catholic gentry, its view of a girl's love as real passion, and its techniques derived from the drama. She considers the first half of the novel to be quite realistic. Tompkins also discusses characterization, asserting that the relationship of the main characters is based on Inchbald's relationship to John Kemble. She also discusses the influences on Inchbald, Inchbald's life, and the critical reception of the book. In addition, she comments on textual problems of the manuscript.

Ty, Eleanor. *Unsex'd Revolutionaries: Five Women Novelists of the 1790's*. Toronto: University of Toronto Press, 1993.
Ty disputes the conventional argument that the theme of *A Simple Story* is the necessity for a proper education. She believes that Matilda "represents a concession to the patriarchal order" and uses biographical and textual evidence to demonstrate this point. She also bases her argument on the linguistic theories of Julia Kristeva and Luce Irigaray. In addition, she points out the resemblances of *A Simple Story* to Frances Sheridan's *Memoirs of Miss Sidney Bidulph* and *Wuthering Heights*. Inchbald's second novel, *Nature and Art*, is unusual in that its protagonists are male. It resembles *A Simple Story* in that it deals with two generations. Ty believes Inchbald's two sets of characters represent acquiescence to the patriarchal order and resistance to it. The rich and powerful do nothing to help the poor, are generally immoral, and abuse their power. Ty points out that Inchbald also criticized the upper classes in her plays. In the novel, two contrasting characters marry—one for money, the other for love. The couple who marry for love are, of course, morally superior to their foils. Ty justifies Inchbald's ending of *Nature and Art* by examining it psycholinguistically. The "good" couple leaves the symbolic order for an "alternative society" in which emotional satisfaction is more important than wealth.

GERALDINE JEWSBURY (1812-1880)

After her mother's death in 1819, Geraldine was brought up by her sister Maria Jane, a writer, and possibly was inspired by her to become a writer herself. She was well educated and acquainted with the important literary figures of the day such as the Carlyles, the Rossettis, the Kingsleys, John Ruskin, and Thomas Huxley. Her first novel, *Zoe* (1845), concerns religious doubt. *The Half Sisters* (1848) argues for the importance of education and careers for women. *Marian Withers* (1851) concerns a self-made industrialist. Her other novels include *Constance Herbert* (1855), *The Sorrows of Gentility* (1856), and *Right or Wrong* (1859. She also wrote several children's books, contributed to periodicals, and was an influential book reviewer and publisher's reader. She died of cancer in 1880.

Clarke, Norma. *Ambitious Heights: Writing, Friendship, Love—The Jewsbury Sisters, Felicia Hemans and Jane Carlyle.* London: Routledge, 1990.
An extremely readable book about the relationship between the ability to be a professional writer and the ability to sustain a marriage. It has been conjectured that the pressures of marriage kept Jane Carlyle from writing professionally. Clarke believes that Felicia Hemans' encouragement helped Mary Jane Jewsbury, just as the encouragement of other women writers, such as Mary Russell Mitford, nourished Hemans. Geraldine Jewsbury and Jane Carlyle were extremely close, perhaps providing Carlyle with the emotional support her marriage did not seem to afford her.

Ireland, Mrs. Alexander, ed. *Selections from the Letters of Geraldine Ensor Jewsbury to Jane Welsh Carlyle.* London: Longmans Green, 1892.
The old-fashioned introduction to this book asserts that both these women were lonely and unconventional. Their lives and Jewsbury's work are described, as is Jewsbury's relationship with Charles Dickens and her work in periodicals. Ireland notes that Jewsbury destroyed Jane Carlyle's letters at Carlyle's request, but Carlyle did not destroy Jewsbury's letters.

MARIA JANE JEWSBURY (1800-1833)

Maria Jane Jewsbury lived in Manchester and published poetry and articles in periodicals such as the *Manchester Gazette* and the *Atheneum*. Her *Phantasmagoria* (1825) contains sketches and poetry. *Letters to the Young* (1828) discuss religion. *Lays of Leisure Hours* (1829) is a book of poetry, and *The Three Histories* (1830) are fiction. When she married, she accompanied her husband to India, where he died of cholera. On her return to England, she met William Wordsworth and became a close friend of his daughter Dora.

Ashfield, Andrew, ed. *Romantic Women Poets 1770-1838*. New York: St. Martin's Press, 1995.
Ashfield provides a selection of Jewsbury's works as well as a brief biographical headnote.

Wolfson, Susan. "Gendering the Soul." In *Romantic Women Writers: Voices and Countervoices*, edited by Paula R. Feldman and Theresa M. Kelley, pp. 33-68. Hanover, N.H.: University Press of New England, 1995.
Wolfson discusses "History of an Enthusiast," which concerns a young woman poet who wants fame rather than domesticity. The young woman lives to regret this, but Jewsbury seems to Wolfson to be ambivalent about the relative merits of fame and domesticity.

ELLIS CORNELIA KNIGHT (1758-1837)

Classically educated, Knight moved to Europe after the death of her father in 1775. There, she published *Dinarbus* (1790), *Marcus Flaminius* (1791), and poetry. After she returned to England, she wrote a guide to Rome entitled *Latium* (1805) and published poems, translations, and histories of France and Spain. She was attached to the English court until 1816, when she went abroad again. There, she wrote a novel, *Sir Guy de Lusignan* (1837), set during the Middle Ages.

Luttrell, Barbara. *The Prim Romantic*. London: Chatto & Windus, 1965.
Based on Knight's memoirs and the memoirs of those who knew her, this readable but old-fashioned biography discusses Knight's parents, childhood, her life in Rome, and her acquaintanceships with Admiral Nelson, the royal family, and other notables. It lists her works, but does not discuss them seriously.

Messenger, Ann. *His and Hers: Essays in Restoration and Eighteenth Century Literature.* Lexington: University Press of Kentucky, 1986.
Messenger compares *Dinarbus* to Samuel Johnson's *Rasselas* and finds the latter more entertaining and optimistic. She describes the plot, which involves intrigue, battles, and love affairs and ends happily. Like *Rasselas*, it is also full of philosophic discussions, but it differs from Johnson's work in its less skilled writing, its greater optimism, and its comments on the author's own concerns. Messenger believes these had to do with the difficulties of life with her eccentric mother, her relationship with Lord Nelson and Lady Hamilton, and the other difficulties of her life at the court of George III.

LETITIA ELIZABETH LANDON (1802-1838)

Born in Africa, Landon attended school in London. She published her first poem in 1820. She reviewed for the *Gazette* as well as publishing several volumes of poetry. These volumes include *The Fate of Adelaide* (1821), *The Improvisatrice* (1824), *The Troubadour* (1825), *The Golden Violet* (1827), *The Venetian Bracelet* (1828), *The Vow of the Peacock* (1835), and *The Zenana and Other Poems* (1839). Her novels include *Romance and Reality* (1831), *Francesca Carrara* (1834), *Ethel Churchill* (1837), *Duty and Inclination* (1838), and *Lady Anne Granard* (1842). Her life was somewhat scandalous, and her poetry was quite popular.

Armstrong, Isobel. "The Gush of the Feminine: How Can We Read Women's Poetry of the Romantic Period?" In *Romantic Women Writers: Voices and Countervoices*, edited by Paula R. Feldman and Theresa M. Kelley, pp. 13-32. Hanover, N.H.: University Press of New England, 1995.
Armstrong supplies a reading for "Calypso Watches the Ocean," in which the story from Homer's *Odyssey* is told from the point of view of the female rather than from that of the male. This perspective, according to Armstrong, causes experiences derived from the senses to be valued, a concept which Armstrong connects to philosophy of David Hume.

Ashfield, Andrew, ed. *Romantic Women Poets 1770-1838.* New York: St. Martin's Press, 1995.
Ashfield provides a selection of Landon's works as well as a brief biographical headnote.

Leighton, Angela. *Victorian Women Poets: Writing Against the Heart.*
Charlottesville: University Press of Virginia, 1992.
Leighton discusses Landon's poetry in relation to her life. She connects
Landon's father's death and the family's subsequent poverty to the
many heroines betrayed by men in her poetry. She also discusses
Landon's work as it was affected by publication in the annuals, popular
literary magazines that paid writers well but expected the melodramatic and picturesque from them. Leighton also discusses Landon's
friends and mentors, her marriage, and her probable suicide. The
unhappy end of Landon's life, Leighton believes, reinforced the idea
that literary success for a woman can be achieved only at the price of
personal misery. Leighton provides a critical evaluation of Landon's
poetry as more realistic and "less domestically sweet" and less religious than Felicia Hemans' work. She also provides readings of *The
Improvisatrice* (1824), *The Golden Violet* (1826), "A History of the
Lyre" (1828), and *The Venetian Bracelet* (1829). She consistently
demonstrates the relationships among the work of Landon, Hemans,
and Elizabeth Barrett Browning.

Mellor, Anne K., and Richard E. Matlak, eds. "Letitia Elizabeth Landon,
Later Maclean." In *British Literature 1780-1830*, pp. 1377-1403. Fort
Worth, Tex.: Harcourt Brace College Publishers, 1996.
The authors discuss Landon's life and work and provide a selection of
her poetry.

Stephenson, Glennis. *Letitia Landon: The Woman Behind L.E.L.* Manchester, England: Manchester University Press, 1995.
Stephenson discusses Landon's relationship to Romanticism, her life,
her orthodoxy and her conflicts with orthodoxy, and her reputation.
Her problems as a woman poet are addressed, as are her attempts to be
a "feminine" writer. Stephenson provides extensive analysis of "Lines
of Life," *The Improvisatrice*, and *The Golden Violet*. She also discusses
Landon's heroines, her relationship to Mme de Staël's *Corinne*, the
importance of Italy in Landon's work, Landon's pessimism about love,
her literary techniques, her fiction, her sense of the female poet as a
prophet, her work for the annuals, and the writing about her after her
death. Stephenson's description of the annuals and their place in the
social and literary life of the age is particularly valuable. Indeed, this
has become the definitive study of Landon's life and work.

MARY LEAPOR (1722-1746)

A gardener's daughter who became a maid, Mary Leapor managed not only to obtain books but also to read and write poetry. Her patron, Bridget Fremantle, arranged for the publication of her work after Leapor's death from measles. Leapor wrote about the difficulties involved in being a poor woman and trying to write poetry. Her poetry is satiric and feminist. She also wrote a tragedy in verse, *The Unhappy Father*, which was never staged.

Greene, Richard. *Mary Leapor: A Study in Eighteenth Century Women's Poetry*. Oxford: Clarendon Press, 1993.

In this definitive work, Greene describes Leapor's life and her reputation, maintaining that her work differs from that of other eighteenth century poets because she does not address abstractions and writes few odes. Leapor writes in octosyllabic couplets as a result of the influence of Alexander Pope and Jonathan Swift, but her stands on social issues understandably differs from theirs. Greene describes Leapor's experiences as a laboring woman who is discriminated against because of her class and her sex. Greene also discusses her attitudes toward marriage, the family, female friendship, beauty, domestic service, agriculture, and literary patronage, as well as her reading and her fear of death. He credits her work with good humor and hopefulness.

CHARLOTTE LENNOX (C.1729-1804)

The daughter of an army officer who served as the lieutenant governor of New York, Charlotte Lennox lived in Gibraltar and near Albany, New York. After her father's death, when she was fifteen, she returned to England. In 1747, she published *Poems on Various Occasions* (1747) and married. She had two children and was the main support of the family. Her career as an actress was short and unsuccessful, but she met some notable literary figures, including Samuel Johnson and Samuel Richardson. Her first novel, *The Life of Harriet Stuart*, appeared in 1750, her most popular novel, *The Female Quixote: Or, The Adventures of Arabella*, in 1752. She did translations and produced a long work on William Shakespeare, *Shakespeare Illustrated* (1753-1754). *Henrietta* (1758), a novel, became an unsuccessful play. Lennox also edited the monthly magazine *The Lady's Museum* (1760-1761) and wrote "On the Education of Daughters" and a novel *Sophia* (1762). Some scholars attribute a novel entitled *The History of Eliza* (1776) to Lennox. In 1775, her play, *Old City*

Manners, was a financial success. Her last novel, *Euphemia*, appeared in 1790. *The Female Quixote* is available in paperback in The World's Classics edition of Oxford University Press.

Barreca, Regina. *Untamed and Unabashed: Essays on Women and Humor in British Literature*. Detroit: Wayne State University Press, 1994.
Barreca provides readings of *The Female Quixote* and Jane Austen's *Northanger Abbey* to demonstrate that Lennox and Austen do not accept male values.

Brophy, Elizabeth. *Women's Lives and the Eighteenth Century English Novel*. Tampa: University of South Florida Press, 1991.
Brophy notes that typical Lennox heroines are more active than other heroines of the time. Their intelligence and education give them another advantage. Nevertheless, they remain submissive and obedient and see marriage as the only guarantee of happiness for women. *Euphemia*, the last novel by Lennox, is an exception. It describes a miserable marriage as it advocates female friendship.

Dalziel, Margaret, ed. *The Female Quixote: Or, The Adventures of Arabella*, by Charlotte Lennox. New York: Oxford University Press, 1989.
Dalziel maintains that Arabella resembles the heroines of French romances and is also a Quixote figure, but she is also the heroine of a serious love story and conventional courtship novel. Arabella is compared to Don Quixote, but Dalziel notes, Arabella rejects the morality of romances. Dalziel believes this novel was much more popular in its day than it is now because readers then were more familiar with the romance genre. She also notes its repetitiveness and its weak ending. She credits Lennox with joining two concepts: a burlesque of an absurd genre with the story of a young girl's entrance into society.

Doody, Margaret Anne. Introduction to *The Female Quixote: Or, The Adventures of Arabella*, by Charlotte Lennox. Edited by Margaret Dalziel. New York: Oxford University Press, 1989.
Doody outlines the eventful life of Charlotte Lennox and discusses her intimate knowledge of French romances. She also points out the importance of these early novels to women authors. She outlines the plot of the novel and notes its relationship to other books whose characters' heads are turned by their reading, and she discusses the ending of the novel as well. A bibliography and a chronology of the life of Lennox (by Duncan Isles) is included, as are explanatory notes.

Isles, Duncan. "Johnson, Richardson and *The Female Quixote.*" In *The Female Quixote*, by Charlotte Lennox. Edited by Margaret Dalziel, pp. 419-428. New York: Oxford University Press, 1989.

Isles describes how *The Female Quixote* was written with the help of Richardson and Johnson and reproduces Richardson's suggestions to Lennox about the novel and her responses to them.

Séjourné, Philippe. *The Mystery of Charlotte Lennox: First Novelist of Colonial America.* Aix-en-Provence, France: Publications Des Annales De La Faculté Des Lettres, 1967.

The author describes the life of Lennox as well as her novels set in America. He explains their historical background and provides additional information on the historical events they describe and the historical characters they depict. Séjourné believes Lennox's originality lies in her descriptions of eighteenth century New York City and the Hudson Valley, with their British, Indian, and Dutch inhabitants. A bibliography of correspondence and historical documents is included, as is a bibliography of Lennox's American works, biographies of her, and comments about her and her contemporaries. The authors also list studies of New York as a colony and studies of the British army in New York during this period. The works he discusses in detail include *Euphemia*, *The Life of Harriet Stuart*, and *Poems on Various Occasions*.

Small, Miriam Rossiter. *Charlotte Ramsay Lennox: An Eighteenth Century Lady of Letters.* 1935. Reprint. New York: Archon Books, 1969.

Small discusses the life of Lennox, *The Female Quixote* in relation to other novels on the same theme, Lennox's other novels, her plays, and her poetry. Two of her poems are included as well as two poems addressed to Lennox. Her works are listed as are works attributed to her. Periodical articles alluding to her are mentioned, and a list of her portraits is provided. The novels are summarized, and Small examines the history of criticism about them.

Todd, Janet. *Women, Writing and Fiction, 1660-1800.* New York: Columbia University Press, 1989.

Todd comments on the difficult life Lennox led. Although Samuel Johnson praised her work, she had few friends and struggled financially all her life. Todd discusses *The Female Quixote* as the story of a heroine who, blinded by reading romances, like the original Don Quixote, thinks too much of herself and her power over men. She thinks she lives in a Romantic world and makes a fool of herself and embarrasses her friends and her lover, until she realizes the error of her ways. Todd believes that the use Lennox makes of male mentor allows her to combine patriarchal and sentimental doctrine without making the lover too strong. Todd comments that Arabella, the heroine, tries to construct her own language and selfhood, but she is not permitted to do this. Arabella can survive, according to Todd, because she is passive and lacks sexual desire. In addition, she is benevolent, sensitive, and prone to crying, blushing, and fainting. Todd points out that Lennox helped change the novel's audience from men, who might have an erotic interest, to women who are educable. The message they will receive has to do with repression and self-sacrifice.

Wilson, Mona. *These Were Muses*. Port Washington, N.Y.: Kennikat Press, 1970.
Wilson quotes from *The Female Quixote* and Samuel Johnson's opinions of Lennox.

JANET LITTLE (1759-1813)

Janet Little began writing poetry when she was a servant in a clergyman's household. She later became a nursemaid and a dairywoman. As a result, her poetry became known as the work of a "Scotch milkmaid" just as Robert Burns was known as "the ploughman poet." With the encouragement of her employers, she published *Poetical Works* (1792) by subscription. Her poetry, in both English and Scots dialect, shows an awareness of class, but most of it is conventionally pastoral and concerned with love and courtship. She wished to meet Burns, to whom she addressed a poem, but he rebuffed her attempts at friendship. She continued to write poetry even after her marriage, during which she had five children.

Ferguson, Moira. *Eighteenth Century Women Poets: Nation, Class and Gender*. Albany: State University of New York Press, 1995.
Ferguson sees Little as one of a trio of eighteenth century working-class poets who defend their gender and their class. Little also defends her Scottish background and resists the hegemony of English culture. Ferguson points out that the poetry of this "Scottish milkmaid" contains many "messages," some overt, some not. She provides readings of many of Little's poems demonstrating this. She also notes that some of Little's poetry refers to current events, particularly Burns's rebuke by the church for fornication. For example, she praises Burns as a Scot and a working man, although she disapproves of his sexual license.

_____. "Janet Little and Robert Burns: The Politics of the Heart." In *Romantic Women Writers: Voices and Countervoices*, edited by Paula R. Feldman and Theresa M. Kelley, pp. 207-222. Hanover, N.H.: University Press of New England, 1995.

Ferguson discusses the life of Janet Little, her use of Burns's name to validate her position as a poet from the lower classes, as well as her criticism of him for his attitude toward women, and her stance critical of the injustices in her society. Ferguson quotes "An Epistle to Mr. Robert Burns," "Given to a Lady Who Asked Me to Write a Poem," "On a Visit to Mr. Burns," and "To My Aunty." In the last poem, she imagines Burns's approval but he did not approve of her poems. She criticizes his libertinism in other poems such as "On Happiness," "From Delia to Alonzo. Who Had Sent Her A Slighting Epistle," and "On Seeing Mr. B___ Baking Cakes." Ferguson notes Little's difficult position as a poor woman assailing traditional values by being a poet who upheld conventional morality.

Harriet Martineau (1802-1876)

The daughter of a Unitarian cloth manufacturer, Martineau was fairly well educated. In her *Autobiography* (written in 1855 and published 1877), she describes her childhood as unhappy. She published her first article, "Female Writers of Practical Divinity," in the *Monthly Repository* when she was twenty. She turned to writing to make a living rather than teaching because of the deafness that troubled her all her life. *Illustrations of Political Economy* (1832-1833) became a best-seller. *Society in America* (1837), published after a trip to America, condemned slavery and the treatment of women. Her next book on America, *A Retrospect of Western Travel* (1838), was even more popular. Her novel, *Deerbrook* (1839), also concerned the aspirations of women. She wrote another novel, less well known, *The Hour and the Man* (1841). Another travel book, on her journey to the Middle East, *Eastern Life, Past and Present* (1848), was well received. She wrote many other magazine and newspaper articles and abridged and translated Auguste Comte's *Positive Philosophy* (1851). She also wrote children's stories and a *History of England During the Thirty Years Peace 1816-1836* (1849-1850). She supported reform of the divorce laws, the education of women and the working class, and woman suffrage. She was acquainted with most of the well-known writers of her time.

Arbuckle, Elizabeth Sanders. *Harriet Martineau's Letters to Fanny Wedgewood*. Stanford, Calif.: Stanford University Press, 1983.
Arbuckle discusses Martineau's life and her Unitarian religious beliefs, which reinforced her political radicalism. Arbuckle also discusses the Wedgewood family and Martineau's opinion of America and of Carlyle. According to Arbuckle, Martineau's letters demonstrate her interest not only in national and international issues but also in the domestic problems of women. A chronology of Martineau's life as well as extensive notes to the letters are included.

Corbett, Mary Jean. *Representing Femininity: Middle Class Subjectivity in Victorian and Edwardian Women's Autobiographies*. New York: Oxford University Press, 1992.
Corbett demonstrates how women writers were excluded from the ranks of professional authors. She then compares the reactions to this of Harriet Martineau and Mary Howitt. The latter wrote only her memoirs, but Martineau, encouraged by her brother, became a professional writer. Corbett discusses Martineau's work as a woman and as a professional writer.

David, Deirdre. *Intellectual Women and Victorian Patriarchy: Harriet Martineau, Elizabeth Barrett Browning, George Eliot*. Ithaca, N.Y.: Cornell University Press, 1987.
David considers Martineau an excellent observer and an excellent analyst of her society who agreed with its values and helped disseminate them. David notes that Martineau was a feminist who wanted to be useful to her society. David reads Martineau's *Autobiography* to show that just as her own life improved, she believed English life would improve. David also discusses the success of *Illustrations of Political Economy* and Martineau's insistence on her own independence. Martineau is a feminist in that she wants an improvement in the situation of women, but she believes that women must become more like men to deserve this. David discusses *Society in America* and provides a reading of *Household Education*, in which Martineau advocates education in domestic science for women. David describes Martineau's antislavery activities and her *History of England During the Thirty Years Peace 1816-1836*, which David finds entertaining. *Eastern Life, Past and Present* had a great influence on Britain's view of the Middle East. David also discusses *Deerbrook*, Martineau's novel.

Figes, Eva. *Sex and Subterfuge: Women Writers to 1850*. New York: Persea Books, 1982.

According to Figes, Martineau supported herself and her mother with her writing. She worked extremely hard, and she may have devoted herself to journalism rather than the novel because she found women's position so painful to write about. In *Illustrations of Political Economy*, Martineau discusses various trades, Figes notes, but she did not discuss the position of women. In *Deerbrook*, however, she examines the difficulties women faced at the time. The plot is summarized by Figes who believes that Martineau could have been a great novelist. According to Figes, Martineau feels that growing up forces women to repress their sexuality and to suffer.

Gillian, Thomas. *Harriet Martineau*. Boston: Twayne, 1985.

Gillian provides a chronology of Martineau's life. He discusses her family, her childhood, her illness, her interest in hypnotism, and her life in the Lake District. He also discusses her travel writings, *Illustrations of Political Economy* and her other works of popularization, her journalism, her fiction, and her children's fiction. He maintains that Martineau saw herself as a teacher.

Lipset, Seymour Martin. Introduction to *Society in America*, by Harriet Martineau. New Brunswick, N.J.: Transaction Books, 1981.

Lipset maintains that Martineau's approach to studying American culture was sociological and therefore similar to that of modern writers and an important influence on public opinion. He discusses her attitude toward the class system and her disagreements with Alexis de Tocqueville as well as her comments on political apathy, conformity, her opinions of religion and socialism, and her concern for others, such as children and slaves.

McDonald, Lynn. *Women Founders of the Social Sciences*. Ottawa: Carleton University Press, 1994.

McDonald provides a brief biography and a list of sources for further reading. She insists that Harriet Martineau deserves credit for founding the discipline of sociology and notes that Martineau was also active in the antislavery movement. She notes, too, that Martineau promoted women's rights and public health reforms. McDonald summarizes and discusses Martineau's "Essays on the Art of Thinking," *How to Observe Morals and Manners*, *Society in America*, *The Martyr Age of the United States of America*, *Illustrations of Political Economy*, and *The Positive Philosophy of Auguste Comte*. She also notes Martineau's collaboration with Florence Nightingale. McDonald's emphasis is on Martineau as a social scientist and journalist rather than as a novelist.

Miller, F. Fenwick. *Harriet Martineau.* Port Washington, N.Y.: Kennikat Press, 1972.
This somewhat dated biography draws upon Martineau's autobiography and discusses her life in relation to her works. Miller believes Martineau's fiction fails because it is too dependent on facts and because Martineau attempts to imitate Jane Austen. She further believes that *Eastern Life, Past and Present* shows Martineau's mastery of thought, mind, and language. Miller maintains that Martineau cared for the truth above all.

Myers, Mitzi. "Unmothered Daughter and Radical Reformer: Harriet Martineau's Career." In *The Lost Tradition: Mothers and Daughters in Literature*, edited by Cathy N. Davidson and E. M. Broner, pp. 70-81. New York: Frederick Ungar, 1980.
Myers cites evidence from Martineau's autobiography to show that Martineau had an extremely unhappy childhood because of her mother's lack of affection for her. Her mother did not prohibit her from reading and writing but insisted that she perform all other domestic tasks as well. Martineau tried to please her mother but her mother caused her great distress from which she attempted to escape by traveling to America.

Pichanick, Valerie. *Harriet Martineau: The Woman and Her Work 1802-1876.* Ann Arbor: University of Michigan Press, 1980.
A detailed biography and a complete analysis and evaluation of Martineau's work. Pichanick discusses Martineau's work on economics, her travels, her deafness, her personality, and her friendships, particularly her friendships with George Eliot and Elizabeth Barrett Browning. Pichanick also writes about her journalism and her works about history. Martineau's status and influence as a writer and as a woman is also discussed.

Sanders, Valerie. *Harriet Martineau: Selected Letters.* Oxford: Clarendon Press, 1990.
These letters were written by Martineau between the ages of seventeen and seventy and were chosen to illustrate Martineau's growth as a writer and the evolution of her interests. A brief biography is included. Sanders believes these letters are particularly important because Martineau's autobiography stops in 1855. The letters discuss her life as an Victorian newspaperwoman and as a deaf person, and they

demonstrate her preoccupation with education. She writes about careers, women, politics, literature, and journalism. Sanders comments on her ideas, her honesty, and her energy, admitting Martineau could be self-righteous. Sanders lists the letters she has selected, includes biographies of people mentioned frequently in the letters, and also includes biographies of Martineau's correspondents. Includes extensive notes.

_____. *Reason over Passion: Harriet Martineau and the Victorian Novel*. Sussex, England: The Harvester Press, 1986.
Sanders maintains that Martineau's important fiction was written between 1827 and 1846, and many of her contemporaries preferred it to her journalism despite its didacticism. Sanders also discusses the history of Martineau's reputation and her current popularity among feminist critics. Sanders wants to show Martineau's relationship to other Victorian writers and to women writers. She discusses Martineau's theory of fiction, *Deerbrook*, the *Autobiography*, her fiction about sick and deformed children and adults, her historical works, and her feminism.

Webb, R. K. *Harriet Martineau: A Radical Victorian*. New York: Columbia University Press, 1960.
Webb focuses on Martineau's deafness, her effect on her contemporaries, her life in Norwich, her relationship to Priestley, her travels to America, and her role as a popularizer. He discusses her interest in education and her role as a journalist, as well as her connection to British radicalism. He summarizes and analyzes her best-known works. His major interest lies in her life as it illustrates early Victorian society.

Wheatley, Vera. *The Life and Work of Harriet Martineau*. London: Secker & Warburg, 1957.
A detailed biography that provides readings of Martineau's most important work, but includes little about her fiction.

Yates, Gayle Graham. *Harriet Martineau on Women*. New Brunswick, N.J.: Rutgers University Press, 1985.
Yates discusses Martineau's life and work. She believes Martineau to be a progressive thinker, a feminist, and a reformer while noting that Martineau displays contradictory attitudes, a situation not uncommon in such a prolific author. Although she considers Martineau to be neither a typical Victorian nor an innovator, Yates explores the ways in which Martineau did influence later feminists. Martineau saw analo-

gies between the position of women and the position of slaves. She believed education and careers should be open to women, and she approved of woman suffrage. Yates provides a selection of her writing on women.

MARY RUSSELL MITFORD (1786-1855)

Mitford was born in 1786 to rather feckless parents. At the age of ten, surprisingly, she recouped the family fortunes by winning £20,000 in a lottery. She attended one of the better girls' boarding schools, where she studied the classics. When her father's gambling lost the fortune she had won, she turned to writing extremely popular stories about village life. A five-volume collection, *Our Village*, appeared from 1823 to 1832. Other collections of her short fiction include *Belford Regis* (1834), *Country Stories* (1837), and *Atherton* (1854). Her *Recollections of a Literary Life* was published in 1857. She also wrote poetry, including *Miscellaneous Poems* (1810), *Christina, the Maid of the South Seas* (1811), and *Narrative Poems on the Female Character* (1813). Her plays include *Julian* (1823), *Foscari* (1826), and *Rienzi* (1828). Her letters, many to her literary friends, have also been collected.

Edwards, P. D. *Idyllic Realism from Mary Russell Mitford to Hardy.* New York: St. Martin's Press, 1988.
   Edwards discusses Mitford's belief that she knew all about her fellow villagers regardless of their social class. He maintains that her use of realistic detail convinced her readers and influenced her successors, including Alfred, Lord Tennyson, Arthur Hugh Clough, Elizabeth Gaskell, George Eliot, and Anthony Trollope.

Johnson, R. Brimley. *Balls and Assemblies from Fanny Burney, Jane Austen, Maria Edgeworth, Susan Ferrier, and Mary Russell Mitford.* London: John Lane, 1928.
   Johnson discusses Mitford's life briefly and maintains that her prose style was damaged by her need to write quickly to support her family. He also notes that she loved the people about whom she wrote and enjoyed her life. Two stories from *Our Village*, "Hannah Had Gotten a Lover" and "There Had Been—An Attachment," are included.

_____, ed. *The Letters of Mary Russell Mitford.* Port Washington, N.Y.: Kennikat Press, 1972.

This collection of letters arranges what the editor considers the most interesting of Mitford's letters chronologically from 1759 to 1854. The introduction discusses her letter writing, which reflects the interests of her time as well as her own individuality. Johnson also discusses Mitford's life and her circle of friends, which included the major literary figures of her day. There is no index.

Lane, Maggie. *Literary Daughters*. New York: St. Martin's Press, 1989.
Lane notes Mitford's emotional dependence on her father as well as the fact that she needed to write in order to support him financially.

Manley, Seon, and Susan Belcher. *O, Those Extraordinary Women!* Philadelphia: Chilton Book Company, 1972.
The authors discuss Mitford along with Elizabeth Barrett as daughters of possessive fathers, and they quote from letters exchanged between Mitford and Barrett. The relationship ended with Elizabeth Barrett's marriage to Robert Browning, of whom Mitford did not approve. Manley and Belcher also discuss the reason for the success of *Our Village*, which they attribute to Victorian nostalgia for rural England in the face of growing industrialism.

Mitford, Mary Russell. *Our Village*. London: J. M. Dent, 1904.
The anonymous introduction to this charmingly illustrated edition of Mitford's stories blames her spendthrift father for the financial difficulties that caused her to write. Her life is discussed, and the writer declares that her "intuitive" descriptions of village life show genius, but a limited one.

Stowall, H. E. *Quill Pens and Petticoats: A Portrait of Women of Letters*. London: Wayland, 1970.
Stowall tells the story of Mitford's winning the lottery and discusses the improvidence of her father. Stowall also quotes extensively from Mitford's stories of village life, but does not discuss her other works.

HANNAH MORE (1745-1833)

Educated by her father to be a schoolmistress like her sisters, Hannah More published a play *The Search After Happiness* (1762) to instruct young ladies. More's *The Inflexible Captive* (1774) was performed in Bath. Other plays include *Percy* (1778) and *The Fatal Falsehood* (1779). She came to know the theater establishment and the literary establishment of her day and wrote *The Bas Bleu* (1786) about the Bluestockings, a group of educated women who wrote and held intellectual discussions. When she also became acquainted with William Wilberforce and other leading Evangelicals, More's works took on a more religious coloring. These works include *Sacred Dramas* (1782), *Thoughts on the Importance of the Manners of the Great to General Society* (1788), and *Slavery: A Poem* (1788). She also began to establish Sunday schools for the poor in order to teach them to read the Bible. She did not believe the poor needed to know anything else. Her charitable work involved her in church politics. To counter pro-democratic sentiment current in the early 1790's, she wrote *Village Politics by Will Chip* (1792) and *Cheap Repository Tracts* (1795-1798). These were widely distributed works of anti-democratic sentiment. She wrote *Strictures on the Modern System of Female Education* (1799), which advocated women's education, but only to ensure that women remained subservient housewives instead of trying to seek their rights. More herself was never involved with domesticity. Her only novel, *Coelebs in Search of a Wife* (1808), envisioned the perfect wife as a traditionally subordinate one. Her involvement in charitable work, however, such as the establishment of schools for the poor, encouraged other middle-class women to do volunteer work among the poor and contributed to their increasing influence of women. Her other works include *The Feast of Freedom* (1819) and *Moral Sketches* (1819). One of the most widely read authors of her time, she died friendless and alone, the victim of servants who mistreated her.

Ashfield, Andrew, ed. *Romantic Women Poets 1770-1838*. New York: St. Martin's Press, 1995.
  Ashfield provides a selection of her works as well as a brief biographical headnote.

Hopkins, Mary Alden. *Hannah More and Her Circle*. New York: Longmans, Green, 1947.
  A rather old-fashioned, but readable biography that discusses More's writing as well as her life.

Jones, Mary Gladys. *Hannah More*. New York: Greenwood Press, 1968.
  This biography is based on letters and the memoirs of More's contemporaries. It discusses her family, their interest in the education of women and her sisters' school in Bristol. Her acquaintance with Edmund Burke, her friendship with David Garrick, and her activities as a playwright are also discussed. More's relationship with the Bluestockings and Samuel Johnson is described, as is her part in the controversy with the working-class poet Ann Yearsley. Her involve-

ment in the antislavery movement and her interest in the Evangelicals is clarified. Jones also clarifies More's contribution to the movement to establish Sunday schools for the education of poor children. Jones describes More's books and their influence.

Kirkpatrick, Kathryn. "Sermons and Strictures: Conduct Book Propriety and Property Relations in Late Eighteenth Century England." In *History, Gender and Eighteenth-Century Literature*, edited by Beth Fowkes Tobin, pp. 198-226. Athens: University of Georgia Press, 1994.

Kirkpatrick compares John Fordyce's *Sermons to Young Women* (1766) with Hannah More's *Strictures on the Modern System of Female Education* (1799) to show the relationship between notions of propriety and the institution of private property. She demonstrates how acts of enclosure caused poverty and how middle-class women lost control of their property and their household occupations. Kirkpatrick notes that More was upwardly mobile herself but condemned such aspirations on the part of others, providing examples from *Village Politics by Will Chip* and *Cheap Repository Tracts*. She concludes that More wanted women to be submissive in order to teach submission to the lower classes and also wanted women to free men to create an empire as the women raised soldiers to arm it.

Kowaleski-Wallace, Elizabeth. *Their Fathers' Daughters: Hannah More, Maria Edgeworth and Patriarchal Complicity*. New York: Oxford University Press, 1991.

Kowaleski-Wallace examines the works of Hannah More because she believes More represents a case of female complicity with patriarchy. Through a psychoanalytic reading, Kowaleski-Wallace finds that More chose older male mentors, such as Samuel Johnson, to gain access to the male literary tradition. She maintains further that More's attraction to Evangelicalism helped her transform her sexual energies into maternal concern, and she notes that More was attracted to the writings of John Milton and to other texts that focused on taming women's sexual nature.

Manley, Seon, and Susan Belcher. *O, Those Extraordinary Women!* Philadelphia: Chilton Book Company, 1972.

The authors connect More with the reaction against excessive sensibility and the Evangelical movement, which eventually produced Victorian earnestness. They also quote a contemporary account of how she was jilted at the altar by a groom who would not marry her and in consequence paid her four hundred pounds a year for life. They also summarize some of the writing on women's education which appeared prior to that of More.

Mellor, Anne K., and Richard E. Matlak, eds. "Hannah More." In *British Literature 1780-1830*, pp. 200-224. Fort Worth, Tex.: Harcourt Brace College Publishers, 1996.
The authors discuss More's life and work and provide a selection of her writing.

Myers, Mitzi. "A Peculiar Protection: Hannah More and the Cultural Politics of the Blagdon Controversy." In *History, Gender and Eighteenth Century Literature*, edited by Beth Fowkes Tobin, pp. 227-257. Athens: University of Georgia Press, 1994.
Myers discusses the importance of Hannah More in her own time, noting that she was highly influential. Although her sentiments were antifeminist, More opened doors for other women as philanthropists and educators. This article concerns her role in the Blagdon controversy, which involved who would choose clergymen for the Blagdon district of England. Myers notes that More used conventional notions of women's sphere and women's virtue to encourage them to undertake social action.

SYDNEY MORGAN (1776-1859)

The daughter of an actor, Sydney Owenson was born in Dublin and spent much of her time at the theater. She published *Poems* (1801), *St. Clair* (1803), and a historical novel entitled *The Novice of St. Dominick* (1806). Her best-known novel is *The Wild Irish Girl* (1806). *Patriotic Sketches of Ireland* and *The Lay of an Irish Harp* (1807) popularized the idea of Ireland as exotic and romantic. Her other books include *Ida of Athens* (1809), *The Missionary* (1811), *France* (1817), *O'Donnel: A National Tale* (1814), *Florence M'Carthy* (1818), *Italy* (1821), *Salvatore Rosa* (1824), *Absenteeism* (1825), *The O'Briens and the O'Flahertys* (1827), *The Book of the Boudoir* (1829), *France in 1829-30* (1830), *Woman and Her Master* (1840), and *Pages from My Autobiography* (1859). She had begun to write in order to earn money. She became famous after she wrote *The Wild Irish Girl*, and was married to Sir Thomas Charles Morgan, a surgeon, in 1812. Although they often advocated better education and more scope for women, her books were popular even when they received unfavorable reviews. She was the first British woman to receive a government pension for "service to the world of letters," and she was a literary celebrity in her time.

Campbell, Mary. *Lady Morgan: The Life and Times of Sydney Owenson.* London: Pandora, 1988.
Campbell discusses Lady Morgan's life and work against the background of Irish history and politics. She also explains the backgrounds and the receptions of Morgan's novels, maintaining that Morgan used the rhetoric of Romantic fiction to argue for her political ideals, which include the necessity for freedom, particularly for Ireland.

Dixon, W. Hepworth. Introduction to *Lady Morgan's Memoirs: Autobiographies, Diaries and Correspondence.* 2 vols. 1862. Reprint. New York: AMS Press, 1975.
Dixon says Morgan wanted her memoirs published to defend her life, which was attacked because of her attachment to civil and religious liberty. She attributes her successes to hard work and common sense. The memoirs were compiled from her own very complete diaries with the help of Geraldine Jewsbury and Morgan's nieces. Her letters are included, as is an index.

Mellor, Anne K., and Richard E. Matlak, eds. "Sidney Owenson, Lady Morgan." In *British Literature 1780-1830*, pp. 806-837. Fort Worth, Tex.: Harcourt Brace College Publishers, 1996.
The editors discuss Morgan's life and work and provide a selection of her writing.

Moskal, Jeanne. "Gender, Nationality, and Textual Authority in Lady Morgan's Travel Books." In *Romantic Women Writers: Voices and Countervoices*, edited by Paula R. Feldman and Theresa M. Kelley, pp. 171-193. Hanover, N.H.: University Press of New England, 1995.
Moskal contends that Morgan used the constraints of a patriarchal society, which included the position of her father and her husband, and her advocacy of another's cause in order to gain acceptance for her work. She describes Morgan's life and particularly the reception of *France*, a successful book but one whose liberal ideas provoked enormous hostility in England. Moskal points out that not only were women writers suspect, but so were women travelers. Moskal contends that to maintain her authority, Morgan used "paratextual" devices, primarily footnotes. She also used these devices in *The Wild Irish Girl*. Moskal also discusses Morgan's attempts to justify Napoleon.

Newcomer, James. *Lady Morgan the Novelist*. Lewisburg, Ohio: Bucknell University Press, 1990.

Newcomer writes about Morgan's life and summarizes and evaluates her fiction. Her characters, he asserts, tend to be abstractions representing her political and social thought. He notes that she was somewhat erratic, but he admires her as an English Protestant who wanted freedom for the Irish, including the Catholics. He believes her reputation as a novelist should be greater than it is.

Sha, Richard C. "Expanding the Limits of Feminine Writing: The Prose Sketches of Sydney Owenson (Lady Morgan) and Helen Maria Williams." In *Romantic Women Writers: Voices and Countervoices*, edited by Paula R. Feldman and Theresa M. Kelley, pp. 194-206. Hanover, N.H.: University Press of New England, 1995.

According to Sha, Lady Morgan used the term "sketches" in her *Patriotic Sketches of Ireland* to take advantage of the fact that sketching pictures was considered a suitable pursuit for women. This descriptive term allowed her to write about politics, a subject which was not generally considered to be suitable for women to discuss. Indeed, in this work, she denies she is writing a political tract but insists she is merely being patriotic as she appeals to the feelings of her readers so that they will help the Irish poor.

Wilson, Mona. *These Were Muses*. Port Washington, N.Y.: Kennikat Press, 1970.

Wilson provides an old-fashioned account of Morgan's life and works enlivened by extensive quotations from her journals and particularly from her acquaintances' opinions of her.

Wolff, Robert Lee. Introduction to *The Wild Irish Girl*, by Lady Morgan. 3 vols. New York: Garland, 1979.

Wolff summarizes the plot of this novel, which he considers an example of "Lady Morgan's passion for the remote both in time and space." He also summarizes and discusses her other novels. Wolff considers Morgan to be "a perceptive, sensitive and talented novelist," who was no more naïve than her contemporaries.

AMELIA OPIE (1769-1853)

An only child of a Unitarian physician, Amelia Opie was taught French and was encouraged to develop her musical and literary talents. She published *The Dangers of Coquetry* anonymously in 1790, and acted in her play *Adelaide* in 1794. She met William Godwin and members of his circle, but later became more conservative than they were. She married in 1798. Her novels include *The Father and Daughter* (1801); her best-known work, *Adeline Mowbray: Or, The Mother and Daughter* (1804), which attacks radical, Godwinian views of marriage; *Simple Tales* (1806); *Valentine's Eve* (1816); and *Madeline* (1820). Although Opie managed to support herself by writing fiction and poetry, *Madeline* was her last novel, because she stopped writing novels after becoming a Quaker. Instead, she turned to poetry and works of self-improvement, such as *Illustrations of Lying* (1825) and *Detraction Displayed* (1828). Her collections of poetry include *Poems* (1802), *The Warrior's Return* (1808), *The Black Man's Lament* (1826), and *Lays for the Dead* (1824). Opie died at the age of eighty-four.

Armstrong, Isobel. "The Gush of the Feminine: How Can We Read Women's Poetry of the Romantic Period?" In *Romantic Women Writers: Voices and Countervoices*, edited by Paula R. Feldman and Theresa M. Kelley, pp. 13-32. Hanover, N.H.: University Press of New England, 1995.
Armstrong compares "The Mad Wanderer: A Ballad" (1808) with Felicia Hemans' "Casablanca" as two poems using the discourse of law. She also discusses Opie's use of language relating to the senses.

Ashfield, Andrew, ed. *Romantic Women Poets 1770-1838*. New York: St. Martin's Press, 1995.
Ashfield provides a selection of Opie's works as well as a brief biographical headnote.

Brightwell, Cecilia Lucy. *Memorials of the Life of Amelia Opie*. 2d ed. London: Longman, Brown, 1854. Reprint. New York: AMS Press, 1975.
Brightwell based this book, which was first published in 1854, on the memories of her father, Thomas Brightwell, as well as on Opie's letters and journals. The result is charmingly frank autobiography joined by biographical commentary.

Mellor, Anne K., and Richard E. Matlak, eds. "Amelia Alderson Opie." In *British Literature 1780-1830*, pp. 556-559. Fort Worth, Tex.: Harcourt Brace College Publishers, 1996.
The editors discuss Amelia Opie's life and work and provide a selection of her writing.

Opie, Amelia. *The Works of Mrs. Amelia Opie*. 3 vols. 1843. Reprint. New
York: AMS Press, 1974.
The anonymous editors provide a brief biography and the texts of
Opie's works.

JANE PORTER (1776-1850)

Porter was brought up in Edinburgh, where she seems to have been a
child prodigy. After moving to London, she met literary figures and
political refugees. Thus inspired, she wrote her first novel *Thaddeus of
Warsaw* (1803), which was a best-seller. The *Scottish Chiefs* (1810) was
also quite popular and helped inspire the historical novels that began to
be published at this time. Porter also wrote *Sketch of the Campaigns of
Count Alexander Suwarrow Ryminikski* (1804), *The Pastor's Fireside*
(1815), *Duke Christian of Luneburg: Or, Traditions of the Harz* (1824),
and *Sir Edward Seaward's Narrative of His Shipwreck* (1831). With her
sister, Anna Maria Porter, she collaborated on *Tales Around a Winter
Hearth* (1826) and *Coming Out* (1828). Her plays, which were unsuccessful, include *Egmont: Or, The Eve of St. Alyne* (1817), *Switzerland* (1819),
and *Owen, Prince of Powys* (1822). Her last days were marred by financial
difficulties, but she remained a literary figure until her death.

Wilson, Mona. *These Were Muses*. Port Washington, N.Y.: Kennikat Press,
1970.
Wilson discusses Porter's wardrobe and her friends, quoting from their
letters and journals. She also describes and quotes from the works.

ANN RADCLIFFE (1764-1823)

Raised in London and Bath, Ann Radcliffe had some education and
claimed she began writing after she was married because her husband,
William Radcliffe, had to work late. Her novels were very popular and
are still in print. They concern isolated, frightened heroines in Romantic
landscapes who seem to be tormented by supernatural occurrences, but
everything is explained naturally by the end of the novel. Her novels
include *The Castles of Athlin and Dunbayne: A Highland Story* (1789), *A
Sicilian Romance* (1790), *The Romance of the Forest* (1791), *The Mysteries of Udolpho* (1794), and *The Italian* (1791). *Gaston de Blonville* (1802)
was published posthumously. She also wrote accounts of her travels and

poems. Radcliffe's novels, except for *Gaston de Blonville* are available in paperback in The World's Classics editions of Oxford University Press.

Ashfield, Andrew, ed. *Romantic Women Poets 1770-1838*. New York: St. Martin's Press, 1995.
Ashfield provides a selection of her works as well as a brief biographical headnote.

Botting, Fred. *Gothic*. London: Routledge, 1996.
Botting discusses the origins of the Gothic novel and its heroes, as well as Gothic wanderers and persecutions. He discusses Ann Radcliffe's life and her popularity, as well as her use of landscape and supernatural machinery. He sees her heroines as derived from those of the sentimental novel. He provides a reading of *The Mysteries of Udolpho*.

Chard, Chloe, ed. *The Romance of the Forest*, by Ann Radcliffe. New York: Oxford University Press, 1986.
In her introduction, Chard describes the Gothic as a genre in which terror is always deferred in order to arouse the reader's curiosity. Radcliffe's work was well received by critics. Chard also points out that Gothic novels concern passion and lack of self-control often on the part of tyrannical figures, such as the Marquis de Montalt in this novel. In Radcliffe's novels, however, the tyranny is always foreign. Chard also notes that the genre's use of landscape connects it with travel writing, which was quite popular, and with aesthetic theory of the time. The novel's publishing history is described, and a bibliography is provided. The edition also includes a chronology of Radcliffe's life and explanatory notes.

Clery, E. J. "The Politics of the Gothic Heroine in the 1790's." In *Reviewing Romanticism*, edited by Philip W. Martin and Robin Jarvis, pp. 69-85. London: Macmillan, 1992.
Clery believes that an early form of feminism led to the popularity of the Gothic novel because their heroines, from the 1790's on, were the centers of the novels. She analyzes *The Mysteries of Udolpho* to demonstrate this. She maintains further that these novels reflected the true horror of the situation of women at this time, but they did not really oppose patriarchy because they ended in happy marriages.

Figes, Eva. *Sex and Subterfuge: Women Writers to 1850*. New York: Persea Books, 1982.
Figes outlines the plot of *The Mysteries of Udolpho*: A young girl caught in Europe when her father dies unexpectedly is locked up in a

castle by her dead aunt's husband and must flee Italy to return to her
family home in France. Figes explains that the only way a virtuous
Gothic heroine can have adventures analogous to those of a hero of a
picaresque novel is to have been abducted so she can escape and grow.
The heroine is also threatened with rape, but she always manages to
escape. The reader is allowed to experience these dangers vicariously.
Figes points out that Radcliffe establishes some distance between the
reader and the heroine's perils by setting the action in a foreign country,
in ages past, and in scenery that seems more like a painting than a real
landscape. She also points out how female imprisonment, a theme of
these Gothic novels, is a reaction to male domination of women. The
novel's didactic purpose is fulfilled by showing how Emily St. Aubert
keeps calm and overcomes her difficulties, which are not supernatural
at all.

Dobrée, Bonamy. Introduction to *The Mysteries of Udolpho: A Romance*,
by Ann Radcliffe. London: Oxford University Press, 1966.
Dobrée discusses the popularity of the novel, which he attributes to
Radcliffe's mixture of horror, sentiment, and the picturesque. Dobrée
also discusses Radcliffe's life and her place in the history of the novel.
The author also explains her rationalization of the supernatural, her
structuring of the novel, and her use of comic elements. Radcliffe's
influence on other novelists is noted, and a chronology of her life is
provided. Although there is a selected bibliography, it is outdated. The
text of the novel is given.

Frank, Frederick S. *The First Gothics: A Critical Guide to the English
Gothic Novel.* New York: Garland, 1987.
This book discusses the influence of Alexander Pope, Edmund Burke,
Horace Walpole, William Godwin, and Ann Radcliffe on the early
Gothic novel. It also discusses the critical reception of the early
Gothics. In addition, it provides synopses of the plots of five hundred
Gothic novels, many by women, and lists available criticism. An
appendix explains terms relating to the Gothic novel.

Garber, Frederick, ed. *The Italian: Or, The Confessional of the Black
Penitents: A Romance*, by Ann Radcliffe. New York: Oxford University Press, 1981.
In his introduction, Garber discusses Radcliffe's interest in the psychology of feeling, maintaining that her novels are primarily concerned
with sensibility and how it must be controlled. He examines her
relationship to other novelists, particularly Matthew Gregory Lewis,

and he notes the careful plotting of the novel and its lack of supernatural machinery. Although Garber admits there are weaknesses in the book, he insists it contains "great scenes." The novel's publishing history is described, and a bibliography is provided, as is a chronology of Radcliffe's life and explanatory notes.

Grant, Aline. *Ann Radcliffe*. Denver: Alan Swallow, 1951.
Grant provides a highly subjective discussion of Radcliffe's life and work, seeing her as sensitive and nature loving. Grant describes the novels and their reception briefly, and she quotes from Radcliffe's poetry and journals.

Johnson, Claudia L. "Ann Radcliffe." In *Equivocal Beings: Politics, Gender, and Sentimentality in the 1790's*, pp. 73-140. Chicago: University of Chicago Press, 1995.
Johnson provides a reading of *The Romance of the Forest*, which she believes is suspenseful, erudite, and critical of society. She analyzes the various households shown in the novel and notes that the household ruled by a "man of feeling" must devalue women. Adeline, the heroine, is placed in an "equivocal" position. Because of her abilities and energy, Adeline is permitted liberties that the other women in the household are not given. The plot is resolved, however, not by the sentimental world, but by the threat of torture by the political authorities. Johnson suspects that the novel seems to withdraw from its criticism of the world, because it was written before the execution of Louis XVI when the French Revolution seemed to be a blessing. Johnson also provides a reading of *The Mysteries of Udolpho*. She believes it privileges male suffering over female suffering. The latter turns out to be imaginary. She also notes gender confusion in the novel and asserts that as sensitivity becomes a masculine characteristic, women are forced to into what was earlier considered "masculine" restraint. Johnson also discusses the stories of murdered women that are found throughout the novel. She believes that Radcliffe implies that all men, the sentimental as well as the tough, are dangerous to women. Radcliffe does not maintain this stance, however, as she reveals that the women caused their own downfalls and the true sufferers were their husbands. Johnson suggests that the war with France caused Radcliffe to become more conservative.

This conservatism is also shown in *The Italian*, which seems to condemn the old regime in favor of domesticity, but ends upholding authoritarian values. Johnson describes the historical events occurring when *The Italian* was written and outlines the novel. In it, female rule

is condemned, and even the Inquisition is rehabilitated. Unsentimental
men are praised, and the heroine, Ellena, is totally passive. Ellena does,
however, exhibit great love for another woman, but since the woman
turns out to be her mother, heterosexuality remains privileged. Johnson
suggests that Radcliffe never published again in her lifetime because
she did not want to renounce her originally progressive ideas to defend
authoritarianism.

Kooman-Van Middendorp, Gerarda Maria. *The Hero in the Feminine
Novel*. New York: Haskell House, 1966.
The author describes Valancourt, hero of *The Mysteries of Udolpho*,
and reveals him to be a descendent of Samuel Richardson's Sir Charles
Grandison, Henry Fielding's Tom Jones, and Hugh Walpole's heroes—
a good-looking, virtuous, generous nobleman who quickly rids himself
of any faults and is worthy of the love of the heroine.

McNutt, Dan J. *The Eighteenth Century Gothic Novel: An Annotated
Bibliography of Criticism and Selected Texts*. New York: Garland,
1975.
This bibliography lists other bibliographies and indexes, covering the
aesthetic, literary, psychological, social, and scientific backgrounds of
the Gothic novel as well as its influence. It lists editions of Radcliffe's
works and criticism written about them through 1970.

Milbank, Alison, ed. *The Castles of Athlin and Dunbayne*, by Ann Rad-
cliffe. New York: Oxford University Press, 1995.
In her introduction to this novel, Radcliffe's first, Milbank asserts that
Radcliffe has combined the novel of sensibility and melancholy with
Scottish history. Her two heroines turn out to be members of the same
family in imitation of the Act of Union, which joined Scotland to
England in 1707. Milbank also discusses Radcliffe's relationship to
Samuel Johnson and to William Shakespeare. She also points out the
importance of the castle, the doubling of character, plot, and emotion
and the fact that Radcliffe is attempting to establish an ethic for survival
in an imperfect world. The book includes a textual history of the novel,
a chronology of Radcliffe's life, and explanatory notes.

_____, ed. *A Sicilian Romance*, by Ann Radcliffe. New York:
Oxford University Press, 1993.
Milbank summarizes the events of Radcliffe's life and discusses her
work. She traces Radcliffe's concept of the sublime to the poet James
Thomson as well as to Edmund Burke. Milbank also asserts that the
concept of the picturesque is more important in this novel than earlier

ones. She explains the importance of the sublime for women's writing and gives a psychoanalytic reading of the plot of the novel, noting the importance of the motif of female imprisonment. The book includes a textual history of the novel, a chronology of Radcliffe's life, and explanatory notes.

Miles, Robert. *Ann Radcliffe: The Great Enchantress*. Manchester, England: Manchester University Press, 1995.
Miles argues that Radcliffe's novels are a product of her background as a middle-class Dissenter and that they not only are interesting and complex but also "possess aesthetic depth." He also discusses her dysfunctional family and her relationship to patriarchy, as well as her relationship to the Romantics and her situation as a woman writer. He provides a thorough analysis of her works and a helpful guide to further reading.

Murray, E. D. *Ann Radcliffe*. New York: Twayne, 1973.
Murray quotes from and analyzes the novels, comparing them with accounts of Radcliffe's travels in England and Europe. He traces an increasing complexity in her work, from her use of sentimental conventions in *The Castles of Athlin and Dunbayne* through *The Mysteries of Udolpho*'s use of counterpoint to the "dramatic confrontations" of *The Italian*. The selflessness of the heroine is compared to the selfishness of the villains. Murray describes Radcliffe's life, her novels, and Gothic novels in general. He evaluates Radcliffe's novels and describes their influence.

Rogers, Deborah, ed. *The Critical Response to Ann Radcliffe*. Westport, Conn.: Greenwood Press, 1994.
Rogers evaluates Radcliffe's contribution to the development of the Gothic novel as she comments on her popularity in Europe as well as in England. Her reputation among critics is summarized chronologically. Early reviews noted her shyness, her lack of a classical education, and even her shortness of stature. *The Romance of the Forest*, *The Mystery of Udolpho*, and *The Italian* were considered her best works. Her poetry was universally condemned, as were her anachronisms and her explanations of the apparently supernatural. Her use of one-dimensional characters, was also criticized. Recently, psychoanalytic and feminist critics have rediscovered Radcliffe's work. A chronology of her life, an anthology of criticism of her work to 1989, and a bibliography are included in this study.

Todd, Janet. *The Sign of Angellica: Women, Writing and Fiction 1600-1800.* New York: Columbia University Press, 1989.

Todd notes Radcliffe's extreme popularity and influence on the later great nineteenth century authors. She asserts that Radcliffe guarded her privacy so carefully that little is known about her life. She seems to have been influenced by Edmund Burke, being against violent revolution and the tyranny of the pre-revolutionary France. She tried to maintain her feminine image and wrote because she had the time, not having children. She cherished her anonymity and said she did not approve of unbridled sentimentality or sensationalism. According to Todd, Radcliffe's "morally reliable" narrators judge the characters, thus controlling her readers' reactions. Todd also outlines the plots of the novels and shows their similarities. Gothic interiors are stressed, and male-female relationships are preferred to female friendships. Benevolence and servant-master relationships are important. Todd also connects the Gothic with the Burkean sublime. She believes Radcliffe's villains are fascinating, but shows how they are different from the Byronic hero-villain. They are always ultimately evil, never admirable. Heroes are passive and feminized. Although there is no real inner life in Radcliffe's characters, there are touches of psychological realism. Nature, rather than eroticism, is stressed.

Voller, Jack G. *The Supernatural Sublime: The Metaphysics of Terror in Anglo-American Romanticism.* DeKalb: Northern Illinois University Press, 1994.

Voller discusses the popularity and influence of *The Mysteries of Udolpho.* He asserts its conservatism is signaled by its insistence on explaining away apparently supernatural events. He summarizes the plot of the novel, noting Radcliffe's emphasis on financial success, conventional religious thought, and empiricism. Only servants are superstitious, and the heroine's maturation involves not yielding to fears inspired by their gossip, "modulating her sensibility by subordinating it to reason."

CLARA REEVE (1729-1827)

Educated by her clergyman father, Reeve published her first book, *Original Poems on Several Occasions,* in 1769. *The Phoenix* (1772) is a translation. *The Old English Baron* (1778) is a Gothic novel, one of the first historical novels, and it was quite successful. Her other books include *The Two Mentors* (1783), *The Progress of Romance* (1785), *The Exiles*

(1788), *The School for Widows* (1791), *Plans of Education* (1792), *Memoirs of Sir Roger de Clarendon* (1793), *Destination: Or, Memoirs of a Private Family* (1795). Her prefaces contain early literary criticism, and she was also interested in the plight of the unmarried woman and the education of poor women.

Brophy, Elizabeth. *Women's Lives and the Eighteenth Century English Novel*. Tampa: University of South Florida Press, 1991.
Brophy notes that the female figures in *The Old English Baron* are completely unrealistic, but she believes that the female figures of novels set in Reeve's own time were meant to be exemplary. They are accomplished and intelligent but never assertive. Although Reeve's views are conservative, according to Brophy, she disapproves of fathers preferring sons to daughters and believes that fallen women can be redeemed.

Kooman-Van Middendorp, Gerarda Maria. *The Hero in the Feminine Novel*. New York: Haskell House, 1966.
The author describes Edmund Twyford, the hero of *The Old English Baron*, whom she sees as another heir of Richardson's paragon hero, Sir Charles Grandison, and a reflection of the sentimentality of the age. She notes that he has much more in common with Reeve's time than the fifteenth century, when he was supposed to have lived.

Luria, Gina. Introduction to *Plans of Education, with Remarks on the Systems of Other Writers*, by Clara Reeve. New York: Garland, 1974.
Luria provides a very brief biography of Reeve, mentioning her other works. She maintains that *Plans of Education* shows the concern the era exhibited over the question of the position of women. She asserts that Reeve must be considered antifeminist.

Mack, Robert, ed. *Oriental Tales*. New York: Oxford Press, 1992.
In his introduction, Mack discusses Reeve's "The History of Charoba, Queen of Egypt," which is included in this book. He discusses her life and the relationship of the story to one translated by John Davies from al-Khafif, Murtada ibnMurtada ibn al-Khafif's history of Egypt. Reeve uses it to illustrate her belief that romances are universal, valuable and that they formed the basis of the novel. "The History of Charoba, Queen of Egypt" echoes Homer and the Bible and is concerned with the plight of women in a male-dominated world.

McNutt, Dan J. *The Eighteenth Century Gothic Novel: An Annotated Bibliography of Criticism and Selected Texts*. New York: Garland, 1975.

This bibliography lists other bibliographies and indexes, covering the aesthetic, literary, psychological, social, and scientific backgrounds of the Gothic novel as well as its influence. It lists editions of Reeve's works and summarizes and evaluates articles written about them up to 1968.

Spector, Robert Donald. *The English Gothic: A Bibliographic Guide to Writers from Horace Walpole to Mary Shelley*. Westport, Conn.: Greenwood Press, 1984.

Spector discusses the reception of Reeve's work and lists criticism of it. He considers her writing dull.

Voller, Jack G. *The Supernatural Sublime: The Metaphysics of Terror in Anglo-American Romanticism*. DeKalb: Northern Illinois University Press, 1994.

Voller maintains that, in *The Old English Baron*, Reeve sacrificed plot, character, complexity, and indeed all narrative interest to didacticism. He believes she also insisted on reducing the supernatural effects in the novel in order to increase its plausibility. Voller attributes this decision to Reeve's conservatism.

MARY ROBINSON (1758-1800)

Born in Bristol, Robinson attended several schools and, with her mother, eventually set up her own school, which her father closed. She married and shared her husband's imprisonment for debt. During her imprisonment, she produced her first book, *Poems* (1775). Robinson had one daughter who survived infancy. In 1775, she began performing on the stage, where she attracted the attention of the Prince of Wales (the future George IV), becoming his mistress for a short time. She was known as "Perdita" to him, as seen in the letters they exchanged. After entering a series of untoward relationships and suffering from poor health, she resumed writing, publishing *Captivity: A Poem* and *Celadon and Lydia: A Tale* (1777). Her 1791 edition of *Poems* attracted many subscribers. She also published *Poems*, *Modern Manners* (1793), *Sight, The Cavern of Woe and Solitude*, *Sappho and Phaon*, and *The Sicilian Lover: A Tragedy* (1796). Her novels include *Vancenza* (1792), *The Widow* (1794), *Angelina* (1796), *Hubert de Sevrac* (1796), *Walsingham: Or, The Pupil of Nature*

(1797), *The False Friend* (1799), and *The Natural Daughter* (1799). She also wrote *Lyrical Tales* (1800) and published *A Letter to the Women of England on the Injustice of Mental Subordination* (1799) under the name Anne Frances Randall. Her poetry for the *Morning Post*, of which she was poetry editor, often appeared under the name Tabitha Bramble.

Adams, M. Ray. "Mrs. Mary Robinson, A Study of Her Later Career." In *Studies in the Literary Backgrounds of English Radicalism*, pp. 104-129. New York: Greenwood Press, 1968.
Adams discusses the superiority of Robinson's mind and her large literary output. He discusses her life and asserts that revolutionary ideas run through her life and work. He mentions her connections to famous men, including the Prince of Wales, and her friendships with Samuel Taylor Coleridge and William Godwin. Adams believes Robinson was influenced by Mary Wollstonecraft. He also discusses her poetry, which he finds perhaps too decorous. During her later life, Robinson's poetry became religious and philosophic, as in "The Cavern of Woe" and "The Progress of Melancholy." He also provides a reading of "The Progress of Liberty" and her novel *Walsingham: Or, The Pupil of Nature*. The attacks on her, primarily because of the reactionary tenor of the times, are also discussed.

Ashfield, Andrew, ed. *Romantic Women Poets 1770-1838*. New York: St. Martin's Press, 1995.
Ashfield provides a selection of Robinson's works as well as a brief biographical headnote.

Curran, Stuart. "Mary Robinson's 'Lyrical Tales' in Context." In *Re-Visioning Romanticism: British Women Writers, 1776-1837*, edited by Carol Shiner Wilson and Joel Haefner, pp. 17-35. Philadelphia: University of Pennsylvania Press, 1994.
Curran discusses Robinson's importance in the literary world of the 1790's and the relationship of her poetry to that of William Wordsworth, Samuel Taylor Coleridge, and Robert Southey. He quotes her poem "The Haunted Beach" to point out her ability to manipulate sound, meter, and stanzaic pattern in her poetry. He also notes her virtuosity and "earthiness."

Ford, Susan Allen. "'A name more dear': Daughters, Fathers and Desire in 'A Simple Story,' 'The False Friend,' and 'Mathilda.'" In *Re-Visioning Romanticism: British Women Writers, 1776-1837*, edited by Carol Shiner Wilson and Joel Haefner, pp. 51-71. Philadelphia: University of Pennsylvania Press, 1994.

Ford notes that these three novels concern father-daughter incest, focusing on the "disruptive connections between sexuality and power," which threatens the individual, the family, and society itself. She summarizes these novels to demonstrate this and also notes that these novels, particularly *The False Friend*, are marked by the absence of the mother and a silencing of the daughter. She speculates on the interest incest itself held for the Romantics and connects it with political revolution and the increasing emphasis on the importance of domesticity.

Luria, Gina. Introduction to *Walsingham: Or, The Pupil of Nature*, by Mary Robinson. New York: Garland, 1994.
Luria provides biographical information, discussing Robinson's life as an actress, her relationship with the Prince of Wales, and her friendships with Godwin and Coleridge. Luria describes this novel as sentimental and notes that it was fairly popular. Luria notes, however, that Robinson was sometimes attacked as a radical. Her other works and her memoirs are mentioned.

Mellor, Anne K., and Richard E. Matlak, eds. "Mary Darby Robinson." In *British Literature 1780-1830*, pp. 317-353. Fort Worth, Tex.: Harcourt Brace College Publishers, 1996.
The editors discuss Robinson's life and work and provide a selection of her writing.

Pascoe, Judith. "Mary Robinson and the Literary Marketplace." In *Romantic Women Writers: Voices and Countervoices*, edited by Paula R. Feldman and Theresa M. Kelley, pp. 252-268. Hanover, N.H.: University Press of New England, 1995.
Pascoe discusses the relationship between Mary Robinson and the *Morning Post*, a London newspaper of the late eighteenth century. Robinson contributed poetry to the newspaper and eventually became its poetry editor. She also found some of her subjects in its pages, and she herself was the subject of many articles.

Peterson, Linda H. "Becoming an Author: Mary Robinson's 'Memoirs' and the Origins of the Woman Artist's Autobiography." In *Re-Visioning Romanticism: British Women Writers, 1776-1837*, edited by Carol Shiner Wilson and Joel Haefner, pp. 36-50. Philadelphia: University of Pennsylvania Press, 1994.
Peterson asserts that Robinson's *Memoirs* (1801) attempted to demonstrate that Robinson was a true Romantic artist. Her readers, and other women writers, however, refused to accept this stance as they refused

to consider themselves as possessing genius, originality, or even superior literary taste. Instead, they saw themselves as transmitters of
superior masculine ideas to inferior women readers. Peterson quotes
the *Memoirs* to show that Robinson considered herself to possess
genius, originality, as well as classical education. Peterson also points
out that Robinson saw herself as following the tradition of Sappho in
being encouraged to write by an older woman. Peterson also notes that
Robinson is ambivalent about the value of Romantic love to the woman
poet. She sees the maternal role as the stuff of poetry. Later women
writers, influenced by Hannah More, represented themselves as lacking genius and as merely extending their domestic role by interpreting
original work by men to women readers.

Vargo, Lisa. "The Claims of 'Real Life and Manners': Coleridge and Mary
Robinson." *The Wordsworth Circle* 26 (Summer, 1995): 134-136.
The gossip of the time saw Coleridge's interest in Mary Robinson as
merely sexual because she had been the mistress of the Prince of Wales.
Vargo believes that each influenced the other's ideas and work, result-
ing in a literary dialogue.

SARAH SCOTT (1723-1795)

Scott was the sixth child and oldest daughter in a family that valued
education. Hers was informal but extensive. Her sister, Elizabeth Montagu, became well known as one of the Bluestockings. After a brief
marriage to George Lewis Scott, from which she was rescued rather
dramatically by her family, she lived with Lady Barbara Montagu (not a
relation), engaged in charitable work, and wrote. With her sister and
friends, she attempted to set up a utopian community similar to the one
she described in *A Description of Millenium Hall*, but she was unable to
do so. Her novels, didactic but not without humor, were published anonymously. They include *The History of Cornelia* (1750), *Agreeable Ugliness*
(1754), *A Journey Through Every Stage of Life* (1754), *A Description of
Millenium Hall* (1762), *The History of Sir George Ellison* (1762), and *The
Test of Filial Duty* (1772). She also wrote history and biography. Although
her works did not retain their appeal, her books were quite popular when
they appeared. Published in America in 1797 as *The Man of Real Sensibility*, *The History of Sir George Ellison* has recently been reprinted.

Brophy, Elizabeth. *Women's Lives and the Eighteenth Century English
Novel*. Tampa: University of South Florida Press, 1991.

Brophy outlines the plot of *A Description of Millenium Hall* and shows how it was an example of the era's need to find a solution to the problem of the "old maid." Millenium Hall is a secular convent in which single women live and do charitable work as well as educate the poor. Brophy points out that these women are able and happy. They enjoy the freedom of their unmarried state. She notes the contradictions in Scott's treatment of women; She nearly always focuses on intelligent, practical heroines, but she insists on daughters obeying their fathers no matter what the circumstances. Brophy considers her radical in her insistence that women's faults are the result of education rather than breeding. She discusses the plots of *The History of Cornelia* and *A Journey Through Every Stage of Life*, as well as *A Description of Millenium Hall*.

Ferguson, Moira. *British Woman Writers 1578-1799*. Old Westbury, N.Y.: The Feminist Press, 1985.
The author describes Scott's books and notes that several of them concern "romantic friendship," which was also exemplified in Scott's life by her involvement with Barbara Montagu.

Perry, Ruth. "Blue Stockings in Utopia." In *History, Gender and Eighteenth Century Literature*, edited by Beth Fowkes Tobin, pp. 159-178. Athens: University of Georgia Press, 1994.
Perry summarizes Scott's *A Description of Millenium Hall* and compares it to Lady Mary Hamilton's *Munster Village* and to utopian novels by Samuel Jackson Pratt and Robert Bage. Perry believes *A Description of Millenium Hall* defends "women's capacity for art and learning and the production of culture." It concerns a group of women who work together and help their community and it is based on the life led by Sarah Scott and Lady Barbara Montagu in Bath. Unlike the utopian novels written by men, it does not mock learned women or seek to maintain the class system.

Rizzo, Betty, ed. *The History of Sir George Ellison*, by Sarah Scott. Lexington: University Press of Kentucky, 1996.
In her introduction, Rizzo describes Scott's life, her upbringing, her education, her charities, her ideas, and her work. Rizzo also explores Scott's relationship with her sister, Elizabeth Montagu, and her relationship with her friends, such as Sarah Fielding. She discusses *The History of Sir George Ellison* in great detail, noting its differences from *A Description of Millenium Hall*, to which it is the sequel, its exposure of corruption in English society, and its concern with education. Rizzo

defends Scott's apparent conservatism by asserting that she is against gender and class distinctions, but does not want to offend her readers by appearing too radical. Rizzo also discusses Scott as an influence on the Gothic novel and on later writers including Mary Brunton, Fanny Burney, and Charlotte Smith. She also discusses the history of a pirated, condensed version of the novel, published in America as *The Man of Real Sensibility*, which contributed to the debate about slavery in America.

Todd, Janet. *Women's Friendship in Literature*. New York: Columbia University Press, 1980.
In this work, Todd discusses Scott's novels in the context of women's friendship.

ANNA SEWARD (1742-1809)

Seward was the daughter of a clergyman-poet who encouraged her reading at first, but then discouraged her writing poetry when Erasmus Darwin, a friend of the family, told him her poetry was better than his. She began publishing poems in 1780, and eventually become known as the Swan of Lichfield. Her first novel in verse, *Louisa*, appeared in 1784. Other poetry appeared in the *Gentleman's Magazine* and other periodicals, sometimes anonymously. She published poems on David Garrick, on Captain Cook (1780), and on Major John André, who was executed for spying during the American Revolution. It is said that after she published the poem, George Washington apologized for André's execution. Her other important books of poems are *Llangollen Vale* (1796) and *Original Sonnets* (1799). Her *Memoirs of the Life of Dr. Darwin* (1804) concerns her relationship with Erasmus Darwin, a biologist and poet who was the grandfather of Charles Darwin. Editions of her poems appeared in 1810, of her letters in 1811. She was admired by many literary figures of the time, among them Sir Walter Scott.

Ashmun, Margaret. *The Singing Swan: An Account of Anna Seward and Her Acquaintance with Dr. Johnson, Boswell, and Others of Their Time*. New Haven, Conn.: Yale University Press, 1931.
This study of a "poetess" whose work was highly esteemed focuses on her relationships with the most important people of her time, including Thomas Day, Richard and Maria Edgeworth, Hannah More, and Sir Walter Scott in addition to those mentioned in the title. It is based on Seward's letters, but it says very little about her poetry.

Manley, Seon, and Susan Belcher. *O, Those Extraordinary Women!* Philadelphia: Chilton Book Company, 1972.
  The authors discuss Seward's dislike of Samuel Johnson and her
  relationship with Erasmus Darwin. They believe her literary criticism
  is superior to her poetry.

MARY SHELLEY (1797-1851)

The daughter of William Godwin, the radical writer, and Mary Wollstonecraft, the early feminist who died within a few days of her birth, Mary
was raised in an intellectual atmosphere. After a childhood made rather
unhappy by her father's remarriage, she met Percy Bysshe Shelley. They
enjoyed reading together, particularly the works of her mother. They
eventually eloped, although he was married and the father of two children.
They married shortly after his first wife, Harriet, committed suicide. Mary
suffered several miscarriages and gave birth to three children, but only
her son Percy lived to adulthood. She spent time with her husband,
stepsister, and Lord Byron in Switzerland, where she wrote *Frankenstein*
(1818). She also wrote *A History of a Six Weeks Tour* (1817). Her husband
drowned in 1822. To support herself and her son, Mary Shelley wrote
Valperga (1822-1823), *The Last Man* (1826), *Perkin Warbeck* (1830),
Lodore (1835), *Falkner* (1837), and *Rambles in Germany and Italy*
(1844). *Mathilda*, a novel dealing with father-daughter incest, was finished in 1819, but was not published until 1959. She devoted herself to
editing her husband's poetry and essays. *Frankenstein* is readily available
in paperback editions. *Mathilda, The Last Man*, and some of her other
short fiction works are available in paperback in *The Mary Shelley Reader*,
published by Oxford University Press.

Alexander, Meena. *Women in Romanticism: Mary Wollstonecraft,
Dorothy Wordsworth and Mary Shelley*. Savage, Md.: Barnes & Noble,
1989.
  According to Alexander, Mary Shelley's life and writing were strongly
  influenced by the fact that her mother died giving birth to her and she
  herself suffered stillbirths and the loss of her babies. To Shelley, the
  female body itself is problematic, but, Alexander believes, the body is
  more important to her than consciousness alone. Alexander also discusses the implications of Mathilda's love for her father in *Mathilda*
  and the relationship of this novel to Percy Shelley's *The Cenci* and
  William Wordsworth's Lucy poems. According to Alexander, in Percy
  Shelley's "Proserpine," the poet connects maternity with nature's

fertility. The loss of a child can cause the end of the world. Alexander notes that in Mary Shelley's *The Last Man* (1826), female work creates the text, although the book is about the exhaustion of (mother) nature and the subsequent end of the world.

Baldick, Chris. *In Frankenstein's Shadow: Myth, Monstrosity, and Nineteenth Century Writing*. Oxford: Clarendon Press, 1987.
Baldick discusses the nature of myth and the development of the Frankenstein myth between 1789 and 1917. She feels that this myth "embraced" important problems of the times. She sees the relationship between parent and child as central to the novel and its development as myth connected to the relationships between men and women, "rulers and ruled, masters and servants, propertied and property-less." She provides a reading of the novel and discusses its critical reception as well as its early stage history. She sees reflections of the work in E. T. A. Hoffmann, Nathaniel Hawthorne, Herman Melville, Charles Dickens, and Elizabeth Gaskell, as well as in Karl Marx, Joseph Conrad, and D. H. Lawrence.

Behrendt, Stephen C., ed. *Approaches to Teaching Shelley's 'Frankenstein.'* New York: Modern Language Association of America, 1990.
Behrendt discusses the differences between the 1818 and 1831 editions of *Frankenstein* and provides a bibliography and filmography of the novel. The essays in the volume discuss the novel in relation to gender, dreams, feminism, language, Marxism, and Romanticism. Although the book is addressed to teachers, the material it presents is quite useful to students.

_____. "Mary Shelley, Frankenstein, and the Woman Writer's Fate." In *Romantic Women Writers: Voices and Countervoices*, edited by Paula R. Feldman and Theresa M. Kelley, pp. 69-87. Hanover, N.H.: University Press of New England, 1995.
According to Behrendt, *Frankenstein* is Mary Shelley's warning that creations such as books or revolutions can injure their creators who may have started out imagining themselves benefiting their society but who are then misunderstood and misinterpreted. He points out that the culture devalued women's writing about what were assumed to be male subjects such as science, politics, and philosophy, causing them to devalue themselves and ultimately to see themselves as monstrous.

Bennett, Betty T. *The Letters of Mary Wollstonecraft Shelley*. 3 vols. Baltimore: The Johns Hopkins University Press, 1980.

Bennett's introduction discusses Mary Shelley's work and her sense of herself as a writer. It also discusses her relationship with her father, William Godwin, and her relationship to her husband. It notes the variety of her correspondents and her many concerns. There are extensive notes to the letters themselves.

Bennett, Betty T., and Charles E. Robinson, eds. *The Mary Shelley Reader: Containing Frankenstein, Mathilda, Tales and Stories, Essays and Reviews, and Letters.* New York: Oxford University Press, 1990. The book's introduction discusses Mary Shelley's life in the context of her times as well as the themes of her works which, according to the editors, involve the creation of a society "based on love, reciprocity with nature, and education, rather than on power and domination." Her novels are described, and a chronology of her life is provided.

Bloom, Harold, ed. *Mary Shelley's 'Frankenstein.'* New York: Chelsea House, 1987. In his introduction, Bloom focuses on the relation of the novel to Romanticism, particularly to William Blake, but also to Percy Shelley and Byron. He also notes the novel's debt to William Godwin's *Caleb Williams* and sees the novel as a questioning of the Promethean ideal. A series of reprinted essays in chronological order written by well-known writers and critics of the novel, such as George Levine, Paul Sherwin, Barbara Johnson, Joyce Carol Oates, Mary Poovey, William Veeder, and Margaret Homans, discuss its relation to domestic realism, artistic creation, and Mary Shelley's life. The bibliography is dated.

Botting, Fred. "Frankenstein and the Language of Monstrosity." In *Reviewing Romanticism,* edited by Philip W. Martin and Robin Jarvis, pp. 51-60. London: Macmillan, 1992. The mob that played so great a part in the French Revolution and in the fears of many that the revolution would spread to England is compared to the monster in *Frankenstein,* who appropriates the language of the established order for the purpose of questioning it. Botting discusses the reversals of power relations between Frankenstein and his creation, and he questions the novel's ending. Botting also compares the novel itself to a monster in that its literary value has never been fully accepted by critics, just as the creature was never accepted by Victor Frankenstein, and he asserts that the novel itself is a monster because it questions authority.

Clemit, Pamela. *The Godwinian Novel: The Rational Fictions of Godwin, Brockden Brown, Mary Shelley.* Oxford: Clarendon Press, 1993.

According to Clemit, the Godwinian novel, a narrative meant to advance a philosophical principle, was expanded by Mary Shelley, Godwin's daughter. Clemit notes that Shelley was familiar with the writing of William Godwin and his circle, and she traces their ideas in *Frankenstein*, *Valperga*, and *The Last Man*. She provides a full discussion of *Frankenstein* showing how Shelley used creation myths, the myth of Prometheus, and her own disillusion with the French Revolution in the novel. She notes similarities between *Frankenstein* and Godwin's *Caleb Williams*, although she finds Shelley to be far less optimistic about the perfectibility of man or the beneficence of nature than her father was. This attitude is made particularly clear in *The Last Man*, a novel in which a plague destroys mankind. Clemit discusses Shelley's use of the apocalyptic theme and notes that Shelley believes that man cannot control his universe and that no political system works well.

Favret, Mary A. *Romantic Correspondence: Women, Politics, and the Fiction of Letters.* Cambridge, England: Cambridge University Press, 1993.
According to Favret, the letters in *Frankenstein* deny the possibility of genuine communication. The narrators are analogous to each other, and they revise each other's stories. Victor Frankenstein does not want to communicate; the monster does. Their voices join Walton's to create the form of the novel. The novel's popularity results from the fact that it never does communicate totally.

Feldman, Paula, and Diana Scott Kilvert, eds. *The Journals of Mary Shelley 1814-1844.* 2 vols. Oxford: Clarendon Press, 1987.
According to the editors, Mary Shelley's journal began as a joint effort by her and Shelley when they eloped. It was soon taken over by Mary and is a record of her development. After Percy Shelley's death, the journal became an outlet for thoughts she could not express aloud. She wanted the journal to survive as both a record of her life and a justification of it, but it does exhibit a certain amount of reserve. Besides the introduction, the editors provide a description of Shelley's notebooks, a chronology of her life, maps of her journeys, and extensive notes. Appendices list the Shelleys' friends, Mary's friends, and their reading lists.

Figes, Eva. *Sex and Subterfuge: Women Writers to 1850.* New York: Persea Books, 1982.

Figes claims *Frankenstein* is an attack on "destructive masculine values on a . . . global level" in favor of more humanist values. She outlines the plot and sees the monster as typical of the uneducated mob. Alexander notes the discrepancy between the ugliness of the monster and his suffering. She also notes that Victor's fault lies in trying to usurp the feminine ability to have children. Figes discusses the case of Justine, who is wrongly executed for murder, as evidence of Shelley's belief that justice does not exist in this world.

Fisch, Audrey A., Anne K. Mellor, and Esther H. Shor. *The Other Mary Shelley: Beyond 'Frankenstein.'* New York: Oxford University Press, 1993.

The introduction to this book summarizes the recent critical history of *Frankenstein*. It also presents biographical information and insists that Mary Shelley's other work deserves critical attention because she is a central figure of Romanticism who believed in the well-being of the community. She was a practical writer cognizant of the demands of the marketplace, but insisted on expressing herself in her own way. She was also a writer who believed in revolutionary ideals and in the reform of society. Brief individual essays concern Mary Shelley in relation to Percy Shelley's poetry, her journals, her transformation of the Byronic hero, her plays, her short stories, her use of everyday phenomena such as the weather, and her novels *The Last Man* and *Valperga*.

Foury, Steven Earl. *Hideous Progeny: Dramatizations of 'Frankenstein' from Mary Shelley to the Present*. Philadelphia: University of Pennsylvania Press, 1990.

Foury discusses the dramatizations of the story that appeared from 1823 onward, changing and spreading the myth. He says that playwrights simplified the novel stressing the moment of creation, the relationship between the Creature and the DeLacey family, the burning of their cottage, the abduction of Elizabeth, and the destruction of the Creature. Most other characters, particularly those in the frame narrative, were eliminated. The text of six nineteenth century versions of the story are supplied.

Gittings, Robert, and Jo Manton. *Claire Clairmont and the Shelleys, 1798-1879*. Oxford: Oxford University Press, 1992.

This biography of Claire Clairmont, Mary Shelley's stepsister, discusses her relationship to the Shelleys.

Glut, Donald. *The Frankenstein Catalogue*. Jefferson, N.C.: McFarland, 1984.

Glut provides a comprehensive list of nearly everything derived from Shelley's novel: short stories, comic books, music, films, and even cartoons. It is particularly informative about representations of film versions of *Frankenstein*. The plot of the novel is summarized.

Hill-Miller, Katherine C. *"My Hideous Progeny" : Mary Shelley, William Godwin, and the Father-Daughter Relationship*. New Castle: University of Delaware Press, 1995.
Hill-Miller explores the influence, both psychological and philosophical, of William Godwin on his daughter, Mary Shelley. Her theoretical stance is both feminist and psychoanalytic. Hill-Miller feels that Godwin's metaphorical seduction of Mary is mirrored in the incestuous emotional entanglements in her books. Her first chapter stresses Godwin's alternating encouragement and rejection of Mary as a writer. The second chapter asserts that *Frankenstein* is a response to Godwin's rejection of her during her adolescence. She reads *Mathilda* with its focus on incest for its biographical significance while she reads *Lodore*, *Valperga*, and *The Last Man* as indicating the daughter's response to her father. She sees *Falkner* as concerned with the duties of a daughter in light of the father's failures. She also reads it as a response to Godwin's *Deloraine*.

Homans, Margaret. *Bearing the Word: Language and Female Experience in Nineteenth-Century Women's Writing*. Chicago: University of Chicago Press, 1986.
According to Homans, *Frankenstein* is about the death of the mother and the son's search for a substitute for her. Frankenstein's sin is his solitariness and self-love. Homans also believes that this novel is about the demands the culture makes on a woman writer as well as a woman's ambivalence about childbearing. Homans believes that when a woman author's books accept the demands of the patriarchal system, they are monstrous.

Joseph, Gerhard. "Virginal Sex, Vaginal Text: The 'Folds' of *Frankenstein*." In *Virginal Sexuality and Textuality in Victorian Literature*, edited by Lloyd Davis, pp. 25-32. Albany: State University of New York Press, 1993.
According to Joseph, the various narratives enfolded in the text of *Frankenstein* resemble vaginal folds. He maintains further that Victor wants to keep Elizabeth—his lover, almost-sister, substitute mother—virginal. This desire is revealed in his dream of Elizabeth after he

finishes the Creature. The worms he sees in the folds of flannel around his mother's body suggest incest with his mother to Joseph.

Ketterer, David. *Frankenstein's Creation: The Book, The Monster, and Human Reality.* Victoria, British Columbia, Canada: English Literary Studies, 1977.

Ketterer sees this book as derived from myth and also as a bridge between early and later Gothic novels. He notes, too, that it is the beginning of science fiction and that Shelley saw her art and Victor's as analogous. He notes that the book is constructed of three rings: the narrations of Walton, the monster, and of Frankenstein. He also discusses the relation of the novel to Romanticism and identifies the issues it engages, including the monster as Victor's double, the conflict between individuality and domesticity, and the problematic nature of knowledge.

Lowe-Evans, Mary. *Frankenstein: Mary Shelley's Wedding Guest.* New York: Twayne, 1993.

This study attempts to explain various facets of *Frankenstein* by relating them to Mary Shelley's life and times, particularly what Lowe-Evans believes is the nineteenth century's concern with the future of marriage as an institution. Lowe-Evans provides a complete chronology of Shelley's life and work, biographical information, a history of the critical reception of *Frankenstein*, its relationship to marriage and family life, the Creature's sensibility, and his relation to Mary and to Percy Shelley.

Lyles, William. *Mary Shelley: An Annotated Bibliography.* New York: Garland, 1974.

Lyles lists works by and about Mary Shelley, including biographies, graduate student research, and foreign works. He also includes fiction about her. This bibliography includes works written up to 1974.

Manley, Seon, and Susan Belcher. *O, Those Extraordinary Women!* Philadelphia: Chilton Book Company, 1972.

The authors discuss, in a perhaps overly dramatic fashion, the origins of *Frankenstein*. They also discuss the lack of attention paid by William Godwin to his daughter, her life with Percy Shelley, and the success of *Frankenstein*. They also mention *The Last Man*, which they consider Mary Shelley's only other readable novel.

Mellor, Anne K. *Mary Shelley: Her Life, Her Fiction, Her Monsters.* New York: Methuen, 1988.

Mellor sees Mary Shelley's life as a search for a family. Quoting extensively from William Godwin's letters, she describes Mary's early life and her relationship with Shelley. She sees *Frankenstein* as a response to Mary's failure to give birth to a healthy child and as a response to her anxiety about her identity as a woman writer. She lists Percy Shelley's revisions and she compares the texts of the 1818 version and the revision. In addition, she demonstrates the influence of Godwinism and Romanticism on the novel. She also discusses *The Last Man*, *Perkin Warbeck*, *Mathilda*, *Lodore*, and *Falkner* as texts that show Mary Shelley's desire for a happy bourgeois family and her recognition that fathers in these families damage their daughters, producing monsters.

Michie, Elsie B. *Outside the Pale: Cultural Exclusion, Gender Difference, and the Victorian Woman Writer*. Ithaca, N.Y.: Cornell University Press, 1993.
Michie argues that Mary Shelley considered women, including herself, as less spiritual than men. In her creation of a protagonist, Victor Frankenstein, who abhors the monster he produced, she sees an example of Marx's concept of the alienation of workers from their labor as well as an example of an idealist who creates something material and cannot control it. Michie discusses other critics of *Frankenstein* whose work she believes bears out her own reading of the novel.

Moers, Ellen. *Literary Women*. Garden City, N.Y.: Doubleday, 1976.
Moers discusses *Frankenstein*'s biographical origins, especially its importance as a birth myth. She analyzes it as a demonstration of the conflict between reason and passion, as a fable about the dangers of science, as a discussion of the divided self, as an attack on convention and prejudice, but she believes its power is attributable to Shelley's experiences as a woman.

Poovey, Mary. *The Proper Lady and the Woman Writer*. Chicago: University of Chicago Press, 1984.
Poovey believes that Mary Shelley tried to resolve the contradiction between her need for self-effacement and her desire for literary fame by following the example of her mother, Mary Wollstonecraft, in reaching for fame in her first four novels (*Frankenstein*, *Mathilda*, *Valperga*, and *The Last Man*) and displaying herself as very proper and domestic in her last three novels (*Perkin Warbeck*, *Lodore*, and *Falkner*). Poovey discusses Shelley's early life and marriage and the critical reception of *Frankenstein*. She provides a reading of that novel in

which she asserts that Victor's denial of femininity and the domestic causes his downfall. She believes that the monster is an objectification of the imagination, disagreeing with her husband that the imagination must be moral. In fact, according to Poovey, Mary Shelley had no faith in religion or in her own reason or feelings. She saw morality only in relationships; they, of course, save Walton. Poovey also discusses the personal and historical context of Shelley's last three novels and provides readings of them. Poovey believes that the financial failure of *The Last Man* as well as Shelley's own inclinations caused her to produce conventional didactic novels at last.

Roberts, Marie. "Mary Shelley: Immortality, Gender and the Rosy Cross." In *Reviewing Romanticism*, edited by Philip W. Martin and Robin Jarvis, pp. 61-68. London: Macmillan, 1992.
Roberts sees Mary Shelley herself as a monster because she has been influenced by such disparate sources as her mother, father, and husband as well as her own desire for propriety. She mentions the Rosicrucian influence on *Frankenstein* and the similarity of the relationship between Victor and his creator to Karl Marx's theory of the alienation of labor. Roberts also discusses the influence on Mary Shelley of her husband, Percy Bysshe Shelley, the artist Henry Fuseli, and Erasmus Darwin. Finally, she asserts that the Rosicrucian influence allowed Mary Shelley to find a female alternative to the split between science and magic and to reconcile the theme of domestic affection with immortality.

Simons, Judy. *Diaries and Journals of Literary Women from Fanny Burney to Virginia Woolf.* Iowa City: University of Iowa Press, 1990.
Simons notes that Mary Shelley's journal is revealing in its silences about the important events in Mary Shelley's life. Simons also believes it is most open and ingenuous during Percy Shelley's life, but after his death it is more guarded and consists primarily of brief jottings. Simons believes Shelley found her journal a source of consolation, and she compares Shelley's life to that of the Creature. They were both unhappy, rejected, and widowed. According to Simons, Shelley's biography also demonstrates and obsession with motherhood and domestic ties and, in certain instances, a disregard for truth.

Smith, Johanna M., ed. *Frankenstein*, by Mary Shelley. Boston: Bedford Books of St. Martin's Press, 1992.
This edition of *Frankenstein* contains the 1831 text and discusses the biographical and historical contexts of the novel in the introduction. It

also provides a critical history of the novel and several critical essays written from the points of view of reader-response criticism, psychoanalytic criticism, feminist criticism, Marxist criticism, and cultural criticism. It includes a bibliography and a glossary of critical and theoretical terms.

Spector, Robert Donald. *The English Gothic: A Bibliographic Guide to Writers from Horace Walpole to Mary Shelly*. Westport, Conn.: Greenwood Press, 1984.
Spector lists, evaluates, and discusses the critical material on Mary Shelley published through 1980.

Todd, Janet. Introduction to *Mary, Maria, by Mary Wollstonecraft; Matilda by Mary Shelley*. London: Pickering & Chatto, 1991.
Todd discusses the similarities in the lives of the two authors and maintains that *Matilda* is a reworking of Wollstonecraft's "The Cave of Fancy" calling both works "subjective," "passionate," and "introverted," although she believes that *Maria* has wider social implications. Todd discusses the lives of both women and asserts that *Matilda* is complex and not merely an incest novel. She notes, however, that Godwin, Shelley's father, would not publish it. Todd maintains that *Matilda* is a birth myth like *Frankenstein*. She also discusses incest and suicide in Romantic literature in general. She asserts that Shelley was less feminist than her mother and more interested in alleviating human suffering.

Vasbinder, Samuel Holmes. *Scientific Attitudes in Mary Shelley's 'Frankenstein.'* Ann Arbor, Mich.: UMI Research Press, 1984.
Vasbinder demonstrates the basis of *Frankenstein* in the scientific knowledge of Mary Shelley's era. He also considers the novel to be "speculative fiction," a term that has replaced "science fiction" in critical discourse. He discusses the critical history of the novel and its textual problems. He also mentions other literature on artificial human beings written earlier than *Frankenstein*. He shows that Victor is neither a necromancer or an alchemist, and he connects Mary Shelley with Priestley and the science of her time, concluding that the novel is "substantially supported by the Newtonian philosophy exemplified" by Victor's life.

Voller, Jack G. *The Supernatural Sublime: The Metaphysics of Terror in Anglo-American Romanticism*. DeKalb: Northern Illinois University Press, 1994.

Voller considers *Frankenstein* a post-Gothic work since it lacks supernaturalism, although the Creature functions the way a supernatural
figure would. He discusses the novel's narrative structure; the interplay
among Walton, Frankenstein, and the Creature, all of whom are sus-
pended from ordinary life; and the DeLacey incidents. He also discusses Victor's guilt and his inability to find solace in nature. Voller
considers the novel "a conservative warning against Faustian/Roman-
tic hubris," and a "vision" of "despair" brought on by contemplation
of a hostile cosmos.

Wolf, Leonard. *The Essential Frankenstein: The Definitive, Annotated
Edition of Mary Shelley's Classic Novel.* New York: Penguin/Plume,
1993.
This edition is based on the 1818 edition of *Frankenstein* rather than
on the 1831 edition, which is more generally used. Wolf discusses how
Mary Shelley came to write *Frankenstein*, its relationship to Gothic
fiction, and its relationship to her life and the life of her mother, Mary
Wollstonecraft. He also mentions the relationship of the Pygmalion and
Prometheus myths to this novel and the interest of the time in automata,
figures that could be made to move as if they were alive. He also notes
that film has increased the novel's popularity. In addition to the text of
the novel, Wolf includes the preface to 1831 edition, selections from
the horror stories the Shelleys were reading in 1818, contemporary
reviews of *Frankenstein*, a chronology of events in *Frankenstein*, and
a selected filmography as well as a bibliography.

FRANCES SHERIDAN (1724-1766)

Born in Dublin, the daughter of a clergyman who did not believe in
educating women, Frances Chamberlaine nevertheless managed to study
Latin. Her first work, a romance, *Eugenia and Adelaide* (1739), appeared
when she was only fifteen. She also wrote sermons. She married Thomas
Sheridan, the manager of the Dublin Theater, in 1747. In 1754, she moved
to London and published her best-known novel, *Memoirs of Miss Sidney
Bidulph*. It is highly didactic. The heroine dies a saintly death in the sequel,
published in 1767. She also wrote *The Discovery* (1763), a successful
comedy for the stage, and *The Dupe* (1764), as well as *A Journey to Bath*
(produced in 1764 and published in 1788) and *The History of Nourjahad*
(1767). *Memoirs of Miss Sidney Bidulph* is available in paperback in The
World's Classics edition of Oxford University Press.

Barker, Gerard. *Grandison's Heirs: The Paragon's Progress in the Late Eighteenth Century English Novel.* Newark: University of Delaware Press, 1985.

Barker points out the resemblances between Sir Charles Grandison, the perfect hero of Samuel Richardson's *The History of Sir Charles Grandison,* and Orlando Faulkland, the hero of Frances Sheridan's *Memoirs of Miss Sidney Bidulph.* He notes that Sheridan solved the problem caused by centering a novel around so static a hero by having the heroine misled into thinking he is a villain and, because of that misbelief, renouncing him. Both the hero and the heroine suffer terribly but they endure. According to Barker, in this novel, the Grandisonian hero plays a supporting role to a heroine who is even more perfect heroine than he is.

Mack, Robert, ed. *Oriental Tales.* New York: Oxford Press, 1992.

In his introduction to this volume, which includes Sheridan's *The History of Nourjahad,* Mack discusses Sheridan's life and her intention to write this tale as a moral fable. He believes, however, that it repeats timeless literary themes such as the dangers of overreaching as in Christopher Marlowe, the magical endings of William Shakespeare's *A Winter's Tale,* and the dangers of wishing for immortality, as in Jonathan Swift's *Gulliver's Travels.* He maintains that Sheridan's tale anticipates the Romantics and Charles Dickens. He also notes its skillful construction and use of language.

Wilson, Mona. *These Were Muses.* Port Washington, N.Y.: Kennikat Press, 1970.

Wilson, whose style is quite dated, provides anecdotes of Sheridan's life, particularly her connections with Samuel Johnson. She also provides summaries of her works and quotes from *Memoirs of Miss Sidney Bidulph.*

CHARLOTTE SMITH (1749-1806)

Because her father, a poet himself, encouraged her to write, Charlotte Smith published a poem on General Wolfe when she was only ten that brought her attention. She married in 1765 to a man who caused them both financial difficulties. She published *Elegaic Sonnets, and Other Essays* (1784) from debtor's prison. An expanded edition appeared in 1787. She had twelve children, but she left her husband in 1787, fearing for her life. Her works included a translation of Abbé Antoine Prévost's *Manon*

Lescaut (1786) and a translation of French crime stories from *Les causes célèbres* published as *The Romance of Real Life* (1787), *Emmeline, The Orphan of the Castle* (1788), *Desmond* (1792), *The Emigrants* (1793), *Beachy Head* (1807), *The Banished Man* (1794), *The Young Philosopher* (1798), *What Is She?* (1799), *Letters of a Solitary Wanderer* (1799), and works for children.

Ashfield, Andrew, ed. *Romantic Women Poets 1770-1838.* New York: St. Martin's Press, 1995.
Ashfield provides a selection of Smith's works as well as a brief biographical headnote.

Figes, Eva. *Sex and Subterfuge: Women Writers to 1850.* New York: Persea Books, 1982.
Charlotte Smith wrote to support herself after her husband's debts ruined them. In *Emmeline*, according to Figes, the heroine who is wrongly thought to be illegitimate is persecuted by her uncle because his son falls in love with her. She resists her uncle's threats and befriends a woman who has had an illegitimate baby, a highly unconventional step for a heroine in an eighteenth century novel. Emmeline triumphs over her wicked uncle, who loses his son and is forced to return her fortune. The unfortunate Adelina refuses to be redeemed, however, although she is really another victim. Feminist comments about the vulnerability of women are made.

McNutt, Dan J. *The Eighteenth Century Gothic Novel: An Annotated Bibliography of Criticism and Selected Texts.* New York: Garland, 1975.
This bibliography list other bibliographies and indexes, covering the aesthetic, literary, psychological, social, and scientific backgrounds of the Gothic novel as well as its influence. It lists editions of Smith's works and the early works about her, all of which were published before 1908.

Mellor, Anne K., and Richard E. Matlak, eds. "Charlotte Turner Smith." In *British Literature 1780-1830*, pp. 225-260. Fort Worth, Tex.: Harcourt Brace College Publishers, 1996.
The editors discuss Smith's life and work and provide a selection of her writing.

Pascoe, Judith. "Female Botanists and the Poetry of Charlotte Smith." In *Re-Visioning Romanticism: British Women Writers, 1776-1837*, edited by Carol Shiner Wilson and Joel Haefner, pp. 194-209. Philadelphia: University of Pennsylvania Press, 1994.

Pascoe notes that several women poets wrote poetry on scientific subjects during this period. Smith's *Rural Walks* (1795), *Rambles Farther* (1796), *Minor Morals* (1798), and *Conversations Introducing Poetry: Chiefly on Natural History* (1804) stress observing details closely and rendering them faithfully. *Conversations Introducing Poetry* and *Beachy Head, with Other Poems* (1807) involve elements of botany. Smith uses the technical language of botany and the scientific names for plants, as well as exact description. During the eighteenth century, women were encouraged to interest themselves in botany, and publication of Erasmus Darwin's *The Botanic Garden* (1791) also heightened interest in this science. Pascoe believes it is important that this interest in botany gave women the right to gaze rather than to be the object of men's gazes.

Rogers, Katherine M. "Romantic Aspirations, Restricted Possibilities: The Novels of Charlotte Smith." In *Re-Visioning Romanticism: British Women Writers, 1776-1837*, edited by Carol Shiner Wilson and Joel Haefner, pp. 72-88. Philadelphia: University of Pennsylvania Press, 1994.

Rogers points out Smith's extremely effective use of landscape to indicate character and to set mood. She notes that Smith differs from the Romantic poets, such as William Wordsworth, in that neither she nor her characters automatically find solace in nature. Rogers also compares Smith to Ann Radcliffe, finding Smith more politically radical, more sympathetic to emotional excess, and more likely to allow her heroine to declare her love. She does not condemn sinning women to perpetual misery nor does she approve of primogeniture or English law relating to marriage, and she never lost faith in the ideals of the French Revolution. She was not an unbridled Romantic, however, stressing the importance of family responsibilities and rational behavior.

Spector, Robert Donald. *The English Gothic: A Bibliographic Guide to Writers from Horace Walpole to Mary Shelly*. Westport, Conn.: Greenwood Press, 1984.

Spector notes that Smith was thought of as an important but imperfect writer in her own time. She and Radcliffe influenced each other. Twentieth century writers have been most interested in her use of landscape, her progressive political ideas, and her possible influence on Jane Austen. A list of critical sources is provided.

Ty, Eleanor. *Unsex'd Revolutionaries: Five Women Novelists of the 1790's.* Toronto: University of Toronto Press, 1993.

Ty maintains that although Smith needed to write to please her audience and earn money, she managed to criticize patriarchy and conventional domestic roles in *Emmeline, Desmond,* and *The Young Philosopher.* In *Emmeline,* the dominant story, that of Emmeline, is conventional, but the narratives concerning Mrs. Stafford and Lady Adelina are not. Ty also comments on the use of Gothic elements in *Emmeline* and compares them with those used by Ann Radcliffe. Ty maintains that *Desmond,* Smith's epistolary novel, is more overtly feminist than *Emmeline,* where republican ideals are upheld and Burkean thought is ridiculed. She also shows that womanly resignation, as advocated by the conservative women writers such as Jane West and Hannah More, leads only to further abuse of women. Ty also discusses *The Young Philosopher* as feminist. It is a two-generation novel in which the mother serves as an example to the daughter rather than a warning as in other two-generation novels. The novel is compared to Mary Wollstonecraft's *Maria* in its dramatization of female suffering.

FRANCES TROLLOPE (1780-1863)

The daughter of a clergyman, Frances Trollope was educated at home. She married in 1809 and had five children including Anthony Trollope, the novelist. She wrote to support them. After a trip to America when she was fifty-two years old, she wrote *Domestic Manners of the Americans* (1832), her best-known work. She also wrote *The Vicar of Wrexhill* (1837), *The Widow Barnaby* (1839), *The Widow Married* (1839), *The Barnabys in America,* (1843), *The Life and Adventures of Michael Armstrong, Factory Boy* (1840) and *Jessie Phillips* (1844). In all, she published a total of 115 volumes, including 35 novels, several travel books, and one poem.

Ellis, Linda A. *Frances Trollope's America: Four Novels.* New York: Peter Lang, 1993.

Ellis focuses on four novels that take place in America: *The Refugee in America, Jonathan Jefferson Whitlaw, The Barnabys in America,* and *The Old World and the New.* She maintains that while Trollope's novels reflect the literary and ideological conventions of her time, they also reflect her own personality. Ellis discusses Trollope's life, the travel literature of her time, the respectability of the novel as a literary form, her use of natural setting, her characters, and her depiction of

America's social institutions. She insists that Trollope may have begun writing out of financial necessity, but she kept on writing out of a need to express her own sometimes unconventional opinions.

Heineman, Helen. *Frances Trollope*. Boston: Twayne, 1984.
Heineman notes that early biographies of Frances Trollope lack objectivity and ignore her writing. She focuses on the "doubleness" of Trollope's life that allowed her to write and do other things at the same time. Heineman notes that Trollope was an innovator in her use of strong and independent heroines and in her use of literary form. She demonstrates this in her discussion of the travel books, her fiction advocating social reform, and her fiction about marriage. Heineman also discusses Trollope's life and provides a chronology.

_____. *Mrs. Trollope: The Triumphant Feminine in the Nineteenth Century*. Athens: Ohio University Press, 1979.
This biography integrates a discussion of Frances Trollope's works with the history of her life. It quotes Trollope's letters and her works as it discusses her stories, her travel books, her social consciousness, and her emerging feminine consciousness. Her novels are summarized and evaluated. The reception of her works is also discussed.

Johnston, Johanna. *The Life, Manners, and Travels of Fanny Trollope: A Biography*. New York: Hawthorne Books, 1978.
Johnston provides a picture of Trollope's life and times, but has little to say about her work. The tone of the biography is rather dated.

Ransom, Teresa. *Fanny Trollope: A Remarkable Life*. New York: St. Martin's Press, 1995.
Ransom insists that Trollope's work has been undervalued and sets out to correct this neglect. Ransom asserts that although Trollope was politically conservative, she was a strong feminist, an early social reformer, and a satirist. Ransom also points out similarities of plot in the work of Frances Trollope and her son, Anthony Trollope. Ransom describes Trollope's early life and education, her marriage and the births of her children, her financial difficulties, her travels, and her later life. Only a few of her works are discussed at any length, but the author does provide a chronological list of them.

Wilson, Mona. *These Were Muses*. Port Washington, N.Y.: Kennikat Press, 1970.
Wilson notes that Trollope not only wrote to support her husband and children, she wrote while nursing them through serious illnesses.

Wilson quotes from various reminiscences of Trollope, including those of her children, her friends, and Trollope herself. She also quotes from the works, which she faults for their too perfect heroines and too evil villains.

JANE WEST (1758-1852)

A self-educated child, West began to write poetry when she was quite young. She married a farmer and had three children. She wrote, she said, to help support them. In all her works, she insisted that a woman's domestic duties should never be neglected. Her works include *Miscellaneous Poetry* (1786), *Miscellaneous Poems and a Tragedy* (1791), *The Advantages of Education: Or, The History of Maria Williams* (1793), *A Gossip's Story* (1796), *An Elegy on the Death of Edmund Burke* (1797), *A Tale of the Times* (1799), *The Infidel Father* (1802), *The Loyalists* (1812), *Alicia De Lacey* (1814), and *Ringrove* (1827). Her conduct books include *Letters to a Young Man* (1821) and *Letters to a Young Lady* (1806). She was highly conservative and extremely didactic. Although West thought very little of men, she felt that their wives were duty-bound as Christians to obey them while trying to protect them from their own folly. Jane Austen in her own letters marvels that West, with so many children, can write such long books.

Ashfield, Andrew, ed. *Romantic Women Poets 1770-1838*. New York: St. Martin's Press, 1995.
  Ashfield provides a selection of West's works as well as a brief biographical headnote.

Figes, Eva. *Sex and Subterfuge: Women Writers to 1850*. New York: Persea Books, 1982.
  Figes describes the plot of *A Gossip's Story* (1797), which involves the travails of a young woman with an excess of sensibility who rejects an unexceptionable suitor for a more exciting young man. They become poor, and Marianne does not behave with what West considers the proper forbearance, so their lives are miserable. Marianne's sister marries the less exciting young man and lives happily ever after. Figes believes this novel influenced Jane Austen's *Sense and Sensibility*.

Luria, Gina. Introduction to *The Advantages of Education: Or, The History of Maria Williams*, by Jane West. 2 vols. New York: Garland, 1974.

In this introduction to the facsimile edition, Luria briefly discusses West's life, lists her works, and locates this work as part of the discussion of women's education that was occurring in the late eighteenth century.

_____. Introduction to *Letters to a Young Lady; in Which the Duties and Character of Women Are Considered*, by Jane West. 3 vols. New York: Garland, 1974.

In this introduction to the facsimile edition, Luria briefly discusses West's life, and lists her works, seeing her as an opponent of Mary Wollstonecraft and others who had begun to champion women's rights during the late eighteenth century. West believed strongly in patriarchy, but also believed that single women may have needed a different social arrangement.

Ty, Eleanor. *Unsex'd Revolutionaries: Five Women Novelists of the 1790's*. Toronto: University of Toronto Press, 1993.

Ty sees Jane West as an exemplar of the conservative woman writer who believes that women should resign themselves cheerfully to male domination. She characterizes her patriarchs as good and wise, and she connects female subservience with the preservation of the British political system. Ty quotes from *The Advantages of Education, Letters to a Young Lady*, and *A Tale of the Times*.

HELEN MARIA WILLIAMS (1762-1827)

Born of Scottish and Welsh parents, Williams was brought up in Dissenting circles in Berwick, an environment which favored cultural activities. She was encouraged to publish by male mentors. Her first work was an antiwar poem, *Edwin and Eltruda: A Legendary Tale* (1782). It was so successful that she was able to move to London where she met the reigning intellectuals. She followed this with *An Ode on the Peace* (1783), on the end of the American Revolution. *Peru: A Poem in Six Cantos* (1784) argues against imperialism. *Poems* (1786) is a collection of her poetry. *On the Bill . . . for Regulating the Slave Trade* appeared in 1788. In 1790, she began writing fiction. Her first novel was *Julia: A Novel; Interspersed with Some Poetical Pieces*. In that year, she traveled to France to witness the French Revolution and produced her *Letters Written in France, in the Summer of 1790, to a Friend in England; Containing, Various Anecdotes Relative to the French Revolution; and Memoirs of Mons. and Madame du F——*. The next year, she published *Sketches of the*

State of Manners and Opinions in the French Republic (1801). Two years later, she published *The Political and Confidential Correspondence of Lewis the Sixteenth; with Observations on Each Letter*. She was unaware that this was a forgery. The need for money led her to produce translations such as *Personal Narrative of Travels to the Equinoctial Regions of the New Continent, During the Years 1799-1804* (1814-1821) and *Researches, Concerning the Institutions and Monuments of the Ancient Inhabitants of America, with Descriptions and Views of Some of the Most Striking Scenes in the Cordilleras!* (2 vols., 1814), both by Alexander von Humboldt. In 1815, she published *A Narrative of the Events Which Have Taken Place in France, from the Landing of Napoleon Bonaparte, in the 1st of March, 1815, till the Restoration of Louis XVIII; With an Account of the Present State of Society and Public Opinion*. Her last book in English, *Letters on the Events Which Have Passed in France Since the Restoration in 1815*, was written out of financial necessity, brought about by the loss of her companion, John Hurford Stone, and the theft of the remains of their fortune.

Favret, Mary A. *Romantic Correspondence: Women, Politics and the Fiction of Letters*. Cambridge, England: Cambridge University Press, 1993.
> After noting Williams' popularity, Favret maintains her letters on the events in France give few clues to her own personality. Because they were about politics rather than her own emotions they were thought to be unfeminine. According to Favret, Williams draws her readers into the letters until they identify with her characters who are also letter readers. She brings out the vulnerability of her correspondents and the revolutionary political implications of their vulnerability. Williams' later letters focus on scenes rather than characters. She herself stays in the background.

Kelly, Gary. *Women, Writing and Revolution: 1790-1827*. Oxford: Clarendon Press, 1993.
> Kelly describes Williams' life and times and gives a complete reading of her works, maintaining that despite a suspicion of women writing on "masculine" subjects such as politics, Williams was successful because she stressed subjectivity, sensibility, and the effects of the revolution on women.

Mellor, Anne K., and Richard E. Matlak, eds. "Helen Maria Williams." In *British Literature 1780-1830*, pp. 500-530. Fort Worth, Tex.: Harcourt Brace College Publishers, 1996.

The editors discuss Williams' life and work and provide a selection of her writing.

Sha, Richard C. "Expanding the Limits of Feminine Writing: The Prose Sketches of Sydney Owenson (Lady Morgan) and Helen Maria Williams." In *Romantic Women Writers: Voices and Countervoices*, edited by Paula R. Feldman and Theresa M. Kelley, pp. 194-206. Hanover, N.H.: University Press of New England, 1995.

Sha explains that Williams called her four-volume work *Letters Containing a Sketch of the Politics of France and of the Scenes Which Have Passed in the Prisons of Paris* to take advantage of the social convention that allowed women to write if they deprecated their work by calling it a sketch. In her later *Sketches of the State of Manners and Opinions in the French Republic Towards the Close of the Eighteenth Century in a Series of Letters*, Williams takes advantage of the fact that letters are part of the private realm and therefore women are permitted to publish them. He notes that Williams connects women's capacity for feeling with their love for liberty and blames France's male rulers for the excesses of the French Revolution.

Wordsworth, Jonathan. Introduction to *Letters Written From France*, by Helen Maria Williams. Oxford: Woodstock Books, 1989.

The author compares Williams' reaction to the French Revolution to that of William Wordsworth. Both approved of the revolution initially, then turned against it as it became violent. He believes Williams influenced Wordsworth's ideas, and he believes Williams' work is important because it shows English attitudes toward the French Revolution.

MARY WOLLSTONECRAFT (1759-1797)

Born in London, Mary Wollstonecraft endured an unhappy childhood as a result of her father's violence and alcoholism. She spent some years as a companion to a lady. In 1783, she established a school. Her first book, *Thoughts on the Education of Daughters* (1787), written to earn money, is much more conservative in tone than her later ones. After spending a year as a governess in Ireland, she wrote *Mary: A Fiction* (1788), *Original Stories from Real Life* (1788), and *The Female Reader* (1789). She also did translations and wrote articles. In answer to Edmund Burke's *Reflections on the Revolution in France*, she wrote *A Vindication of the Rights of Men* (1791). The next year she wrote *A Vindication of the Rights of*

Woman, her best-known work. She traveled to France at the time of the French Revolution and recorded her reactions in *Historical and Moral View of the French Revolution* (1794). She fell in love with Gilbert Imlay, an American businessman, and had a daughter with him. She then traveled to Scandinavia and wrote *Letters Written During a Short Residence in Sweden, Norway and Denmark* (1796). Although her relationship with Imlay soured and she attempted suicide, Wollstonecraft recovered and had an affair with British author William Godwin. When she became pregnant, they married. She gave birth to a daughter who became a novelist herself, but she died of childbirth fever shortly thereafter. *Maria: Or, The Wrongs of Woman* (1798) appeared a year after her death. Her reputation among most of the British public suffered because of the irregularity of her personal life, but during the twentieth century her works have been rediscovered and are now seen as prophetic. A combined edition of *Mary: A Fiction* and *Maria: Or, The Wrongs of Woman* is available in paperback in The World's Classics edition of Oxford University Press. *A Vindication of the Rights of Woman* is available in paperback in a Critical Edition from W. W. Norton.

Alexander, Meena. *Woman in Romanticism: Mary Wollstonecraft, Dorothy Wordsworth and Mary Shelley*. Savage, Md.: Barnes & Noble, 1989.
    Alexander quotes William Godwin, Wollstonecraft's husband, saying the French Revolution affected her greatly, by transforming her personal anger into anger at social and political repression. Alexander states further that Mary Wollstonecraft read and admired the works of Hester Chapone, Sarah Trimmer, and Anna Laetitia Barbauld, who tended to be religious. Wollstonecraft, on the other hand, came to believe in the sublimity of nature rather than religion. Alexander also compares *Thoughts on the Education of Daughters* (1788) with a well-known conduct book by a male writer, Dr. Gregory, noting that Wollstonecraft stresses the importance of the mind over the appearance. Alexander notes Wollstonecraft's use of biblical diction. When she comments on *Original Stories from Real Life* (1788), Alexander points out that didactic fiction for children was quite popular during the time. William Blake provided six plates for the first edition. According to Alexander, through Mrs. Mason, the governess and storyteller, Wollstonecraft picks out maternity as the vehicle for women's power. In *Mary: A Fiction*, however, the heroine's mother ignores her, while devoting her time to reading trashy fiction and improving her appearance. Mary writes because she is very unhappy. *Maria: Or, The Wrongs of Woman*, according to Alexander, is Woll-

stonecraft's most radical work questioning eighteenth century rationalism. Her heroine is shut up in a madhouse, a victim of male oppression. Female friendship literally supplies her with the means to write. *A Vindication of the Rights of Woman* is indebted to Catherine Macaulay's *Letters on Education* (1790), which advocated the same education for women as for men.

Conger, Syndy McMillen. *Mary Wollstonecraft and the Language of Sensibility*. Rutherford, N.J.: Fairleigh Dickinson University Press, 1994.
Conger wants to resolve the paradoxes that she believes pervade Wollstonecraft's work. Wollstonecraft believed in reason, but was emotional; she was a Romantic, but didactic, and she was a feminist who was attracted to "unreliable" men. Conger believes that the language of sensibility corrupted her mind. In this regard, she discusses *Maria: Or, The Wrongs of Woman*, *Mary: A Fiction*, and "The Cave of Fancy." She also discusses the history of sensibility and Wollstonecraft's relation to it, myths of sensibility, and Wollstonecraft's knowledge of the literature of sensibility. Conger believes Wollstonecraft begins to criticize sensibility in her articles in the *Analytic Review*. When she wrote the *Vindications*, she blamed abuses of sensibility and the language of sensibility for oppression. By the time she wrote *Letters Written During a Short Residence in Sweden, Norway and Denmark*, however, she credited sensibility with the power to stimulate the imagination and civilize the world. Conger believes that Wollstonecraft would have shown how sensibility can liberate in *Maria*, but died before she could accomplish this. A bibliography is provided.

Detre, Jean. *A Most Extraordinary Pair: Mary Wollstonecraft and William Godwin*. Garden City, N.Y.: Doubleday, 1975.
Detre combines the letters of Wollstonecraft and Godwin with a fictional journal in order to tell the story of their relationship.

Favret, Mary A. *Romantic Correspondence: Women, Politics and the Fiction of Letters*. Cambridge, England: Cambridge University Press, 1993.
Wollstonecraft's *Letters Written During a Short Residence in Sweden, Norway, and Denmark* remain spontaneous and "feminine" but at the same time attempt to be philosophical and political. Favret notes that Wollstonecraft writes about financial matters as well as political events, which Favret attributes to Wollstonecraft's need for money. Her later letters become even less personal and more political as her

concern moves from the individual to society and she sees women as guarding the world of the imagination from the pressures of commerce.

Ferguson, Moira. Introduction to *Maria: Or, The Wrongs of Women*, by Mary Wollstonecraft. New York: W. W. Norton, 1975.

Ferguson maintains that Wollstonecraft's fiction echoes the ideas she expressed in *A Vindication of the Rights of Woman*. Ferguson describes the legal situation of women in the late eighteenth century and how their lack of rights affected women of every class. In addition, she describes the particular suffering of the poor. Ferguson further demonstrates how Wollstonecraft's life caused her to be open to revolutionary ideas, and she describes Wollstonecraft's works and their reception. She also discusses the history of the novel and novels by and about women. She maintains that *Maria* is a compendium of all Wollstonecraft's ideas about women and that parts of it are autobiographical. She admits that Wollstonecraft had trouble with the form of the novel and that she asks more questions about the plight of women than she answers.

Ferguson, Moira, and Janet Todd. *Mary Wollstonecraft*. Boston: Twayne, 1984.

The authors discuss Wollstonecraft's life and the reactions to her work, but the emphasis is on her work itself. They note that she was familiar with the work of earlier feminists and was influenced by the American Revolution, the French Revolution, and the growing urbanization of England. They maintain that Wollstonecraft's writing was didactic because she believed that education must lead to reform. They describe her religious beliefs, her attitude toward authority, her feminism, and her distrust of marriage. They also discuss her literary style and the influence she had on her successors.

George, Margaret. *One Woman's "Situation:" A Study of Mary Wollstonecraft*. Urbana: University of Illinois Press, 1970.

George summarizes Wollstonecraft's works in the context of her life. She quotes extensively from the works. George believes Wollstonecraft's principle contribution to political philosophy was to insist that liberal thinkers take gender into account. In addition, her work provided a theoretical basis for later feminists. George admits, however, that Wollstonecraft's fiction is merely conventional, her history writing amateurish, and her ideology impractical. George also describes the condition of women during the second half of the eighteenth century.

Holmes, Richard. Introduction to *Mary Wollstonecraft's 'A Short Residence in Sweden, Norway and Denmark' and William Godwin's 'Memoirs of the Author of the Rights of Woman.'* Harmondsworth, Middlesex, England: Penguin Books, 1987.
Holmes discusses the relationship of Wollstonecraft and Godwin, their lives, and their work, as well as the reaction to Wollstonecraft's death. He describes *A Short Residence* and discusses its relation to other travel literature, and concepts of nature. Holmes believes that Godwin's *Memoirs* sheds further light on this work in its discussion of Wollstonecraft's relationship with Gilbert Imlay. He also explains that Wollstonecraft hoped to transact business for Imlay. He discusses the book itself, details of its publication and reception, and its influence on other work. It was highly popular despite the effect Godwin's *Memoirs* had on Wollstonecraft's reputation. Holmes discusses the *Memoirs* and Godwin's strengths and weaknesses as a biographer.

Johnson, Claudia L. "Mary Wollstonecraft." In *Equivocal Beings: Politics, Gender, and Sentimentality in the 1790's*, pp. 23-72. Chicago: University of Chicago Press, 1995.
Johnson reads *A Vindication of the Rights of Woman* as more a republican text than a feminist one. She maintains that Wollstonecraft denounces the feminization of men and their exaggerated sentimentality, seeing upper-class men as decadent and wishing to return to the republican manly virtues. Johnson contends that *A Vindication of the Rights of Men* attacks Edmund Burke's concepts of the sublime and the beautiful. Wollstonecraft denies that either political entities or women need to be beautiful, rather they need to be rational. Johnson also discusses Wollstonecraft's disgust for the body and her insistence on heterosexuality. Johnson believes that the culture responded to the feminization of men by requiring the hyperfeminization of women so as to differentiate between the sexes. Wollstonecraft, she believes, advocates the hypermasculinization of men to allow for the rationality of women and to maintain sexual difference. Johnson also finds a strong homoerotic subtext in *Mary: A Fiction*, noting that Mary's first love is a woman. Mary has all the attributes of a sentimental hero, while Ann resembles a sentimental heroine. To avoid further homoeroticism, Mary falls in love with Henry, who is exactly like Ann except that he is male. Like Ann, Henry dies. Mary tries to return to her husband, but she cannot involve herself in a heterosexual relationship. *Maria: Or, The Wrongs of Woman* shows how women's minds and bodies are imprisoned by patriarchy and reflects Wollstonecraft's despair at the direction of the French Revolution and political repression in England.

Johnson notes that unlike Wollstonecraft's earlier writing, this novel urges the solidarity of all women regardless of social class. Indeed, Wollstonecraft's final image of the perfect family consists of two women and a child.

Kelly, Gary. Introduction to *Mary: A Fiction and Maria: Or, The Wrongs of Women*, by Mary Wollstonecraft. London: Oxford University Press, 1976.

Kelly describes Wollstonecraft as an English Jacobin who lived in an age of revolution. He believes she was reacting against the ideas of Rousseau and the valorization of sensibility, although she agreed with the advocates of sensibility about the natural goodness of man, the necessity of judging by experience, and the idea that education can keep a child good. He describes *Mary: A Fiction* as didactic and pre-Romantic, noting that it makes use of several autobiographical forms. The heroine wants to escape the condition of women but can do so only through death. He goes on to say that the French Revolution caused Wollstonecraft to write both *Vindications*. He believes she was deceived both by Gilbert Imlay and the French Revolution. He also believes that *Maria: Or, The Wrongs of Women* is a revision of *Mary* in light of other Jacobin novels, particularly Godwin's *Caleb Williams*. *Maria* examines the condition of women and explores the dangers of both too much and too little sensibility. He notes the parallels between her work and her life and notes that she might have revised *Maria* in order to make it less gloomy had she lived. He notes the limitations of her novels but he asserts they are "a record of the imagination's quest for wholeness in life and in art."

_____. *Revolutionary Feminism: The Mind and Career of Mary Wollstonecraft*. New York: St. Martin's Press, 1992.

Kelly begins with a thorough, detailed, and clear description of the cultural revolution taking place in England during the eighteenth century, including the change in the role of women. He demonstrates how the rise of the professional classes and the spread of their values to most of the population provided the opportunity for Wollstonecraft to write. He discusses Wollstonecraft's works in the context of her life, analyzing her literary style as well as explaining her ideas. He provides a detailed discussion of her minor articles as well as her well-known books. He notes that she demanded that women be permitted to use their mental powers, and he insists that the poor writing some of her work exhibits is the result of her experimentation with form. An extremely valuable book for students of Wollstonecraft or her time.

Lorch, Jennifer. *The Making of a Radical Feminist.* New York: Berg/St. Martin's Press, 1990.

Lorch believes that Wollstonecraft's feminism derived from her own sense of grievance. She notes that unlike other women authors of the period, Wollstonecraft wrote mainly polemic and history rather than novels, further noting that she wrote to support herself and others. Lorch views Wollstonecraft's life as a search for independence and integrity. She reviews the changes in late eighteenth century culture and shows how those changes affected Wollstonecraft. In addition, she traces Wollstonecraft's work to show how it changed from "prim radicalism" to an outlook which was both socialist and feminist. She provides readings of *Original Stories from Real Life, A Vindication of the Rights of Men, A Vindication of the Rights of Woman,* and *Maria: Or, The Wrongs of Women.* Lorch also discusses Wollstonecraft's work in relation to nineteenth and twentieth century thought. Includes a bibliography.

McDonald, Lynn. *Women Founders of the Social Sciences.* Ottawa: Carleton University Press, 1994.

A brief biography of Wollstonecraft is followed by a list of sources for further reading. McDonald believes Wollstonecraft should be better known as an advocate of empiricism and for her contributions to political theory. In addition to discussing *A Vindication of the Rights of Woman* and *An Historical and Moral View of the Origin and Progress of the French Revolution,* McDonald also discusses *Original Stories from Real Life,* which told children to be kind to animals, and *A Vindication of the Rights of Men,* which argued for human rights and against class barriers.

Manley, Seon, and Susan Belcher. *O, Those Extraordinary Women!* Philadelphia: Chilton Book Company, 1972.

The authors explore the reasons for the disrepute Wollstonecraft's work suffered after her death. They also discuss Wollstonecraft's life, her involvement with the publishing industry of her time, and her relationships with Henry Fuseli, Gilbert Imlay, and William Godwin. They do not discuss her writing.

Mellor, Anne K. "A Revolution in Female Manners." In *Romanticism: An Anthology,* edited by Duncan Wu, pp. 408-416. Oxford: Blackwell, 1995.

Mellor notes that Wollstonecraft was influenced by the ideas of other revolutionaries, but she worked for a revolution in the situation of women, insisting they were rational. Mellor believes Wollstonecraft was influenced by Catherine Macaulay, who had advocated the education of women earlier. She notes that Wollstonecraft attacked John Milton and Jean-Jacques Rousseau for their misogyny, and showed how their ideas harmed men as well as women. Mellor asserts Wollstonecraft's ideas were well received despite the scandal caused by Godwin's *Memoirs* published just after her death.

Mellor, Anne K., and Richard E. Matlak, eds. "Mary Wollstonecraft, Later Godwin." In *British Literature 1780-1830*, pp. 366-429. Fort Worth, Tex.: Harcourt Brace College Publishers, 1996.
The editors discuss Wollstonecraft's life and work and provide a selection of her writing.

Moore, Jane. "Sex, Slavery, and Rights." In *The Discourse of Slavery: Aphra Behn to Toni Morrison*, edited by Carl Plasa and Betty J. King, pp. 18-39. London: Routledge, 1994.
Moore asserts that Wollstonecraft links rights to duties thus acquiescing to "enslaving" women. She also feels that Wollstonecraft's work was too utopian and too oriented toward religion. Wollstonecraft's writings are compared to those of Jacques Derrida and Luce Irigaray.

Nystrom, Per. *Mary Wollstonecraft's Scandinavian Journey*. Göteborg, Sweden: Kung.Vetenskaps-och Vitterhets Sam Hallet, 1980.
Nystrom writes about Wollstonecraft's life and work, focusing on her journey to Sweden, Denmark, and Norway. His sources are her work, *A Short Residence in Sweden, Norway and Denmark*, as well as letters she wrote during that time. He describes the political situation in Europe and the personal relationship between Gilbert Imlay and Wollstonecraft that motivated her travels. He notes her interest in the different governments of the Scandinavian countries and the condition of women in the different Scandinavian countries. He also notes her sympathy for the British princess who became queen of Denmark and died at the age of twenty-four. He also discusses Wollstonecraft's life after her return to England. He maintains that her book encouraged others, such as Thomas Malthus, to travel to Scandinavia.

Poovey, Mary. *The Proper Lady and the Woman Writer*. Chicago: University of Chicago Press, 1984.
Poovey asserts that Wollstonecraft craved the emotional satisfaction of being loved and needed, but was highly suspicious of emotional ties. She describes Wollstonecraft's life and her career, which initially seemed to offer her freedom. Poovey also describes how Wollstone-

craft's reactions to the writings of Edmund Burke ultimately led her to write *A Vindication of the Rights of Men*, and also led to the evolution of her ideas about religion. Poovey also provides a reading of *A Vindication of the Rights of Women* that emphasizes Wollstonecraft's attacks on authors such as John Milton and Jean-Jacques Rousseau. Wollstonecraft asserts that women's inferiority is the result of their social situation and is not natural. Poovey argues that Wollstonecraft distrusts female sexuality and fears the physical. Poovey also provides a detailed reading of *Letters Written During a Short Residence in Sweden, Norway, and Denmark*, and *Maria: Or, The Wrongs of Women*. In the latter book, Wollstonecraft argues that marriage imprisons women and dehumanizes them. Poovey asserts, too, that Wollstonecraft distrusts the imagination and is ambivalent about the effects of novels on the reader. Poovey asserts that Wollstonecraft was not able to reconcile her feelings with her intellect.

Poston, Carol. Introduction to *Letters Written During a Short Residence in Sweden, Norway, and Denmark*, by Mary Wollstonecraft. Lincoln: University of Nebraska Press, 1976.
Poston believes that this, the last book published in her lifetime, is Wollstonecraft's "most delightful work," containing moving passages on the self and on nature, this despite the fact it was written when she was very unhappy that her relationship with Gilbert Imlay was unravelling. Poston describes the *Letters* as travel literature, showing her interest in social criticism and in the treatment of women. Influenced by the Enlightenment and by Romanticism, Wollstonecraft seems modern in her desire for reform. A bibliography is included.

St. Clair, William. *The Godwins and the Shelleys: The Biography of a Family*. New York: W. W. Norton, 1989.
St. Clair focuses on the life of William Godwin, but he discusses the significant events in the lives of his wife, Mary Wollstonecraft, and their daughter Mary Godwin Shelley. He notes that Shelley's descendants were embarrassed by their elders. In appendices, he discusses the Godwins' sexual relationship, conduct books for women, and the illegal publication of some of Percy Shelley's poetry.

Sapiro, Virginia. *A Vindication of Political Virtue: The Political Theory of Mary Wollstonecraft*. Chicago: University of Chicago Press, 1992.
This study is written from the point of view of a political scientist rather than from that of a literary critic. Sapiro discusses various subjects discussed by Wollstonecraft, including reason, passion, God, virtue,

and nature. Sapiro also summarizes Wollstonecraft's thoughts about the structure of society, particularly how class and gender inequalities can lead to tyranny. She analyzes Wollstonecraft's political thought, and her ideas about the relationship between the individual and the wider community. Sapiro maintains that Wollstonecraft's work was not limited to writing about women or to writing about "rights," and it should be integrated into the field of political science. Her bibliography is extensive.

Scheuermann, Mona. *Her Bread to Earn: Women, Money and Society from Defoe to Austen*. Lexington: University Press of Kentucky, 1993. Scheuermann provides a reading of *Maria: Or, The Wrongs of Women* that supports her assertion that Wollstonecraft believed women were victimized because they were women.

Solomon, Barbara, and Paula S. Berggren, eds. *A Mary Wollstonecraft Reader*. New York: New American Library, 1983. This anthology contains excerpts from Wollstonecraft's works to do with female education, women's plight, human rights, travel, and the French Revolution. The editors discuss her life, stressing her unfortunate experiences with her father, brother, and lovers. They also discuss her acquaintances in London radical circles, such as Joseph Johnson and Mary Hays, and her relationships with Gilbert Imlay and William Godwin. In addition, they evaluate her influence. A chronology of her life and a bibliography are also included.

Sunstein, Emily W. *A Different Face: The Life of Mary Wollstonecraft*. New York: Harper & Row, 1975. Sunstein's readable biography stresses Wollstonecraft's modernity as well as her often self-defeating independence. Sunstein discusses Wollstonecraft's background, particularly her resentment of her father. Sunstein believes Wollstonecraft was misunderstood after her death because she was so exceptional in her originality, passion and optimism. Her ideas had to wait to be rediscovered.

Todd, Janet. "Aphra Behn—Whom Mary Wollstonecraft Did Not Read." *The Wordsworth Circle* 26 (Summer, 1995): 152-158. Wollstonecraft, presenting herself as a rationalist who abhorred sentimentality, never acknowledged the existence of Aphra Behn or other early women writers. Todd attributes their differences in language and tone to the different historical situations and their different attitudes toward sexuality. Most of all, however, she believes that Wollstonecraft would have benefited from reading Behn because of Behn's sense of humor.

_____. *Gender, Art and Death*. New York: Continuum, 1993.
Todd discusses Wollstonecraft's attempted suicide after Gilbert Imlay deserted her, giving the historical and personal context. According to Todd, Wollstonecraft believed a "rationally" motivated suicide was not connected to sexuality or female emotion.

_____. Introduction to *Mary: A Fiction*, by Mary Wollstonecraft. New York: Schocken Books, 1977.
Todd maintains that Wollstonecraft's originality lies in the fact that she insisted the mistreatment of women harmed all of society. She writes out of her own experience but is able to make her ideas apply to all of society. Todd outlines the legal position of women in eighteenth century England, the attitude toward women, and women's reading. She notes that women internalized feelings of inferiority. She maintains that Wollstonecraft shows women's problems in *Mary*, not their solutions. She also discusses Wollstonecraft's life in terms of her wish for independence.

_____. Introduction to *Mary, Maria by Mary Wollstonecraft; Matilda by Mary Shelley*. London: Pickering & Chatto, 1991.
Todd discusses the similarities in the lives of the two authors, and maintains that *Matilda* is a reworking of her mother's "The Cave of Fancy." She discusses the lives of both women and considers *Maria* as a novel of sensibility. She notes that Wollstonecraft believed women were imprisoned by their society and wanted to raise women's consciousness of this, while Shelley, less a feminist, wanted to alleviate suffering.

_____. Introduction to *A Wollstonecraft Anthology*. Bloomington: Indiana University Press, 1977.
Todd discusses Wollstonecraft's life and work. She believes Wollstonecraft's ideas about woman's condition sprung from her own experience and from her reading. She discusses Wollstonecraft's relation with Fuseli, her visit to France, and her position as a moderate in regard to the French Revolution. She notes that Godwin ruined her reputation in the nineteenth century by his frankness about her after her death. Her reputation did not recover until the end of the century. Todd notes that Wollstonecraft always supported herself and managed to overcome depression and passivity. She includes excerpts in this anthology from

Wollstonecraft's courtesy books, works of commentary, controversy, fiction, and letters. She also provides a bibliography.

_____. *Mary Wollstonecraft: An Annotated Bibliography*. New York: Garland, 1976.
Todd lists works by and about Wollstonecraft written from 1788 to 1975, including some in foreign languages. The criticism is divided chronologically. Biographies and historical and critical studies are discussed.

_____. *The Sign of Angellica: Women, Writing and Fiction 1600-1800*. New York: Columbia University Press, 1989.
Todd sees the cult of sensibility as a force in Wollstonecraft's life as well in *Mary: A Fiction*. She contrasts this with the rationality of Wollstonecraft's nonfiction. She believes that Wollstonecraft outgrew and repudiated this entirely impotent sensibility, attacking it in *A Vindication of the Rights of Woman* as a part of the cultural oppression of women. Todd believes *Maria: Or, The Wrongs of Women* again engages the cult of sensibility through a dialogue with Rousseau's *La Nouvelle Heloïse*. Emotions ruin Maria's life, causing her to marry a villain who imprisons her to get her wealth. She falls in love with another unworthy man in prison. Sexuality is described in religious terms and for the first time in these novels is accepted as enjoyable, although it still leads to disaster. Todd believes the new element in the novel is the character of Jemima, a lower-class woman who has experienced terrible suffering, a prostitute, yet Maria's mainstay. Todd notes that if more were made of her story, it might have opened new pathways for Wollstonecraft's writing. She asserts that *Maria: Or, The Wrongs of Women* rewrites *Mary: A Fiction*, but is still too subjective and tends to make fiction into therapy for its authors.

Tomalin, Claire. *The Life and Death of Mary Wollstonecraft*. New York: Harcourt Brace, 1974.
A readable, sympathetic biography with wonderful illustrations. Tomalin stresses the life rather than analyzing the works, but she supplies an annotated bibliography. Her appendices include a list of eighteenth century references to woman suffrage, Wollstonecraft's review of Mary Hays's *Appeal to the Men of Great Britain in Behalf of Woman*, and a note on Charles Dickens' allusion to Wollstonecraft in *Bleak House*.

Ty, Eleanor. *Unsex'd Revolutionaries: Five Women Novelists of the 1790's*. Toronto: University of Toronto Press, 1993.

Ty believes that Wollstonecraft wrote with two voices: a rational one influenced by William Godwin, her husband, and the nonsymbolic, literal voice believed to be feminine by feminist language theorists such as Julia Kristeva and Nancy Chodorow. Maria suffers all the wrongs of women and is literally imprisoned, mirroring the plight of all women in a male-dominated society.

Wardle, Ralph M., ed. *Godwin and Mary: Letters of William Godwin and Mary Wollstonecraft*. Lawrence: University of Kansas Press, 1966.
Wardle discusses the provenance of the letters and the relationship of Mary Wollstonecraft to William Godwin: how they met, her unhappy love affairs and suicide attempts, their courtship and life together.

_____. Introduction to *Collected Letters of Mary Wollstonecraft*. Ithaca, N.Y.: Cornell University Press, 1979.
Wardle notes some missing letters and copying errors in the extant letters. He describes Wollstonecraft's life in great detail and provides thorough discussion of her works, noting that *A Vindication of the Rights of Men* made her a celebrity.

_____. *Mary Wollstonecraft: A Critical Biography*. Lincoln: University of Nebraska Press, 1966.
Wardle discusses Wollstonecraft's era and her life. He discusses her work, quoting extensively from it, in the context of her life. He mentions how Godwin's writing about her affected her reputation and the influence her work had on his.

Whale, John. "Preparations for Happiness: Mary Wollstonecraft and Imagination." In *Reviewing Romanticism*, edited by Philip W. Martin and Robin Jarvis, pp. 170-189. London: Macmillan, 1992.
Instead of seeing a conflict between reason and emotion in Wollstonecraft's work, Whale sees an attempt to harmonize them. He traces the contradictions in some of her views and in her treatment of Rousseau's work. He sees religious hope in her work, but he asserts she retained the most faith in the workings of the imagination to provide mankind with the insight that leads to happiness.

Wordsworth, Jonathan. Introduction to *Original Stories from Real Life*, illustrated by William Blake. New York: Woodstock Books, 1990.
Wordsworth discusses William Blake's affinities with Wollstonecraft and her interest in education. He believes she was influenced by Richard Price and Joseph Priestley, and he discusses other books of the era meant to educate, such as Thomas Day's *The History of Sandford*

and Merton (3 vols., 1783-1789) and Hannah More's *Cheap Repository Tracts*. He notes that Wollstonecraft's book is less religious than More's and notes that Wollstonecraft's main character, Mrs. Mason, is implacable as she cures the very minor sins of Mary, who is fourteen, and Carol, who is twelve.

Ann Yearsley (1756-1806)

The daughter of farm laborers, Yearsley learned to write—an accomplishment which in itself was quite unusual for the time. She married in 1774 and had six children in six years, but she retained her desire to learn and her desire to write. Hannah More, the Evangelical philanthropist and writer, became Yearsley's patron but they quarreled. Before their quarrel, More helped interest subscribers in Yearsley's first book, *Poems on Several Occasions* (1785). Another edition appeared the next year. *Poems on Various Subjects* (1787) followed. Yearsley attacked slavery in *A Poem on the Inhumanity of the Slave Trade* (1788) and in *Stanzas of Woe* (1790). A play, *Earl Goodwin*, was published in 1789. It defended the rights of peasants. Yearsley published a novel, *The Royal Captives* (1795), and a collection of poetry entitled *The Rural Lyre* (1796). She died in seclusion after the deaths of her sons and her husband.

Ferguson, Moira. *British Woman Writers 1578-1799*. Old Westbury, N.Y.: The Feminist Press, 1995.

Ferguson describes Yearsley's quarrel with More and her constant battle for the rights of the poor, slaves, and other subordinated people. She ascribes this to the poet's personal experiences, which caused her to flood "her poetry with powerful feelings, a quest for justice and an evolving ideological perspective." To demonstrate this point, Ferguson provides readings of *Poems on Several Occasions*, *Stanzas of Woe*, *Earl Goodwin*, "Reflections on the Death of Louis XVI," and *The Rural Lyre*. She also discusses Yearsley's unpublished work, speculating on why they were never published. Ferguson's analysis constitutes the definitive assessment of Yearsley's life and work.

Mellor, Anne K., and Richard E. Matlak, eds. "Ann Cromarty Yearsley." In *British Literature 1780-1830*, pp. 261-271. Fort Worth, Tex.: Harcourt Brace College Publishers, 1996.

The editors discuss Yearsley's life and work and provide a selection of her poetry.

Tompkins, J. M. S. "The Bristol Milkwoman." In *The Polite Marriage*,
pp. 58-102. Reprint. Freeport, N.Y.: Books for Libraries Press, 1969.
In this work, which was first published in 1938, Tompkins describes
the life and work of Ann Yearsley, her relation to the Bluestockings,
her patronage relationship and dispute with Hannah More, and the
difficulties she encountered. Tompkins maintains that the reading
public was less interested in Yearsley's *Poems on Several Occasions*
than it was in the circumstances of her life and her struggle to write
despite her poverty and lack of education. In Yearsley's *Genius Unim-
proved*, she advises a young poet to substitute feeling for education,
and in the advertisement for *Felix Farley's Bristol Journal*, she expresses similar sentiments. Tompkins also discusses *Address to Friendship* and the circumstances of its rededication as well as her play, *Earl
Goodwin*, the critical reception of her work, and the circumstances of
the remainder of her life. Tompkins concludes that Yearsley's sensibility was religious. Her early work uses Christian diction; her later work
depends on "Christian parable and iconography." She also discusses
Yearsley's novel, *The Royal Captives*, and its critical reception, which
noted Yearsley's force and sincerity but deplored her style and technique. Tompkins believes the novel's main characters express
Yearsley's "mind and experience." She also analyzes its themes and
imagery. Tompkins also discusses *The Rural Lyre*, the lack of critical
attention it received, and Yearsley's silence afterward.

SUBJECT INDEX

AUTHOR INDEX

AUTHOR INDEX

About the Author

Barbara Horwitz, an Associate Professor of English at the C. W. Post Campus of Long Island University, received her Ph.D. from the State University of New York at Stony Brook. She is the author of *Jane Austen and the Question of Women's Education* (New York: Peter Lang, 1991). Her essay, "The Wicked Mother in Jane Austen's Novels" appears in *Jane Austen: The Beginnings*, edited by J. David Grey (Ann Arbor: University of Michigan Press, 1989). She has also published articles about Jane Austen's influence on Anthony Trollope and her interest in education. In addition, Horwitz has written on Fanny Burney and Josiah Wedgewood, as well as on current fiction.